THE FEELING CHILD

Arthur Janov, Ph.D.

A TOUCHSTONE BOOK
PUBLISHED BY SIMON AND SCHUSTER

SBN 671-21584-1 Casebound
SBN 671-22022-5 Paperback
Library of Congress Catalog Card Number: 73-3784
Designed by Irving Perkins
Manufactured in the United States of America

1 2 3 4 5 6 7 8 9 10

ACKNOWLEDGMENTS

I wish to thank Barbara McAlpine, my library aide, who has spent many hours chasing down obscure references for me, has brought special articles to my attention, and generally has been a great help in helping find relevant material for this and my previous books.

My special thanks to the person who literally put this book together, Janet Seefeld, my secretary. Finally, my thanks to my wife, Vivian, my best critic and editor.

A. J.

To Rick and Ellen,
and to the world's
largest oppressed minority—
children.

Contents

Introduction

Generally, a book should stand on its own. It should be understood on its own terms without relying too heavily on other works. I think *The Feeling Child* can stand on its own, but the reader should understand that it is based upon Primal Theory, and a thorough knowledge of that theory, as detailed in *The Primal Scream*, would be helpful as preliminary reading. This book is a result of observing patients relive their childhoods. What they feel and experience enables us to know the many ways parents can harm children and make them neurotic. Perhaps their suffering can provide lessons which will help prevent hurt to other children. The purpose of this book is to help stop the hurt of children. We cannot redo parents, but we can offer guidelines for those who are floundering with their children.

I have searched out the scientific literature and combined what I have found in my research with my observations to draw certain conclusions about the rearing of children. What Primal patients experience about their youths is primary. Any research is but an adjunct to what they learn about children through becoming the feeling children they never were.

I shall use the term "a Primal" throughout this work. This refers to the total reliving of early experiences in Primal Therapy. A Primal is a painful reliving, often an agonizing experience where patients return to feel what they dared not feel when they were too young and fragile to withstand the Pain. They feel now the hate from their parents, their indifference, and their deadness. They feel the terror of being sent away to school, being sent to surgery alone, being abandoned by one parent or another, being pulled in two by parental dispute, or being left to cry it out in the crib. They feel the need to suck at mother's breast as they never have before. In short, they feel the Pains of their lives which have been stored in their bodies for a lifetime, producing tension and its symptoms.

Each Primal by a patient is another pinpoint on the map of parenthood, which tells what to do and what not to do, what to avoid, what to encourage, what to say, and what to leave unsaid. After seeing many thousands of Primals, our map is studded, so much so that it seems almost impossible to do right by children; and it may well be impossible. The only real protection a child has is for his parents to be healthy mentally. In our terms, this means to be bereft of Primal Pains themselves. We know from our research that there is a "feeling brain" and a "thinking brain," and the thinking part has very little control of the feeling part, especially when that feeling brain is overloaded with Pain. What this means in practical terms is that lectures and education for neurotic parents usually cannot make a profound difference in how they treat their children, but it may help some.

This is not a traditional "how to" work. There are already many of those in existence. The problem with them is that one would have to list a separate rule for each occasion in order to be effective, and that would only appeal to compulsives who have the problem of living by rules instead of feelings. Parents treat their children in terms of their own hidden feelings, and it is the feeling parent who can sense what is right in situations involving the children.

It can be argued that if the wrong knowledge of child care, as taught in early child-rearing manuals, could do harm, then the right knowledge should be helpful. Unfortunately, this is not entirely true. Wrong information in those early books was part of a neurotic view of human development. It fit into the general neurotic outlook (crying children should not be picked up, infants should be fed on a strict schedule, etc.) and thus was easily embraced. Primal views do not coincide with those neurotic ideas and will therefore not so easily be accepted.

The general view in decades past was that it is a cold, hard world and that children should not be pampered lest they become unprepared for it. So child manuals stressed the necessity of not spoiling children, of not indulging them—seeing to it that there were plenty of chores to do to build character. It was the Horatio Alger myth brought into family life. Primal theory indicates that children cannot be spoiled; that it is *lack* of proper indulgence of need that produces "spoiled," demanding behavior. For those of us who grew up the hard way, believing that struggle builds character, the notion of indulgence is not an easy one to accept.

A child is predestined to become neurotic if his parents are. I do not expect that the guidelines set forth herein will counteract parental neurosis, but there are things that parents can do for their children, nevertheless. Parents should know that crying babies should be picked up and not left to "cry it out." They don't have to overcome their neuroses to comfort children who have been hurt.

I will follow the child from his conception to his adulthood, indicating each step of the way the kinds of things that bring about neurosis. I will concentrate on uterine life and the moments around birth because these are neglected areas of discussion in the child-rearing field. What I am saying is that the seeds of neurosis may well begin before birth, and that experience by the fetus in the womb may be as important, if not more so, than subsequent social events. A child's neurosis begins in the mind of the parent—in the very reasons why he or she wants a child. Sometimes the reason may be to have someone all to himself for the first time in his life, or it can be to prove the parent's feminity or masculinity. Whatever the reasons, they will determine how the child is treated from the day he first enters this world.

By and large, it is the parent who shapes the child and makes him sick or well. But there are subtleties. Suppose a child is born with poor eyesight, and grows up taunted by neurotic playmates as "four eyes." This must produce Pain. Probably not what taunting by a parent can do to a child, but nevertheless there are experiences just in living that help make a child neurotic. It is not the isolated experiences that produce neurosis, however. It is the accumulation, the load of one bad experience after another that does it. And this is accomplished by living day in and day out with parents who do harm, who are hostile, indifferent, or openly rejecting. After seeing the dramatic changes in children after their parents have Primal Therapy, I am convinced that it is the only sure way to give children a chance in life. We have treated child experts, authors of books on children, and nothing they knew helped them be decent parents until they could get some of their own needs and tensions out of the way. Primal parents do not need lectures. They have felt what their parents did to them and know what they must not do to their children. Those who have never felt the subtleties of the Pains inflicted by their parents can never know how they keep their own children sick. Feelings are the answer both for the parent and the child. Feeling parents do right by their children, and a feeling child does right by himself.

It is much easier for a philosopher to explain a new concept to another philosopher than to a child. Why? Because the child asks the real questions. . . .

JEAN PAUL SARTRE (interview with
John Gerassi, *Le Monde*, October 1971)

I

Reasons for Having Children

How a child is going to be treated may already be predestined in the planning stage. If a mother wants to have the family she never had in her lifetime, then the child is going to have to make her feel that she has a warm, loving family. Later, when the child wants to do things on his own, independently, whether it be to go away to school or to get married, it will be perceived as an unconscious threat to the mother. What is unconscious in the mother is the *old* feeling of not having had a real family for herself, a Pain so great that it has been blocked from consciousness. Any sign of independence by the child and of not needing "momma" produces first, a vague tension in the mother, and then defensive behavior to quell the Primal feeling. She will rationalize why her son should not go away, why she needs him, etc. For the same Primal reasons this mother will not permit her children to show anger toward her. She will denigrate her son's boyfriends because they threaten her position as the sole loved one. In short, mother is acting out against an old hurtful feeling that she could not and still cannot face. She is manipulating her present life continuously to keep away Pain. She can't be straight with her children because she is using them in the service of her need.

I am introducing this concept of acting out denied, pained feelings because this is the essence of neurosis. It is inescapable in neurotics, and having children is one more way neurotics act out their needs. There are a host of neurotic reasons for having children, none of which have to do with producing a new human being on this earth.

One of the key reasons neurotics have children is to produce someone who will be loving, someone the parent can have all to himself. A person who grew up in a large family and who had practically no attention or affection may tend to be possessive about his child. The child's value will lie in his making the parent feel loved. Again, this is not a conscious procedure. The parent may become anxious at a child's occasional indifference, or there will be a disproportionate display of anger when the child doesn't pay attention to his parent. "Look at me when I am talking to you!" can be one way neurotic parents will express it. The emotional overreaction (anger, in this case) is an old feeling toward this parent's own parents which has been suppressed and now erupts inappropriately. The great denied anger is over being treated indifferently. Any indifferent treatment, then, arouses this Primal feeling and the suppressed old reaction as well.

Let us look at how complicated this can get. One patient was so furious over being neglected that she used to wish her mother dead. The child became so fearful of this feeling that she blotted it out of consciousness and got headaches instead. When this person grew up and was treated indifferently, she was immediately seized with inexplicable headaches. She had no idea why, no idea that she was being slighted, and no idea that she was suppressing a wish that the offending person would die. By now it was all an unconscious neurologic sequence, run off without the intercession of consciousness. It was, in short, an old Primal sequence, finally uncovered in Primal Therapy with screams and convulsive fury about wanting her mother to die. The scene that triggered this sequence was when her own daughter would not pay attention to her.

Now we see what produces neurotic reactions to children's innocent responses. Children sense this soon enough and learn how to keep that parental Primal wrath away. They cower, placate, keep quiet and remain attentive. They become neurotic because the parent is. The child is being rigidly molded because the unresolved Primal feelings in the parent cause the same kind of neurotic reactions time after time, year after year. The child must then also placate in the same way, year after year. If it is his mother who needs him to make herself feel loved, then it may take the form of a secret conspiracy against father. Mother subtly denigrates the father so as to have the child's love exclusively. This is a double-barreled neurotic ploy. It robs the child of his father and presses the child into a neurotic bond with his mother. The child doesn't have a chance. It is very easy to manipulate defenseless children into this position. Phrases such as "John is such a good boy, he can't do enough for me" do the damage because it is a literal statement—John will never be able to do enough for his mother, who has a lifetime of deprivation to fill.

Another reason for having children is to hold together a faltering marriage. This is especially true of women who desperately want to bind their husbands to them. The child, himself, is the least consideration. The child will soon enough be used as a pawn in his mother's efforts. He will have to beg and plead and be the go-between during arguments. He will soon come to feel responsible for their happiness—and unhappiness. Simply the general demeanor of the parent, say sadness, automatically throws the child into a struggle to ameliorate and pacify. No amount of advice to a melancholy parent about rearing children is going to help if everything he does with his child, even if it is done according to the "book," is done sadly.

Of course, many pregnancies are accidental, leaving the parents with nothing but resentment toward their offspring. From the time he is born he will have to pay for his intrusion and demands upon his parents who still are and want to be fun-loving children. He will be spanked for his interrupting and irritating crying, hushed, and given a number of chores to earn his right to exist. He will pay for the impulsiveness of his parents, an impulsiveness which usually derives from two young people so deprived of love that when they find it in sex, they throw precaution to the wind.

There are as many reasons for having children as there are neuroses. A man who doubts his masculinity may want children, preferably male children, to prove his manhood. When his children show fear, his exaggerated image of masculinity will be threatened and their fear will be squelched. A woman may want to have children to prove her femininity, or at least so as not to feel barren. She may still want to go to parties, to go to nightclubs and social gatherings to prove her feminine attractiveness. Having a child was just a ploy in the game with no thought that a separate, needing human being was being created. Mother is neglectful for the same reason that she had a child—to be pretty, attractive, and "feminine."

The last thing many neurotics want is to have to take care of someone constantly. *They* are really the children who long to be taken care of. Having a baby for these people is a fantasy. The woman only sees the care and attention she gets while pregnant. Or having a baby may be the only way she can ensure having a husband who will remain with her to support and direct her. These parents do not understand that *a baby is total need and total demand*. No wonder that parents soon become agitated and irritable nearly all the time at having to give up more of themselves in deference to the baby. Thus, the reflexive reaction to the baby's cries is to suppress the crying and the demand rather than to take the time necessary to cater to the child's needs. When a parent cannot fulfill needs he must suppress them. The process is somewhat as follows: As an infant, the parent who was not catered to had to shut down the recognition of his intolerable unmet need. Having shut down awareness, he now has a child and cannot recognize the child's need either. The infant's constant wails (reminders of needs) become intolerable to the parent and the cries are suppressed. There are many ways to suppress. Distracting him with rattles, noise, games, etc. are some ways. Shaking him roughly is another, more crude way. The end result is the same.

The main point of all this is that the reasons we give ourselves for having children are often not congruent with the unconscious motives. Those motives are needs and they are unconscious because the needs are buried. A child will be incorporated into those unconscious needs from the day he is born because those needs exist in the parent from the day he is born.

One of the more general reasons why people have children is because they cannot face the finality of death. They need to feel that part of them will live in the hereafter, and either they adopt a *concept* of a hereafter or produce one via the child. Having nothing in this world that lasts beyond us means to accept death as the very end of our existence.

Clearly, one of the best methods for preventing unwanted (hence neurotic) children from coming into the world is to prevent unwanted pregnancy. The best insurance for this is for the woman to be open to herself, and to use contraceptives intelligently. Primal women can often feel when ovulation begins in them; they are not suddenly surprised by the condition of pregnancy, as sometimes happens to neurotic women. Being well means that a woman is not desperate for love and therefore is less likely to act out compulsively with sex. Being well means that a woman will not bring a helpless human into the world for the sole reason of keeping a man around who will take care of *her*. Obviously, a major factor in producing well children is to produce *wanted* ones. Accidents, by definition, are not wanted.

II

Intrauterine Life

Research on life in the uterus is sketchy, but there is clear evidence that the mother's condition has an effect on her fetus. In other words, the seeds of neurosis begin with whatever one experiences in life, and life experience begins in the womb. By the second month of life in the uterus, the brain is already functioning and transmitting impulses which coordinate the organs of the tiny body. It is a rudimentary brain which very soon can register its sensations from the uterine environment. I emphasize the term "register," since that tiny nervous system lives in a world where there are outside influences which may eventually contribute to neurotic development long before those influences can be conceptualized. If a mother takes a drink of alcohol, some of it may find its way into the fetus. If she injects heroin, it will help addict the fetus. If she smokes, the fetus may have retarded development and come into the world smaller than it should be.

Let us take the simple act of smoking by a pregnant woman. Research in monkeys indicates that nicotine moves quickly from the mother to the fetus.* It adversely affects the circulatory system of the fetus, reducing oxygen. It also depresses the heart rate and blood pressure of the fetus. In other words, the injection of nicotine into a pregnant monkey puts her fetus under stress, and it is not unwarranted to assume that this holds true of the human fetus.

A study of seventeen thousand British children indicates that the child of a heavy smoker (ten cigarettes or more per day after the

* "Effects of Nicotine on the Unborn," *The Stethoscope* XXIV, no. 4 (April 1969): 1.

fourth month of pregnancy) is in poorer physical condition and has inadequate social development.* There is evidence that smoking depletes Vitamin C levels and that this can affect the cellular structure, as well as adversely affecting the synthesis of collagen in the body. It turns out that smokers need twice as much Vitamin C as nonsmokers.

The study of the seventeen thousand British school children will continue so that they will be surveyed every four years.† One late finding of the survey is that mothers who smoked during pregnancy lost their babies 30 percent more often than those who did not. The babies who survived were measured at the age of seven. They were one-half inch shorter on the average than children of nonsmoking mothers. They also tended to be less skilled in reading and presented more psychological problems in school. They seemed less physically coordinated and showed impairment in copying simple drawings.

Obviously, there is much that we don't know about the effect of smoking on the fetus, but enough is known to indicate that pregnant women must not smoke. What we don't know is how much more anxious and tense smoking mothers are than nonsmoking ones and how this affects the results attributed to smoking. Another way of saying this is that smoking is just another side effect of tension and that it is tension that we must deal with and eradicate in order to insure healthy pregnancy. Since the nervous system is already fairly well developed by mid-pregnancy, can you imagine what kind of sensations the fetus undergoes when it is bombarded every hour by nicotine, which reduces its oxygen levels?

At a recent meeting of the American Association for the Advancement of Science (Spring, 1970), there was a report on pregnant rats who were exposed to loud noises. These experiences produced smaller offspring. This suggests that stress (or fear) has a direct effect on fetal development. Pregnant rats exposed to noise stress not only had a faster heartbeat, but the heart rate of the fetus

* "Gravida's Smoking Seen Handicap to Offspring," *Obstetrics-Gynecology News* 5, no. 12 (June 15, 1970): 16.

† R. Davie, N. Butler, and H. Goldstein, *From Birth to Seven* (London: C. Longman, 1972). Also reported in London *Times*, June 4, 1972, p. 27.

was stepped up as well. This means that stress on the pregnant mother can precondition the offspring toward neurosis. There is some evidence that sound is transmitted directly to the fetus. In an experiment where an audiotape of a heartbeat was played in a hospital nursery, there was less crying among the babies. What this may indicate is that the mother's heartbeat registers on the fetus, and its regularity (or irregularity) has an effect on it. Mother's heartbeat while carrying can have a later effect on the child.

It would seem that a steady heartbeat in a pregnant woman helps counter neurosis. Steady tones are reassuring. We all can go to sleep by them. But irregular noise is disquieting. If this inbuilt factor is true of adults, why should it not be true of the fetus? Not only is sound perceived by the skin, but there is evidence that the location of the sound can be detected by different areas of the skin. Skin is the eyes and ears of the fetus.

One Primal mother reported that when she was eight months pregnant, she went to a park which had a rifle range. Each time a shot was fired, the baby jumped in the abdomen. When the baby was eight months old she returned to that park, and when a shot was fired, the baby had a startled reaction more inordinate than might be expected, according to her.

Experiments in Sweden have shown that the fetus responds to mild noises by increasing its heart rate; this is an indicator of a stress reaction. Just because the fetus cannot conceptualize the stress does not mean that it isn't being hurt by it, or that the stress is not having a lasting effect on later behavior. What is happening throughout pre- and postuterine life is that there are stresses which are leaving their marks on the organism, forming a Primal pool which one day overflows into symptoms.

Research carried out by S. Rosen, a New York ontologist, is instructive: "When a sudden noise strikes the ear, the heart beats rapidly, the blood vessels constrict, the pupils dilate, and the stomach, esophagus, and intestines are seized by spasms . . . you may forget the noise, but your body never will." (Life, June 1970)

Dr. Rosen is discussing a stress or anxiety reaction. An infant who is unable to focus on the source of noise or to do anything about it will undergo this stress reaction. Whether the human organism is inside or outside the uterus makes little difference in terms of its physiologic response to noise stress.*

What is happening during gestation is that we are preparing to become feeling human beings. Sensations on the fetus become elaborated into total physiologic events affecting secretions, hormone development, brain elaboration, and so on. That is, sensations are becoming elaborated into the precursors of feelings. Catastrophic sensations can begin the shutdown which evolves into a full-blown neurosis after birth. What has seemed to be genetic temperamental differences among newborns may be the "personality" which has already developed due to life experiences in the womb. Certainly, if a smoking mother produces a smaller offspring, somehow, somewhere that stress helped shut down whatever hormonal development was necessary for growth. Since hormones are so intricately a part of feelings, it is logical to assume that adverse hormonal development will affect our ability to feel.

Sometimes these catastrophic sensations are not so apparent. For example, if a pregnant woman climbs a high mountain, flies in an airplane that is not pressure regulated, or if her circulation is constricted due to tension, the baby may suffer oxygen deprivation. This must be an uncomfortable sensation. Though the placenta will tend to compensate for this lack, the point remains that oxygen deprivation is sensed by the fetus in some way. Continued discomfort automatically shuts down or distorts the sensitivity of the system in some way (producing an overdeveloped placenta, in this case) without any necessary conscious perception that there is Pain. The fetus can have the sensation of discomfort (which I term Pain) without conscious perception of it. Sensations are the key elements of consciousness. Blunted sensation, then, may well have a later effect on the consciousness of the newborn. The baby may be less acute, alert, and alive, have retarded conceptual development, or whatever.

---

* Young rats, for example, who were put under stressful noise for a prolonged period of time were susceptible to convulsions and respiratory failure. Others died from the stress. (American Association for the Advancement of Science, Spring, 1970, proceedings.) Other research found that noise-stressed rats were more prone to have virus infections.

There is an argument that even these sensations cannot have lasting effects because many of the brain cells necessary for their interpretation are not myelinated.* However, as Delgado points out, the
newborn rat moves about days before birth even though myelinization of the necessary brain structures does not take place for days
after birth.†

If ever a woman should take good care of herself, it should be
during pregnancy. Improper nourishment, drinking too much alcohol, etc., affects the baby. The pregnant woman already is having
a relationship with her child. If she cares about the child, she will
make sure she is in good shape, not racing around and driving herself to work up until the last minute, not screaming and yelling
every few minutes at her other children and, generally not doing
those things which increase tension. She needs a relaxed system.

Oxygen insufficiency is not the only kind of deprivation a fetus
can experience. Improper nourishment on the part of the mother is
another crucial factor. A healthy mother feels the needs of the fetus
inside her as part of her own need. She will fulfill those needs intuitively through proper diet when she is pregnant. She will not
starve herself to keep thin out of vanity. A mother who is not eating
properly is producing an adverse effect on her fetus. It becomes
need-deficient, and eventually this subtle deficiency will become
translated into physical vulnerabilities later on. Starvation can subtly
affect the nervous system at a time when it is developing rapidly in
the yet-to-be-born.

All of us are aware of how improper diet can affect our bodies.
What we may not fully appreciate is how improper diet by a pregnant woman can cause suffering in her baby, even though a full-
blown consciousness is not yet developed to apprehend that suffering.

One of the ways that the mother's neurosis affects her baby is in

* Myelin is a fatty sheath covering nerve fibers, which signifies the nerves
readiness to function. The fetus can be conditioned to a mother's heartbeat.
The fact that the presence of a heartbeat after birth is reassuring means that
some kind of systemic memory has occurred while in the uterus.

† José Delgado, *Physical Control of the Mind* (New York: Harper & Row,
1969). This point will be discussed in detail in a forthcoming book by the
author, *Primal Man: The New Consciousness*.

producing either delayed or premature birth. I believe that both of these conditions are affected by neurosis. For example, the chemical serotonin is heavily concentrated in those areas of the brain involved with repression. One of the concomitants of increased serotonin is constriction of the blood vessels. This chronic constriction resulting from neurotic repression contributes in some cases to either spontaneous abortion or premature birth. Excess serotonin can also decrease the blood flow to the placenta and thus starve the fetus. There are many deleterious effects of premature birth, but what is rarely discussed is the psychologic trauma of such an event. One Primal patient who was a premature birth had a birth Primal of being thrust abruptly into the world before he was ready, and came out of it with the insight that all of his life he has been holding onto things, trying for permanence in his job and living arrangements, and being panic-stricken when making a change. He strongly felt that the prototype of such panic came from premature birth and the need to hang on longer until he was ready for a proper birth.

I am sure that there are many biochemical factors producing premature birth of which we are not aware. I am equally certain that those factors are intimately associated with neurosis. Primal patients who have been mothers who gave birth prematurely knew that they ejected their babies into the world because they couldn't stand pregnancy and didn't want to carry their little ones. There are any number of studies indicating the harmful effects of prematurity, ranging from retarded mental development to the greater likelihood of respiratory disease. Of course, much of this may be due less to the prematurity and more to the fact that premies are put in incubators and thus do not have the greater amount of stimulation, warmth, and touching they must have in order to develop—especially considering that for all intents and purposes they are still fetuses requiring all the stimulation provided in the womb.

If the premie is to have any chance at all of normal growth, it must have a greater than usual amount of tactile stimulation. As we shall see later, that stimulation has a direct effect on the growth of the cells in the brain. One study by Freedman, et al., of twins is instructive. These twins were of low birth weight (considered premature). One group of them was rocked and the other was not. The rocked group gained weight faster than the unrocked group.*

Denial of the baby's natural self is also accomplished by delayed birth—the baby cannot be allowed to do what comes naturally, be born at the proper time. Previously neurotic Primal mothers also feel that one way they rejected their children was to delay their entrance into the world because they did not feel ready to take care of them. One of the mothers said that she became pregnant so that *she* could be taken care of and she wanted to hold onto that state as long as possible. The very act of holding a baby back from being born is neurotogenic, foreshadowing, possibly, a more general retardation of the development of the baby by the mother.

The trauma of late birth is attested to by the fact that the mortality rate of late-term infants is twice as high as for normal ones. Because the head and pelvis are often larger than ordinary (due to the extra weeks of life inside), birth becomes more difficult and traumatic. In a very direct way, a mother who does not feel ready to be a mother, who is tight and constricted and tends to hold things in, may unconsciously hold her baby in too long.

The kind of research we need is to take measurements of the tension levels of pregnant women and then to correlate the amount of tension with the kind of birth which occurs. Do more tense women have delayed birth? Is higher tension in the mother associated with greater incidence of brain damage and other serious ailments in the child? Does it affect the mortality rate of the baby? We have evidence that such is the case in animal research. Pregnant rats who are fondled and stroked a lot during pregnancy have a greater number of surviving offspring than those rat mothers who are not touched.† Stroking evidently produces a feeling of well-being, a relaxed system which functions at optimum levels. Of course, humans are a bit more complicated, but I think that the principle is the same. If a mother had a lot of stroking and fondling when she was an infant, she will tend to be a more relaxed person with a more fluid, well-

* D. G. Freedman, H. Boverman, and N. Freedman, "Effects of Kinesthetic Stimulation on Weight Gain and Smiling in Premature Infants" (American Orthopsychiatry Association presentation, San Francisco, California, April 1960).

† J. Werboff, et al., "Handling of Pregnant Mice," *Physiology and Behavior*, 3 (1968): 35–39.

functioning system for her baby. The mother's experience as an infant helps set the stage for how she will do as a mother.

It is also important to know whether a pregnant woman's tension produces a greater likelihood of a colicky or eczemic baby. When we speak about tension, we are describing a total physiologic state of hormone output, muscle systems, blood systems, and so on. Tension is merely the term, the index for all these integrated physiologic systems. The reason that touching rat mothers changed the survival rate of their offspring is that the sensation of touch became elaborated physiologically, producing changes in many key systems.

Imbalance in the mother's hormone system may produce lifelong effects on the fetus. It may help determine how aggressive or passive the child's temperament is. Male hormones administered to pregnant primates resulted in more aggressive offspring than a control group of primates whose mothers did not have the hormone injections. The offspring were unusually aggressive, and this character trait seems to be lifelong. The point is that neurosis can accomplish a hormone situation in which there is an overabundance of androgen (male hormone) in the mother. One implication of this is that neonate females can be born unusually aggressive and masculinized so that they meet the world in a "tough" way. In humans this kind of situation may set the stage for later sexual deviation, such as lesbianism. Of course, many other social factors would have to be present for that to happen, but a general predisposition set up during gestation is a possibility.

It has been demonstrated, for example, that the female hormone estrogen administered just after birth to male rats feminizes them for a lifetime. That same hormone administered later on does not produce such changes. There are critical times when hormone imbalance can be catastrophic. Nature somehow understood all this, because during pregnancy in humans there is a sharp rise in progesterone levels. This is a key hormone which accomplishes many things—it tends to relax the mother, reduces the irritability of the uterus, and ultimately may help to moderately sedate the fetus. Its most important contribution, however, has been pointed out to me by Dr. Oscar Janiger.* He has searched the literature and dis-

* Personal communication, Dr. Janiger is administrator of psychiatric research, University of California, Irvine.

covered that rarely, if ever, has there been a psychotic episode (nervous breakdown) during pregnancy. However, the literature is replete with notations of postpartum psychosis—a time when progesterone levels drop radically. So automatically during pregnancy there is an inbuilt mechanism which gives the mother's defense system extra protection; this must be part of our survival mechanism —something that insures that the mother will stay sane during the time she carries and will give the baby the best chance at life.

There are reports that minor surgery has been done on individuals who have been given large doses of progesterone, which seems to act as an anesthetic.

And here we return to the Primal hypothesis. A chemical which diminishes the experience of Pain is secreted during pregnancy, and thereby bolsters the defense system. The absence of active psychosis during this time seems to indicate that this internal painkiller is an enormous help—further, that psychosis is related to undefended Pain. The vulnerability of the postpartum mother must in some way be attributed to lowered progesterone levels.

Progesterone has other functions, not the least of which is to help the differentiation into male or female. Here again, alterations in progesterone during pregnancy may shift that differentiation so that the neonate's basis orientation to life events is askew. Women who have had trouble keeping their babies during pregnancy have sometimes been given massive doses of progesterone (to quiet the uterus), which has resulted in masculinized female offspring (with excessive body hair, etc.). In other words, hormone changes in the mother do get transmitted to the fetus, and we must account for that when considering the origins of neurosis. We have been looking to genetics to provide the answers when we should have been studying the gestation period in minute detail.*

For example, I have pointed out that an excess of serotonin may produce spontaneous abortion or premature birth. Perhaps in some way body hormones such as progesterone may when released, feed back to the brain hormones such as serotonin and these hormones

---

* It is not entirely clear whether the enhanced defense system is a direct effect of progesterone increases or whether these increases have an effect on other biochemical elements.

then affect bodily processes. The body has a complex hormone chain, and interference or alteration in any part of the chain may ultimately affect the rest of it. If we do not look at the whole person, we may be misled into believing that a single hormone substance is the "cause" of this condition or that. I believe that neurosis distorts the entire interacting system, causing slight imbalances all down the line, which in turn may affect growth rate, hair development, sexual drive, blood sugar levels, and so on.* Progesterone may be only one part of an antipsychotic biochemical system which mediates defenses. Serotonin is another. In psychosis, for example, serotonin levels are depleted. Once we understand that defenses are not just what the mind does, such as project ideas onto others, but involve our complete neurochemistry, then we can see how neurosis affects the entire system.

Life in the uterus constitutes a relationship of mother to baby. It is not unlikely that a straight mother who is straight internally is going to have a better relationship to her fetus than a nonstraight one.

Helen

Last night in Group I had a very odd Primal where it felt like I was back in the womb, and I suddenly got a terrible jarring and I actually became slightly more conscious than is usual while in that phase of life. Today, just now, it comes to me what that Primal was all about. I remember my mother telling how when she was nine months pregnant with me she tripped over a croquet arch in the dark front yard late at night. She said she fell flat on her face and was immediately afraid she might have injured me, so she called her

---

* The manner in which neurosis alters hormonal output has been discussed in *The Anatomy of Mental Illness.* For those interested in a more technical discussion, I refer them to a new work, *The Neurobiology of the Amygdala*, a Bar Harbor, Maine, Symposium, Plenum Press. Evidence from this work indicates that the amygdala modulates the hormonal output of the hypothalamus and also may have a more direct effect on the endocrine system. Thus, when Pain is blocked by the limbic system (of which the hypocampus and amygdala are key structures), the energy of the blocked feeling is rechanneled back into the system via the hypothalamus, producing hormone-related diseases.

doctor and he assured her that I would be okay and that no injury would have occurred. I now realize that the Primal I had last night was a reliving of that experience. Toward the end of the Primal, after experiencing the feeling of being in the womb, which was like a total suspension of all thinking and bodily processes, even breathing, I suddenly felt a jolt which created in me a sharp awakening or forced awareness and accompanying pang of fear, and like a grabbing on to myself or a pulling inward of my body. And that was the end of the Primal. I lay there for awhile afterward totally unaware of time or place or anything else. In fact, if it hadn't been for that sudden, sharp jolt, I would never have been able to remember that being-in-the-womb feeling, because it was at such a deeply unconscious level. I might have, though, if I had simply fallen asleep. I know as a child I lapsed into this state often, and I later thought it was a way of escaping my pitiful childhood, but now I see it as my body trying to relieve that first original traumatic experience. The panicky feeling at the end of the Primal wasn't even a cognitive experience; it was purely a body response.

Another reaction to that "womb Primal" is that when as a child I would lapse into that state of being suspended or in a trance, it provided a way for me not to feel the Pain that my mother inflicted upon me; but once I was in that womb feeling for awhile, I would become intensely panicky and fearful and my body would clutch itself inward, probably in anticipation of that sharp jolt. I was the first-born also, which probably compounded her fear and apprehension.

Feeding was an immediate battle because I was breast-fed on a schedule rather than on demand. So, when I got hungry and showed my need by crying, I never got satisfaction from my efforts (crying). Instead, my feelings would come at what seemed to me like crazy times, either when I wasn't even hungry or when I was sleeping. My need and the actual meeting of the need (feeding) seldom were coordinated. They didn't match. When I experienced need, I didn't get, but when I didn't feel the need, I got. It just didn't make sense, it seemed crazy and confusing to me and like being out of synchronization with life at an early age. I realize now the same thing was true when I needed to be held and loved. I would show this need in the only way I could as an infant, by crying; and rather than being held or getting attention, my mother would get mad at me and leave me alone in my room. So you see, I would get what seemed to me like punishment for showing I needed, and my need would never get answered in the way I wanted, but rather it got answered in just the opposite way: by being left alone and isolated. No wonder I wanted to go back to the womb. But once I got back into the womb feeling, it wasn't safe there for long either, for that sharp jolt might occur at any time and I'd become anxious and fearful even there. That's how I remember my whole childhood, as being anxious and fearful *all the time*.

Other ways my mother hurt and crippled me were by being angry and spanking me a lot. She used to brag that I was the most spanked kid on the block. She was always afraid she'd spoil me. Well, let me tell you now that I know you can't spoil a kid by giving him too much love. I, in turn, used to spank my son liberally and scold him a lot, but I have finally gotten down to the bottom of that anger. A few weeks ago I had a Primal about getting mad at my son over some petty little thing, and as I was experiencing the anger it suddenly became much more intense, to the point where I was in a total state of rage. The anger at my son immediately became anger at my mother for all that I had to endure as a child. I now can see that whenever I feel anger in the present it is always triggered by old unexpressed anger at my mother from the past. My poor son has had to bear the brunt of far too much of this kind of anger, as I had to from my mother . . . and she had to from hers.

I could actually write a book-length report on the ways my mother fouled me up and the ways I did it to my son. To sum it all up, you can't be good parents if you are still hung up in your past, which most of us are.

III

Labor and Delivery

I have just discussed how the mother's condition can affect the child she is carrying inside her. The precursors of neurosis can begin soon after conception. The next critical point is the delivery itself. I am going to spend some time discussing labor and delivery because I believe that these processes frequently add not only quantitatively to neurosis, but produce qualitative leaps in terms of the amount of Pain and residual tension implanted in the system.

Childbirth is a rhythmical process. Labor pains have a rhythm to them; the fetus coming down the canal and out into the world is, by and large, part of an orderly sequential event—*when* birth takes place in a natural person in tune with her own bodily rhythms. Menstruation and gestation both are rhythmical. Rhythm is very much a part of human life. Neurosis is antirhythm. In neurosis, things no longer "flow." Life becomes fragmented and disjointed. And birth for neurotics often becomes an "unnatural" process—no longer smooth and flowing, but agonizing and disjunctive.

In the socialization process, a woman no longer has an instinctive birth as animals do. She has a "trained" birth. She is processed, taught, and prepared for something that should come naturally. The idea of producing an offspring naturally usually isn't even discussed. She is brought into the hospital and drugged so that she cannot fully participate in her own bodily processes during childbirth. She therefore does not flow with her own rhythms because she cannot feel her body. Her body cannot be used to "help" her newborn out of the canal. Often, it must be dragged out of her with the use of instruments. While all this is going on, the fetus is sensing disruptions in birth rhythms and is already out of rhythm with himself before he has seen the light of day. Thus, at birth, the newborn is no longer a naturally free-flowing organism. He is someone "held back" from being himself—from developing at his own natural pace. He has had to "defer" to the truncated, disjunctive rhythms of his mother.

So the first point to be made is that Pain takes place on different levels, some of which are conceptual and some of which are not. Physical Pain stays in the system just as any conceptualized Pain does. Secondly, Pain (discomfort) can begin in the uterus and become compounded during birth.

This does not mean that one experience, being held back at birth, will make a child thereafter deferent. It means that there exists in his *life* a crucial experience where he had to defer and that experience coupled with many more later experiences where he had to defer to another's needs may produce a deferent character structure. The initial birth experience may be prototypic of how the child will respond to stress later on. The notion of prototypic trauma and prototypic defense will be discussed in detail later on. What is important now is that we see that having a natural, flowing, uninterrupted childbirth is crucial if we are to avoid inculcating neurosis in a child.

The baby is nurtured in the uterus, a muscular sack which expands with the growth of the fetus. At a certain critical point, the fetus is expelled. The process is much the same as with other visceral organs, such as the bladder and the rectum. A person all tight inside may be chronically constipated and unable to respond to his natural rhythms. A "tight" mother may be unable to let go of her baby. We know that tension tightens muscle fibers and so it is to be expected that during neurotic birth the circular muscle fibers of the uterus may not be relaxed enough to permit free passage of the fetus into the vaginal canal. The vagina, too, is elastic, and under normal conditions should stretch to accommodate a rather large baby. But due to tension, there may be a "clamping down" instead of an "opening up." I am not talking about tension due to apprehension over childbirth. I am discussing residual tension in the mother's body—the load of Pain she customarily carries inside her which causes her to be a chronically tight person internally.

I am indicating that the great Pain of childbirth may be mostly a function of neurosis—of an unnatural system closing down against a natural process, in much the same way that Pain is produced when an unreal system shuts down against real feelings. Certainly, I can think of no other *natural* process which produces such Pain. Indeed, it would seem that being natural is what avoids Pain. Lack of flexibility in neurotics, then, is not simply a personality trait, but is a total neuromuscular event.

Persistent tension in the muscles of the uterus prevents relaxation between birth contractions. This slows down the flow of venous blood, thus inhibiting labor. The result of this is added pressure on the baby and a restricted oxygen supply. Both of these must have an affect on the newborn's system. In a kind of vicious cycle, neurosis produces Pain in the mother, which interferes with natural childbirth, thus producing more Pain and more interference; so labor is long because it is painful and painful because it is long.

CAESAREANS

Sometimes, labor is so difficult that a Caesarean operation is necessary to take the baby out. This again may traumatize the newborn, for the contractions during birth have a function—to stimulate the baby's skin, which in turn stimulates many crucial bodily systems, including the respiratory and genitourinary. Contractions serve much the same function as animals licking their young. Licking helps newborn animals in their use of their bowels and bladder.

One of the problems with both Caesarean and premature birth is the lack of physical stimulation. (Premature babies usually have shorter labor times). There is evidence that these babies do have more breathing problems and achieve sphincter and bladder control later than would be expected. "Hurrying" a baby out of the mother's body or delaying his departure both are inimical because they are out of rhythm. In many cases, I submit, these aberrations of natural birth are functions of neurosis in the mother, and by fiat of her neurotic system the baby is traumatized at birth and thus begins his own neurotic process.

There are critical times in our lives when needs must be met in order to avoid lifelong problems. One of the needs, I believe, is the compression and massive physical stimulation during birth . . . something lacking in Caesarean sections. I doubt that any later physical comfort or handling can erase that need. There is evidence, for example, that Caesarean babies are more emotionally disturbed than babies born normally.* They are more fearful and restless. In response to stimuli they tend to be more passive—which makes sense when we consider that they did not actively participate in their birth. A study of Caesarean-delivered infant monkeys showed this same passivity.† There are biochemical differences in Caesarean babies—lower serum proteins, etc. They have a higher mortality rate. In other words, being born naturally, at the proper time, is a developmental need, just like walking, and when that need is deprived or hindered, profound and permanent changes occur. Contraction of the uterus against the baby in order to expel it stimulates peripheral nerves, which in turn conduct impulses to the brain, which then affects all of the key systems of the body. Without that critical happening, there is inadequate activation of the nervous system. There are key times in the development of the brain when, in order for it to grow properly, it must receive certain kinds of stimulation. "Key times" is emphasized because if the kind of massive stimulation and compression which occurs at birth were to happen to the child at the age of three months, it might well be unwelcome and traumatic and produce a shutdown in the brain.

There is another way we know about the harm of Caesarean delivery; and that is by observing Primals in patients who were born in that manner. These birth Primals lack the fluid rhythm of the usual birth contractions. Their movements are more random and usually more violent than others. It is as though by their wild movements and thrashings they were trying to make up for some developmental deficit; their Primals seem to be trying to fill some biologic lacunae which occurred when they were robbed of the

* W. J. Pieper, et al., "Personality Traits in Caesarean–Normally Delivered Children," *Archives of General Psychiatry* 2 (1964): 466–71.
† G. W. Meier, "Behavior of Infant Monkeys: Differences Attributable to Mode of Birth," Science 143 (1964): 968–70.

compression of normal birth. They never got their initial "rhythm" experience; they lacked that initial experience which would have primed their bodies. In this sense, it is just as Primal in the Pain it produces as being strangled by the cord at birth. As one Caesarean patient put it: "Ever since that birth experience I have been waiting for something big to happen. Each new day I thought that a key phone call was going to change my life. Now I know what big experience I have been waiting for."

What we are learning is that Pains are produced by the *omission* of events; that is, depriving a child of a necessary developmental experience can be just as catastrophic as overloading him with too much of an experience. Thus, breech birth and Caesarean birth both contribute to neurosis in their own way.

One Caesarean Primal patient told me that when he had his birth Primal, he felt wrenched "out," not up or down. He felt disoriented because at birth he had no concept of up or down, simply feeling that he was jerked out of a safe matrix into space. He remembered being overwhelmed by people falling in space in the movie *2001*. When the little girl, Kathy Fiscus, fell into a well some years ago, he could not sleep from anxiety. He had to know if she could be safely pulled out. After his Primal he understood his anxiety very well. In a sense, the absence of a necessary experience remained in his system, producing specifically related, though unconscious, anxieties later on.

Birth itself is not necessarily traumatic to the newborn unless the birth process is traumatic. It isn't as though the fetus has an idyllic life inside and is rudely thrust out of his "cocoon" one day against his will. Rather, coming into the world is part of the development of life. It is a stage in growth, comparable to sitting up and walking. We wouldn't think that the change from being carried around serenely to having to propel ourselves around this earth was traumatic; nor should we consider the change from total dependency on the mother to partial dependency as intrinsically upsetting.

So much of the current "natural" childbirth movement has to do with diverting women away from their Pain. While natural childbirth notions represent a giant leap ahead, I think we should not overlook the fact that we cannot entirely train away inner Pains in a neurotic mother, allowing for truly natural childbirth.

Perhaps the belief that Pain is endemic in any childbirth has led the movement toward the avoidance of Pain. Certainly, there is discomfort in childbirth, but there is no reason why in normal mothers they could not be encouraged to "go with" that discomfort, to feel whatever Pain there is and to scream out their agony if it exists. I reiterate: agony and screams occur when something real has to be wrenched out of an unreal system; whether feelings or a baby, I think the principle is the same. Training does help but we must not delude ourselves that we can "train" a neurotic to be normal and be without inner Pain. It is a contradiction in terms to "train someone to be natural."

Better to have a labor room full of screaming women than a room filled with docile, drugged mothers who are deprived of experiencing the most important event in their lives: the birth of their child. It is not only a nice "ideal" to keep mothers off anesthetic, but many patients who have undergone birth Primals report feeling numbed at some critical point in their labor process and have Primals where they come out more dead than alive, totally unaware of what has happened to them. Instead of entering this world alive and bouncy, full participants in their birth process, they arrive "fogged and numb." (more on this later)

An orientation to "going with" pain for neurotic mothers helps uncomplicate the birth process and avoids some of the neurotogenic factors for the child. If women knew they should scream freely, some of the guilt and tension might be eased. What happens instead is that mothers are encouraged to "be brave," "act their age," and so on. They get into a literal "double bind." They are in Pain and need to scream out, and then they are in Pain again from suppressing the expression of the original Pain. This suppression compounds the tension and adds to the trauma of birth. Just the screams would aid relaxation, and there would be less over-all Pain, not more. Pain would be much more tolerable if expressed. Stiffening against its expression is harmful.

Doctors need to fight off their own reflexive use of painkillers whenever they hear shrieks. They, too, need to "go with" a mother's pain. These painkillers help keep the tension inside, and so many of the subsequent Pains surrounding birth, the headaches and backaches, for example, may be the result of tension suppression, either from the disapproval of hospital personnel or from the drugs given to the mother to "calm" her down. The price one must always pay for suppression is a later reaction. Suppression means that there is an ascending force, and that force, when bottled up, must find outlets.

Madelyn

Today I have made a connection that has plagued, troubled and depressed me for six and a half years! After my crying and screaming over the horror of my baby's death and experiencing some of the sadness, and then the misery that has come over my relating to her, my body went into the position of delivery. I had hard pains in my abdomen and my legs spread apart and my hands and arms came down and my body pushed and experienced some of the pains of labor. Then like someone had flicked on a light bulb in my mind the connection was made: I was induced into labor when my little girl was born and never experienced any of the labor because my doctor gave me Scopolamine which is a memory block-out drug. I was awakened in the recovery room not having had any of the *good, normal* pain of bringing a baby into the world. They [the doctors] deprived me of my pain by blocking out my memory and therefore I went into a severe mental depression after my baby was born. With my other three children I could feel and experience their births fully. It has always been my pattern that unfelt pain leads itself into depression.

For me there's no such thing as postpartum depression; my depression was caused by drugs which kept me from feeling. The repressed, *un*experienced pain of labor due to the drugs caused a severe depression to occur. I was already very close to my pain when I became pregnant, for a good friend's child had been killed and she went into her pain. Seeing and being with her brought mine dangerously close to the surface. Then to be deprived of my labor gave me an *over*load of *un*felt pain and spiraled me into a depression.

IV

The Birth Primal

What we in Primal Therapy know about the relationship of birth traumas and later neurosis comes from observing, recording, and filming many birth Primals.* A patient may be reliving an experience of helplessness at school at the age of seven and suddenly find himself having a birth Primal involving a feeling of helplessness. That early Primal tells us a great deal about his later reactions to situations and whether they will be neurotic or not. Birth Primals leave little question as to the powerful effect of early physical trauma on later general behavior. I lay such stress on birth trauma not because it alone "causes" neurosis, but because looking back from the point of view of birth Primals we can see what a tremendous impact these traumas have in terms of laying down stored tension. Their contribution to neurosis is much more than we have previously thought existed. That contribution is not a "theory" I made up but derives from seeing how many Primals it takes just to resolve that single trauma. Also, the amount of systemic blockage involved in birth traumas can be inferred from observing the great psychophysical changes which take place in patients once they are through those experiences in Primal Therapy.

Otto Rank built an entire theoretical system out of the birth trauma, which he believed to be universal. Essentially, it was believed that birth was intrinsically traumatic because a child was being ejected out into a hostile environment. Leaving the security

* For a full description of a Primal, see *The Primal Scream*.

41

of the womb, according to birth-trauma theorists, is in itself over-whelming. Births are traumatic when they are traumatic and only then—strangulation by the cord, breech birth, excessive labor time. Birth can be harmful when excessive pressure with forceps has been applied. These traumas, combined with subsequent physical and psychological hurts, produce an eventual overload and a split or disconnection. Perhaps the most frequent birth trauma is inordi-nately long labor. I have discussed the concept of disconnection in my previous works. Basically, overload means that a feeling is so painful that it cannot be smoothly integrated into the system. Therefore, there is a disconnection between consciousness of the feeling and the feeling itself. That is, consciousness is split and the person becomes unaware of his hurts.

We have had two births in Primal mothers and both were quick and easy. I can only assume that this wasn't fortuitous, but the re-sult of a relaxed mother who psychophysiologically welcomed her infant into the world and caused it no struggle. One can imagine the trauma laid down in the nervous system of a neonate who has been struggling some twenty to thirty hours to get out. We need not imagine it, however, since we have seen patients twisting, hunching, and thrashing in these Primals which go on for hours at times. They are completely exhausted after the experience, and some patients finish up feeling "depleted" and connect that feeling to the one of being constantly exhausted throughout life, scarcely having enough energy to undertake any difficult task. A number of Primals have to do with being strangled by the cord; and still others involve breech birth.*

What we have seen thus far is that a mother's neurosis is a literal adversity for the fetus. Just to come alive he must overcome it. He is in the struggle before he breathes his first breath. No matter how many facts are in her head, no matter how well-trained she is for childbirth, her neurosis will put the fetus in the struggle. If a mother has shut down and repressed many different kinds of early traumas of her own, and if those repressions are mediated by a tense musculature, then when Pain strikes again in childbirth, the

* For a full description of birth trauma relived during birth Primals, see descriptions by patients in Appendices A and B.

musculature (of which the uterus and vaginal canal are a part) will automatically respond by clamping down. This is particularly true of frigid women who respond sexually by "closing down." It is my observation that women who have had sexual problems, who defend automatically in sexual situations by constriction, will suffer longer labor times.

Some Primal mothers believe that when they started into labor, their rhythmical contractions set off their own original birth pains and the subsequent shutdown which occurred back then. So we might say that one way to insure a good delivery in a pregnant woman is for her to have had a good birth herself. If the mother did have a traumatic birth, then she will have to relive it in order to be free enough to produce a good delivery of her own.

No birth Primals are ever trammeled by words. There are only groans and grunts and, finally, upon birth, the infantile wail. The birth trauma is set down into the nervous system even before the development of those critical areas of the brain which could interpret the experience. No wonder then that it remains an unconscious force. What then is trauma? Any amount of Pain that cannot be smoothly integrated into the system; a quantity of Pain that overloads our integrative capacities, causing fragmentation and disintegration. The surplus that cannot be integrated becomes stored tension.

Tension, then, is a feeling disconnected from consciousness. Consciousness need not mean something conceptualized, such as "I am afraid." It can be strictly a physical experience of which we are aware; the awareness of sensation. When the sensation, such as birth Pain, becomes overwhelming, consciousness (and sensation) is blunted. That is why we say that neurotics do not feel. What they do feel is gradations of tension. Actually, there is no such thing as "neurosis." Neurosis is a term, an interpretation we put on people who have split away from feeling many of their early experiences and who are therefore left with significant degrees of tension. For each feeling not felt the person has become a less-feeling "neurotic." That is, each repression of experience widens the gap between what is real and the amount of symbolic, unreal behavior adopted. The degree of neurosis depends on the amount of real

Pain repressed; and this is measured by the amount of residual tension in the body. The higher the tension level, the more repressed feelings there are.

Repressed birth Pain often shows itself early in life in the form of agitation or irritability. The young child cannot sit still, or he is cranky most of the time unless he is soothed by constant holding and rocking. But the soothing is only ameliorative, like a tranquilizer. It cannot remove the early Pain. After a patient has had his birth Primals he is no longer automatically irritable. *The point is that we defend against preverbal and preconscious hurts just as we defend against remembered ones. Defenses are automatic and reflexive, not choices we make.*

Indeed, there is very little difference subjectively between the preconscious physical hurt we have experienced and the postconscious psychological ones we have. The Pains are felt in much the same way; that is, the *experience* of Pain is mediated by the same physiological and neurological processes. It doesn't matter, for example, whether one hurts from a feeling of "Don't be mad at me, Daddy!" or "Why can't you hold me, Momma?" The subjective experience would be similar, only the mental labels change. The hurt is unfulfilled need, and that is what causes the agony.

The following is a case history of an actor, who was delivered three weeks prematurely. It is instructive in terms of the profound effects the premature delivery had on the most diverse kinds of social behavior—from what career he chose, acting (to merge into someone else), to why he was impotent (he wasn't ready to grow up). Wrenched prematurely out of his mother left him "not ready" for life. He was continuously acting out, trying to get back to that "safe place" . . . trying once again to be "part of." That one great trauma robbed him, in the most existential sense, of his identity. He was "her," never fully him. He woke up in the middle of the night (when undefended) feeling female. Initially he could only feel in therapy when he could live through the feelings of some female in group. Here we see the profound effects very early trauma has on sex life. He truly felt "impotent" and helpless since that birth and that impotence was reflected in his social life, where he was a "loser," to his sex life where he was also inadequate.

Brian

According to my parents, I was premature by three weeks.

I woke up this morning with pains in my neck and shoulders. My left hand was partially paralyzed; I couldn't move my fingers. As I lay in bed, I could hear a high-pitched noise inside my head—like there was too much pressure inside. Gradually I could move my fingers, but I felt exhausted and slightly nauseous. I felt as I had for a few months now—paralyzed socially and unable to let go and to sink into my birth feelings.

I walked around, ate something, sat down and listened to some music, John Lennon's Plastic Ono Band, which I had bought a few days before. Periodically I would lie down on the living-room floor and try to sink into the feelings. I got up and went into my little soundproof room. I began thinking of a girl in therapy with whom I have often struggled. I began feeling I was she and that if I were she, I'd want to have my own friends and not have to share them with her (my) daughter, Jean. I had to tell this to Lynda, who remained in the living room. When I told her "I felt I was the girl from group," Lynda commented (as she had in the past) that it was so easy for me to absorb myself into other people—be another person—by imitation or feelings. (I'm an actor.) The pressure in my neck and shoulders increased—as did the nausea. I lay down on the floor and started to quiver; then my hands and arms, feet and legs started to flap around uncontrollably (like I was a puppet on a string). My limbs felt almost weightless. I didn't know what was happening. I was sinking deeper into it; the spasms and flapping increased. I was a very tiny thing not fully formed, but I was moving, being tossed around mercilessly. I felt relieved somewhat that at last after months of paralysis I was moving.

After an hour or so I pulled myself off the living-room floor and staggered into the Primal room. I sank deeper and yet earlier into my birth. Now I felt even smaller, something very primitive, like in the pictures of the fetus at six or seven months I had seen in the book *A Child is Born*. I felt almost as tiny as a rat. But something was happening. There was no me. I was feeling that I was her. That these quiverings and spasms were really her and that she was trying to force me into existence. I didn't want it! I hated it! Terror! Screams! I only had known myself as *her*. At least that's where I was at when the spasms struck. So that I felt there was something new about her I was becoming aware of. Before I had only known her from this tube that went from the middle of me to her and from the warm liquid of her I had lived in. Now I had to know her from the outer limits of me, and yet even with the quivering and spasms, I couldn't tell where I left off and she began or where I began and she left off. But why did I have to learn this? Why? I didn't ask for this! The spasms and the flopping increased, and I found that to survive soon I would have to assume and feel that it *was* me. She was making me be me even though I didn't want it. All right, if I have to be me, I've got to get out. I had to be me, but I didn't want to be me. As I flopped about, like on a rough sea with no control over movement, I felt terror and helplessness. I screamed and screamed—this time for her to recognize me. Later on I yelled out to Lynda, who was sitting by the door, "Do you know what's happening to me?" She replied, "I have no idea." I screamed, "You have no idea? You have no idea? Unbelievable!!" The feeling swept over me that mother had no idea what was happening and what was happening to me right then and there. I was being tossed around violently and she couldn't feel me, feel what was happening. Incredible! She couldn't even feel her own body. (She was drugged.) I was scared I might die. I had to be me if I was going to stay alive. I had to get out and be my own boss from then on. Now it was me, really me coming out. I screamed and screamed. I felt my neck choking, and I was still a tiny, undeveloped thing. Something was around my neck, and I could feel my head coming through an opening into cold. I was choking on fluids and there were hands around my neck. A big gasp—and then a terrible pain in my chest. My chest was going up and down, and with each movement—terrible pain. Breathing with my lungs! Awful! I screamed and screamed with each new gasp. I never asked for this. Why do I have to do this? It was so painful being out—alive, breathing. I felt I didn't have the strength to keep up this breathing. Would I ever get beyond the pain of breathing to feel where I was, what was happening to me? I lay there for a long time screaming, wheezing, hoping I could keep up with the air going into my body, feeling great pain in my lungs with each new breath. (After a while thoughts came into my head: "I'm out. I'm alive.) I still felt the longing, though, to be back where I belonged.

As I was coming out of the Primal, I dreamed of looking at the flowers and the trees, taking a walk in the night air to really see the earth for the first time. (The Primal started at 1:30–1:45 in the afternoon, and it was already dark.) I had been Primaling for nearly seven hours. I called Art. Art answered the phone. The pain along with the speed of breathing increased. I was mixed with elation along with pain as I told Art that I was born. Art said, "Sounds like you're still in it." He was right (or was it a cue from my mother?).

I staggered back to the room and sank back into the quivering and spasms. I was back inside struggling to get out. Then the hands on my neck, the choking, the cold and light (this time), the gasps and the awful pain of breathing—using my lungs for the first time (with the fear, "Would they hold out?"). I screamed again with all of my guts. That felt good. I lay there feeling I didn't want anything but *to get used to breathing so the pain would stop*. I found myself so into *just trying to make my body work*. Later on, as I came out of the Primal, I joked with Lynda how silly it is to breathe, to have to use your lungs (what a strange planet!). I looked at the plants in the apartment and felt a comradery with life struggling to live. Also, I felt "How could I have eaten meat all these years?"

During portions of the Primal, the haunting, driving pulses of John Lennon's song, *Remember*, augmented and blended with the spasms and the quivering. For me those beginning spasms bringing me into chaos and confusion were the beginning of time for me, time I wasn't ready for. For me, Lennon's song is about the beginning of it all for me. On my way out, too, I felt the feelings in his song: "Don't feel sorry for the way it's gone; don't you worry for what you've done." I was sorry, but that's the way it *did* go! The fifth of November—a bomb explosion—was really March sixth, my birthday.

Even though I'm out, I still long to be where I was when the shock came, which was then to be her, a part of her, sucking her through my umbilical cord. For the past thirteen years I have been conscious of trying to feel my body (also, I have been mostly impotent, without real sexual feeling through these years), but underneath it all, I didn't really want to. This created a struggle for me in therapy, too—a struggle to get into my body.

Before therapy the only escape from this pain was masturbation (which didn't happen easily), pornography (watching), voyeurism (I was a compulsive "Peeping Tom" until age twenty-four), smoking, and sleep. I slept a lot in the past few years, often falling asleep with my clothes on after returning home to my one-room apartment after work. While teaching spaced-out, home-bound, handicapped kids, I lost myself in them and the role I was playing. I often found myself falling asleep while with them.

Within the past ten years I've awakened in the middle of the night feeling that I was a woman with tits and a cunt—horrified. Often, too, I'd be fearful of wearing clothes that were too feminine. In feeling movies I often cry with the sorrow and loneliness of the female characters (this is a recent insight). I've often found relief in sinking into imitations of well-known personalities (Frank Sinatra, John Kennedy) or someone I know—this for others or for me alone. When acting in plays, I became the character, even offstage. I've often dreamed of being like other people, if not being them.

Whenever someone whom I like grows to like me, I have found reasons to flee. I've often gotten people to like me and then I space out, or bust them, or just split to be alone (afraid of being straight with them, too). Often I find (more recently) I am absorbing myself into their rhythms, personality—becoming them. Before Therapy, going to a party or on a date spaced me out. I often spent a lot of money on dates without feeling it. I could only look forward to walking the streets of New York alone looking for whores or pornography shops or going home to smoke and sleep. In high school, even after a date with a girl, I felt driven to look in windows.

In group (therapy), it's often hard to sink into my own feelings and Primals (at least it's been that way for the last few months). Someone else's feelings or Primals pull me away. My biggest Primals have occurred in the presence of one or two other people who weren't into their own feelings.

Most of my struggles with my mother in my early life seem to have something to do with not being ready to take the next step or to do what she requested. I wouldn't eat solid food until after two years of age (this I did after compulsory training at a baby's hospital for ten days at the age of two). I refused to learn how to walk until I was eighteen months. Again, I never asked for this. Also, I never felt my mother knew what was happening to me.

Even when into deep feelings, in Primals, I didn't quite believe it was happening to me, to *my* body. Now I'm really beginning to connect up why. All during this Primal, I *was* my feeling.

PROTOTYPIC PRIMAL TRAUMA

What is the significance of the birth Primal? It tells us a good deal about the way experience later in life will be handled. Birth trauma may be a significant factor in the development of neurosis. The birth struggle may be *prototypic* of how the person will respond to a situation of threat later on. This can only be true if the birth event was indeed traumatic.

The concept of prototypic Primal trauma and its ubiquitous companion, prototypic defense, is important in understanding later neurotic responses to stress. In another work (*The Anatomy of Mental Illness*), I pointed out that congestion by fluids during a protracted labor and birth could cause the neonate to reflexively constrict his bronchioles in order to save his life. That experience becomes frozen in time (in the form of a Primal memory circuit) so that any later stress which is life-endangering or is interpreted as life-threatening—an argument between one's parents which is violent and portends divorce—will automatically set off the prototypic trauma and its defense of constricted bronchioles. The result may be an asthmatic attack. Instead of the organism being saved by this defense, as it was at birth, it is in danger of death from the attack. This, in essence, is neurosis: a defense that has outlived its function. The asthma occurs because the parents' argument sets off the original, Primal trauma at birth.

In the case of asthma, we can only talk about cure (in this example) when key prototypic traumas which set the constriction defense in motion are relived and resolved.

Jeff

I've had asthma all my life. Just before I started therapy I was in the Veterans Hospital, and when I was there, I was getting a lot of different medicine for it—shots of adrenalin (.3 cc's), amenopheline (intravenous and suppositories). Since I started therapy I've been taking both Choledyl and Tedrol. At night I take Tedrol S.A. I included all this as sort of credentials to establish myself as an expert in my field, choking.

On the last day of my three-week period of individual therapy I had a Primal. I'll try and describe it. I had taken my medicine that morning before I went to the Institute, and when I arrived there I wasn't wheezing. I lay on the floor and started to tell my therapist about this phone conversation I'd had with my girlfriend. I missed her, I thought about her all the time, and I couldn't wait to see her again. I had asked her out and she had said yes, and we were going to go to a show. But I don't have a job or any money and my parents are sending me money. When I started talking about my money situation, Bob said, "Why don't you sell your truck?" As soon as he said that, I tensed up and I said so. He said, "Yeah, I noticed." "I thought about getting an old VW," I said. "They cost too much; why not an old junker?" "Why bother, it's such a hassle . . . it's better with something . . ." I was getting real uncomfortable. "I don't want nothin' . . . (I started crying) . . . I want something . . . it's nicer with something . . . (more crying and I had started to wheeze and I felt just like a little kid) . . . I want it . . . don't take my trucks . . . Guy . . . Guy . . . don't take my toys, I won't have anything if you take 'em . . ."

Then I thought of Daddy. "Daddy, Daddy . . ." I pictured myself in a crib and my daddy was standing over me, and I reached up for him and he just sneered at me and walked out of the room (heavy wheezing and I had begun to sweat plus some coughing). "I didn't do anything . . . my daddy doesn't love me, he hates me, he wants me to die." Then I screamed. Just before I screamed I had started to choke, but as soon as I screamed, the choking went away and the sweating went away and I was comfortable again.

The scream was like a shot of adrenalin, only faster. The adrenalin usually takes anywhere from two to five minutes to work. The scream did it immediately.

My reactions to the whole thing are centered not so much with the breathing thing as with the train of thought—my daddy doesn't love me, he doesn't want me, he wants me to die. I instinctively fight that sort of childish feeling, it's dumb, what a stupid thing to say, etc. All my life that sort of thing was met with scorn until I "learned" that the only way to make it was to try and be something else, something acceptable, something more sophisticated, something more grown-up, anything except what I was—a little boy.

Now, prototypic traumas can be psychological as well as physical. However, the physical traumas are crucial because they usually occur so early in life and are often in reality life-endangering. But one patient who had a normal birth came home from nursery school one day to find his parents were not getting along. They were totally indifferent to him that afternoon; he was four years old at the time. This was a terrible shock because ordinarily they were happy to see him. It turned out to be a prototypic trauma in which he spent years trying to make people happy to see him. He became an ambulance driver because it was a situation where everywhere he went people were happy to see him.

It may seem an unwarranted extrapolation to connect ambulance driving with that early experience. But the connection was made during a Primal about that nursery school. It was set off by a situation in which someone was not glad to see him on his ambulance rounds. We must remember that the early trauma sets off an overload which keeps it unintegrated into the system. The system thereafter keeps trying to master that situation. So, earlier he delivered papers in order to make others happy to see him. Later it was ambulance driving. The connection between those decades of time was an encapsulated Primal trauma.

One more example of a prototypic response: One patient came

in one day feeling giggly. Just before he got into any hurtful feeling he would giggle. It was only when the therapist blocked those giggles that the energy of them turned into sobs and tears. As the patient got deeper into his feelings, he relived scenes from his first year of life when his father was playing with him by throwing him up in the air over his head and catching him. The baby was terrified, but could not express it; so he giggled out of anxiety. This kind of play went on for many months and traumatized the infant, who was powerless to stop it. Thereafter, any fear would set off the giggles. When a feeling would come up that would be embarrassing, the child would giggle instead of cry or show fear. Giggling became a prototypic response. It lasted all the way into adulthood.

In the past week I have seen two Primals which produced very different prototypic responses. The first was a female patient who relived the first days after birth of being unattended, except to be fed by bottle every few hours. She "decided" to "tough it out." Obviously, it was not a conscious decision, but the organismic response was to act as though she didn't need anything or anyone. We shall see in a moment how this early trauma dictated so much of her life.

Another patient relived a scene in the crib. (We put him in the crib at our Institute.) The therapist left him in the dark and went out of the room. When she returned, he had fallen asleep. This pattern was repeated several times over the next few Primal sessions until he could finally bear the Pain and feel it, instead of using a sleep defense. The feeling was of being left unattended to cry it out in his crib time after time and being slapped when he cried. He became a "good boy" and stopped crying out his needs; instead he feel asleep. The insight after he could bear the Pain of the feeling was that his prototypic response to later trauma, particularly rejection, was to take the passive way out. His prototypic response was shaped for him. He was left almost no alternative behavior other than sleep. It took many Primals to get to this feeling because it happened so early and so many times that the Pain was shattering. We had to allow him his defenses and proceed slowly.

Another example of a psychological prototypic trauma is illustrated in a Primal by a former call girl. She relived the time in her crib, very young, when she was given crayons and she put them into her vagina. Her grandmother slapped her very hard and said "Bad girl!" This memory was lost until she had been in Primal Therapy for over one year. She realized afterward that the trauma had set a fixed response in her; namely, to use her vagina to be "bad." Obviously, it wasn't that one event that turned her into a call girl later. But that event together with being molested at age five by an uncle, plus a general home atmosphere where parts of the body were dirty and bad, plus no love and affection from her father while she was growing up all helped turn her to prostitution. The use of her vagina, however, was a prototypic response whenever she was going to be "bad" later on.

There are many things which go into prototypic responses. A particular kind of nervous system (fast firing, for example), which I believe can be inherited; experiences prior to the event, such as intrauterine events which shape later behavior; and the kind of alternatives permitted during the prototypic trauma itself. But once the response is made during a prototypic trauma, it develops a force all its own which remains and tends to become fixed and persevering.

Anita

When I learned that my mother was having shock treatments, I felt very lonely and abandoned. As I began to feel that loneliness, it suddenly occurred to me that my father was dead and my mother was as good as dead, so there was no one for me. My feeling of abandonment went back to when I was just born and my mother wasn't there to hold me and reassure me, as she didn't want anything to do with me after the "ordeal" she had just been through. I wouldn't have my father to hold me for another five days and, as he was the only one who knew how to take care of me, I had nothing for those five days. I got born by not giving up, no matter what happened. I learned in birth that by pushing harder, I could make it. Therefore, in those five days of deprivation I got tough rather than give up, which is the lesson I had learned in my birth struggle.

My toughness has shown itself in many ways in my life. I have always taken care of myself and have never looked to others for any help of any kind. I don't expect anything from anyone, and I don't ask for favors of any kind. If I don't have something I want, I either get it myself or do without it, but I never look to someone else to supply it for me. I keep people I don't know at a distance and am cold and unapproachable if I feel that they are threatening to me. I only warm up and show myself when I feel safe with a person. I cannot lie, because if I lie then I am in the wrong and at the other person's mercy to punish me as he pleases. I have always been very careful never to step out of line for that very reason. If I am hurt, I don't let on in any way to the person who has hurt me that whatever he said or did had any effect on me whatsoever. I never cried in front of my parents when scolded or punished by them. In this connection I have noticed that when Jodey would bust me for something, I would let him finish and then change the subject and go on as if nothing had been said. I would feel it when he wasn't around, but I couldn't let him see that I had heard him. I couldn't let my daddy see that he could get me.

My father reinforced my prototypic behavior by rewarding me for never giving up and castigating me for showing any signs of weakness. I once took a music appreciation class and, as I am tone deaf, I had incredible difficulty with it and worked twice as hard as anyone else. He saw me struggle through it and he kept telling me not to take it so hard, that it wasn't worth so much pain. However, when I brought him my report card and showed him the "A" I got in that class, his face softened and lit up and he said, "See what happens when you just keep trying harder and never give up!" He never gave up either; he was rewarding me for his own behavior.

One major reason for the stability of defenses, the "characteristic personality," is that the system continues to defend against the early, internalized Pains. These Pains overload the system at the time of trauma and "fixate" the person in terms of how he will handle stress. So, a child rejected in the schoolyard may have an asthmatic attack. We each differ on where we first feel a twinge of anxiety when we are upset. Some of us get "butterflies in the stomach," others get a tightness in the chest or a shortness of breath. I believe those areas are prototypic and indicate where the first major trauma of our lives took place. Being starved in the crib, for example, may make the stomach a target organ for all later stress, just as suffocation at birth may cause us to feel the first felt anxiety in the chest and respiratory system.

The overload event becomes the key repository for all similar traumas which occur later. They are connected neurologically and stored together as associated memory circuits. For example, enduring a long, arduous labor where the neonate must "wait" an intolerable length of time to get out may be reactivated later whenever the child has to wait for anything—waiting in line, waiting for dinner, etc. His reactions will be terrible anxiety and impatience all out of keeping with the current waiting situation because the original trauma has been triggered. When it is set off, the *entire unit* of waiting experiences will be activated as well. That is why feeling the first prototypic trauma sets off all the later associations with it.

There is not a single prototypic experience. There can be many kinds of early traumas. A birth trauma can be followed by inadequate breast feeding where the child is systematically starved for weeks. The trauma would be in the area of the mouth and possibly caused by a curtailing of the time needed for sucking. The need to suck, coupled with later deprivation of father's love, could turn into homosexuality and the need to suck penises. Of course, I am simplifying the thousands of daily experiences that also contribute to the problem, but homosexuality in such a person could not be reversed until the person felt his great need for his father and the early need for sucking. The notion that he could be urged to go straight without feeling those experiences is specious. Having any number of heterosexual experiences or having a "big brother" to help out will also not undo that history. If a child were to deceive himself and go straight in order to please his mother or a therapist, he would be made doubly sick by being forced to pretend that his needs do not exist. Sucking for this kind of homosexual is a prototypic Primal need. No *analysis* of that need can eradicate it, and that is doubly true of trying to punish that habit away.

Let us take another example of prototypic trauma—circumcision.

Circumcision traumatizes the child in the genital area. We know this from observing dozens of Primals about it. A tyrannical mother combined with circumcision at the age of one or two can produce first, an anxiety about the genitals, and secondly, fear of the use of genitals in relationships with females. Again, I am simplifying to make the point about prototypic experience. Circumcision may later come to be interpreted as punishment so that sexual desires activate fear and produce impotence. The added physical trauma at a very critical age may be one significant factor in determining why one person with a tyrannical mother becomes homosexual, while another does not, given the same kind of mother.

Let us examine a case of an epileptic who suffered from seizures for years and who recently entered therapy. During the first week of treatment he went into a birth Primal where he felt his head crashing against something. After two hours of this Primal he began wailing like a newborn. He later explained that his was a very hard and long labor and that his mother told him he came out wailing. The impact of the pressure on his head in trying to get born may not have been physiologically traumatic, but it certainly was the focal point of a psychological trauma. After a few months of life, when he was left alone in the crib without being fed or picked up, he began head-banging against the end of his crib. In his teens he began seizure activity.

Since the day he entered therapy he has not had a single seizure, despite the fact that he took no Dilantin from his first day. What does this mean? One thing that it means is that the tension set up *at birth* was significant in terms of its over-all contribution to his general tension level later on. The high level of tension would spill over into an epileptic symptom, focused in the key area of his early trauma, much in the same way that patients develop a skin rash under adult stress—that is, they develop a symptom in the area of early trauma (in the latter case, the trauma was that of not being touched sufficiently in the earliest months of life) under any stress situation.

If the epileptic had had a decent early life, he could have had a birth trauma and never developed epileptic symptoms. The *sum total* of all the traumas produced the overload. It is my observation, however, that birth traumas carry a large valence in their contribution to the general level of chronic tension. This is partly due to the newness and fragility of the organism in terms of its ability to cope with stress, and, most importantly, because birth traumas are often life and death matters—a neonate strangling on the umbilical cord will really die unless something is done. This life-and-death struggle goes on in many of us even before we come into this world.

The tension resulting from a birth trauma can be so catastrophic that effective psychologic functioning is no longer a possibility, as in the case of infantile autism. The autistic child syndrome has baffled experts because they have found neither organic brain damage to account for the child's total inability to relate to those around him, nor have they discovered a particularly deleterious psychologic environment as a major cause. After all, in households with autistic children other siblings are often fairly well adjusted. One would imagine that a home environment so terrible as to produce infantile autism would also adversely affect the other siblings.

What the experts may have overlooked is a shattering birth experience which encased the infant deep into Primal Pain, rendering him unable to function. That is, there is massive suffering continuously going on, but the youngster has no way to understand or conceptualize it. He is too immersed in his trauma to help himself out of it. He will need to relive that trauma in small measured doses under the guidance of a Primal expert.

Here is what a research investigator wrote in the *Journal of the American Medical Association*: "The hazards confronting the fetus mount to a climax during the hours of labor. Birth is the most endangering experience to which most individuals are ever exposed. The birth process, even under optimal, controlled conditions, is a traumatic, potentially crippling event for the fetus."* Towbin, the investigator, goes on to say, "Cerebral damage present at birth frequently is incurred latently, often in the period prior to delivery." His point is that subtle brain damage occurs more often than we think and derives from hazardous (because it is neurotic, in my

---

* Abraham Towbin, "Organic Causes of Minimal Brain Dysfunction," *Journal of the American Medical Association* 217, no. 9 (August 30, 1971): 1213.

view) birth processes. He believes that one central reason for the damage is hypoxia, or deficient oxygen supply.*

As a result of many autopsy studies, hidden lesions were found in deep brain structures in many premature newborns. The point Towbin is making is that deficient oxygen can have subtle effects which only show up later under additional stress; and the kind of effect which occurs will depend upon which brain cells were affected at birth. It may be in later speech, in emotional instability, or in the inability to think abstractly.

At the 1971 meeting of the Society for Neuroscience, a Los Angeles psychologist, Virginia Johnson, reported on her studies, which included analysis of more than 25,000 hours of interviews. She found that patients given a drug, methlyphenidate, were able to recall experiences from the first weeks of life. Such recall, she said, was frequently related to neurotic symptoms later in life. She believed that certain of these experiences were schizophrenogenic— contributing factors in the development of later psychosis. "The experiences that most often correlated with symptoms of schizophrenia tended to involve a deep or extended altered state of consciousness shortly before or after birth."†

She found that specific behavioral patterns manifested by schizophrenics were determined by the nature of the original trauma. "This," she says, "is because the disorganization experienced during one of these states is imprinted on the memory and is thus subject to recall under the proper conditions." I believe that those conditions are what occur in Primal Therapy. What she indicates is that there are many different kinds of traumas which are schizophrenogenic and that these later determine the kind and quality of the psychosis, indicating, quite properly, that psychosis is not a single, monolithic entity but is variegated.

Dr. Johnson believes that auditory hallucinations, for example, derive from certain prenatal auditory experiences of the fetus. She believes that the fetus can hear during the final weeks of pregnancy

* Quoting Towbin, p. 1212: "The conclusion is inescapable that lesser hypoxic lesions occurring in the fetal-neonatal period are correspondingly responsible for the appearance later of lesser patterns of clinical disability, for varied subtle forms of attenuated distorted Central Nervous System function."

† Virginia Johnson, "Does Schizophrenia Get Its Start Early in Life?" *Science News* 102, no. 17 (October 21, 1972) p. 263.

and what he hears can become part of the schizophrenic process. I think that it is a possibility only when the auditory experience is traumatic, such as a gunshot near the pregnant mother, as I discuss elsewhere. That trauma in aural modality (plus many other ones later on) can lie sequestered and play a later part in the "hearing of voices" so common to many schizophrenics.

The lasting and subtle effects of birth trauma were documented in the *American Journal of Obstetrics and Gynecology* (1972). A group of Indianapolis medical researchers matched the obstetric records of 1,698 babies with their progress in school, as well as other information about their physical and mental adjustment when they reached the age of nine. One fourth of all children breech-born had flunked at least one grade by age nine and one in five needed academic remedial help.

One other example. Recently a woman came to therapy because of a lifetime of "pressure headaches," as she called them. In her second month of therapy she underwent a birth Primal which I supervised. For two and one-half hours she was curled in a ball, spitting up fluid and butting her head against the (padded) wall. The butting process was clearly automatic and involuntary, and it is doubtful that anyone could continue to butt her head against a wall for more than two hours without exhaustion. Her head twisted and turned constantly. She explained later that she was "trying to get out." She discovered days later that she underwent an unusually long labor. That trauma became the prototype of a specific reaction pattern; namely, that under any later stress she would develop a "pressure headache." Neither she nor I could ever have guessed the origin of her headaches. If we were to try to understand her symptom within the conventional analytic mode, we could have posited guilt over her not helping her sick mother enough, suppressed anger at her father, and so on—all of which could be true. But none of which would explain how guilt or anger became transmuted into a headache which put her in bed for days.

It is my observation that the *severity* of the symptom is usually commensurate with the severity of the trauma. A few aspirins might assuage some guilt or anger, but would be powerless against the pressure of the birth trauma.

It would seem that during traumatic birth the organism splits *right then* (from feeling fully) so that further psychologic traumas only widen the split. In other words, the soil for neurosis begins at birth for those who have had birth traumas. I might add that in a neurotic world with neurotic mothers, it is difficult to avoid traumatic birth. When the organism splits at birth, there is a lifeless, "dead" quality to the person's personality thereafter. The most lifeless patients are often the ones to go through a severe birth Primal at some time in their therapy. The reason for the lifelessness is that there was no time in this world when the person was totally himself and feeling.

The importance of this discussion is that if we look at a child's behavior and symptoms, we have a point of reference—a place to look for origins. Later stress becomes focused in the area of original pain, as though under each stress the body returns to its first catastrophic event in order to repair itself. This is the miracle of human existence! The body can go back fifty years in time to undo a trauma which occurred then. Undoing is the proper term, for after having these Primals, patients not only change their behavior but many profound changes take place in the system, such as alterations in hormone output.

Let us return to an earlier example of a delayed birth and see how being born out of one's natural rhythm affects later behavior. First, the birth trauma means that the neonate had to defer or "acquiesce" to his mother's needs. This acquiescence *in the womb* is a life experience—a relationship—every bit as meaningful as when mother later scolds the child and makes him behave. The womb experience is the prototype of acquiescent behavior. There are other factors, as well. If the neonate thrashed and fought his way out aggressively instead of "giving up" and acquiescing during his birth, the prototype would be different. That is, later on under similar conditions of being controlled by his mother he would act aggressively.

Obviously birth trauma and later childhood behavior is not a one-to-one affair. Many experiences go into producing behavior. But if a child is born out of rhythm and then intellectual parents lay great stress on speech, the focus of the early disharmony may end up in the speech area, thus producing stammering or stuttering. Speech would be arhythmical, nonfluid, and halting. An unwarranted extrapolation? Keep in mind again that each experience is *preserved* and that those experiences exert a constant effect on us. When the early effect is great (birth trauma), the force of its effect on later behavior will be great. Its effect is not only quantitative but qualitative, as well. That is, it has a certain *degree* of effect on later behavior, but it also has a directive quality which determines the kind of behavior which occurs—nonfluid birth to nonfluid speech, is an example.

Acquiescence during birth will not automatically make a child acquiescent in later life. But when his parents constantly control him, when they caution "What will the neighbors think?" every time he makes a move, when the child must defer to his father's every mood and whim, *then* we have a combined experiential force for producing acquiescent behavior.

There are other aspects of delayed birth, and many of our patients who suffered unusually long labors have reported similarities in certain aspects of their personalities. It has to do with waiting. Being made to wait so long during birth has made many of these patients intolerant of waiting. Usually the parents were the kind who would not give into the wants and demands of the children. Their reluctance and indecision—the "we'll see later" in response to all of the child's requests—made these children feel that if they didn't get something "now" they would never get it. What produced a monumental impatience was the life-and-death wait during some 30–50 hours of labor, added to the parental attitudes later on. One patient said, "I always made impulsive decisions in my life because I could not wait—that is, I could not stand to feel that early waiting; so I married the first girl I met, I rented the first apartment I saw, I bought the first car I looked at, all because I can't stand waiting." His mother made him wait for life, and then made him wait for anything enjoyable thereafter. She seemed to think that to put off pleasure helped build his character. What it helped build was a rash and impulsive adult.

The reason that I lay such stress on the prototypic traumas is that they shape the response patterns of the infant; they help form his personality. And, because he starts out by not acting in accordance with the desires of the parent (he may be jumpy and jittery, or too

weak and passive for an aggressive father), he gets rejected very
early in life, which simply compounds the problem. When other
children come along who have an easier birth, for example (because
later children are less apt to have protracted labor times), they may
start out in life less colicky, less demanding and irritable, and so get
more from the parents in the way of patience and kindness. If, for
instance, a parent wants an athlete, he is going to be disappointed if
a traumatic birth sets up faulty physical coordination in the infant.
Let us examine this in greater detail.

The preserved arhythmicity (of being born out of rhythm) may
just as well affect a child in terms of jerky, uncoordinated movements or nonfluid gait. This may be true when parents put great
stress on early walking and throwing. That is, when parents again
provoke out-of-rhythm behavior by forcing a child to do things
physically before his natural bodily and neurological processes are
ready, they are reactivating the early arhythmicity which then results in poor physical coordination. A "funny" walking style is just
one more sign of a total system that cannot be smooth—that is, a
system that has not smoothly integrated early experiences. High-
pitched, nasal, stammering speech is another indication of lack of
physiologic unity. Distorted facial set is yet another example, and
finally, it shows in the lack of unified physical growth, so that the
torso is too large for the legs, or the legs are too long for the torso,
etc. Arhythmicity is something learned as anything later might be
learned. A difficult birth "teaches" the child that life is a struggle,
that one is helpless, that life is dangerous, and so on. These learnings
are contributing factors, the matrix for future learning; so that
when a person later embraces a philosophy positing the necessity
for struggling as a *sine qua non* of life, we can understand that there
are complex factors stemming far back into his history that went
into the making of that ideology. To talk someone out of an "irrational" idea, then, is tantamount to talking him out of his history.

I want to cite a few more examples of the effects of the prototypic birth trauma in order to indicate the widespread ramifications
of a single trauma and to point out the lifelong effects of an early
event. These examples are taken from patients' Primals. Several patients were held back in the mother because the doctor arrived late
at the hospital. One understood from his birth Primal that he had

always been "on the go" as a drive away from containment at birth. Another finally got in touch with her rage at being "held back" and noted that at birth she "gave up" and had reacted later to restriction with resignation. After her birth Primal she could feel and express her rage; that is, she was finally able to make a significant change in her "passive" personality.

One female patient used to tell me that since adolescence suicide was "her thing." Under stress she'd want to kill herself as some others might want to eat. She had a birth Primal in which she was in excruciating Pain for hours, feeling she wanted to die to end her agony. After her Primal she understood that all later stress reactivated that wanting to die from birth. Suicide entered her mind when she was upset because it was a prototypic response which began with her life on this earth. It may be that the so-called "death wish" that Freud wrote about was simply this "wanting to die" response that so many neurotics have whenever they get into hurtful situations. Only the death wish isn't genetic or innate; it is a response of an infant who can do absolutely nothing to shut off his excruciating Pain at birth.

It is my observation that there are some introverted patients who often think of death under stress and others who never do. Those who do not are the "doers," the ones who struggled mightily to get out during birth; for them to stop doing means "to die." So their activity is a defense against that death-wish feeling. They must keep going. Or they must keep thinking. These people tend to act tough under stress, keeping those primordial fears deeply buried and hidden. They will be the ones who act counterphobically in fearful situations—plunging in, acting brave, and denying fear.

Life experience tends to make these defenses convoluted. They ramify and become more complex with age. For example, one patient had a birth Primal and found out why he could never compromise or "give in." He came from a home where no one gave in to him; where orders and demands were given and never altered. But these life experiences lay on top of a birth trauma where letting up and giving in (to the struggle) unconsciously meant death. He had to plunge ahead, to maintain his position, so to speak, and not let down.

When a patient gets close to those early death feelings later on in Primal Therapy, he needs special help, because he will try every one of his defenses to stay away from them—staying busy, pretending they don't exist, etc. This is a dangerous time for the patient, because as these tremendous Pains ascend, the patient has the feeling that he is going crazy . . . which means there is more coming up than his mind can integrate. With non-Primal people who take marijuana or LSD, which opens the gate of Pain and prematurely allows birth Pains to arise out of their natural sequence, they often do go crazy. Pain fragments their minds, producing disjointed thinking and lack of coherence. We have to understand that prototypic defenses that develop around the birth trauma are the cement which holds personality together. They must be dismantled carefully, not summarily obliterated. We see that disjointed thinking is a necessary defense . . . one we often see in those who have had many acid trips. They must not "put it all together" because total comprehension and understanding means to feel Pain.

So we have certain preverbal traumas constituting a steady stream of unconsciousness, and later behavior based on those early experiences which is irrational because it is based, not on current reality, but on those past experiences. So when a person is stubborn and will not compromise, even when a situation calls for it, he is behaving neurotically because his mind is thinking, "I am a person of principle," while the real reason lies in different events. The mind, in short, develops concepts to rationalize what the body cannot feel.

What neurotics do later in life is to recreate the birth struggle in order to master it, at least in a symbolic way. For example, many of us cannot function unless we are under pressure. We need a deadline (an apt phrase) before we can produce. Some patients have had Primals in which they realized that working under pressure was a way of recreating the birth trauma—of being under terrible pressure to get out—and that the struggle in that situation was necessary in order to live. Later in life they externalized the pressure, pretended that there were many demands on them, so that they could deal with it in some way. These people created five things to do at once so that they could unconsciously maintain that (early) state of pressure. They always felt "under pressure," but having no way to understand where that feeling came from, they had to believe it was from outside.

Others who have had quite similar birth traumas cannot take any pressure without collapsing. Perhaps the birth struggle was all for naught, because in the end the mother (and indirectly the baby) was finally drugged and the baby dragged out. What was "learned" was that struggle avails you nothing. "Pressure" was too much to struggle against. So when this child becomes a student, he may fall apart when he has two assignments due at once. Again, it is not only the birth situation that creates that reaction. The birth situation *directs* future reactions. Parents who constantly pressure their children to clean up, to study, to know the answers, etc., are adding to the load of birth-trauma pressure. Later on, the adult cannot take pressure because he is already overloaded with it.

A different example of this same thing is in the case of mothers who are in a hurry to get rid of their fetus. They have a physician prematurely induce labor because someone told them that the birth should have happened on a certain date and the mother becomes anxious when that date comes and goes and the baby is still inside. A number of Primal patients have relived this trauma of being shoved into the world too soon and know after the Primal why it is they could never be rushed. In their childhoods, as soon as their mothers would call for them to come home for dinner, they would find reasons to stay where they were for a little while more. They were hurried up at birth and no one could ever do that to them again.

Another way we continuously recreate our birth traumas is in our dreams. A recurring dream of being suffocated may occur because the unresolved traumatic sensations at birth are constantly vying for access to consciousness. Those traumatic sensations and their derived symbols are "frozen" into the system for a lifetime. One patient had a constant nightmare of being in a *pink* prison, being suffocated by his uniform, which was too tight; a nightmare that ended when he felt the real nightmare—his birth. Recurring dreams clarify the whole nature of neurosis for us because we see how past experience is imbedded permanently into our nervous systems, constantly requiring repeated symbolization of those buried Pains; and that is neurosis—constant inappropriate symbolic behavior where the organism is responding to its past instead of its present.

Here are the words of a Primal patient about his birth trauma, strangulation by the cord, and its subsequent lifelong effects:

"So far as I've been able to perceive to date, the main patterns of acting out which have resulted from my birth trauma are those of fear, helplessness, and deadness. I have always tended to be anxious, particularly with people, and I think now that the most fundamental source of that anxiety is the terror I experienced while being strangled in the uterus. There have been times in the past when I have been able to repress that fear for awhile.

"The main birth Primal I'm having currently consists of my hunching my shoulders so as to bring my head and body as close together as possible, while at the same time my back makes as full an arc as possible, bending backward. This brings a lot of pressure both on the small of my back and on my head. Actually, it's a pre-Primal, since I'm still aware of my surroundings. An additional movement is that my head turns toward the left. The arcing movement sustains itself until I run out of oxygen; my mouth is closed tight in a grimace during the movement.

"Recently I have also had birth Primals in which I make gurgling noises. This occurs when my shoulders are hunched, but there is no arcing of the back. In this Primal I seem to be trying to get my mouth open, with only limited success.

"Sometimes in the crying which intersperses these Primals, I expel air through my throat as if it is attempting to open up, but this also goes only so far.

"Earlier birth Primals have included lying on my back with my arms above me in a fetal position and shaking with fear and crying. These Primals went on for six months, deepening in intensity. Also, I've had a type of Primal in which I simply lay on my back in a state of muscular rigidity and vibrated. The vibrations began in my jaw and neck and gradually included more of my body. I also brought my head and body as close together as possible during these Primals, which went on for five months.

"I believe the fear Primals and the muscular rigidity Primals involved two tenacious lines of defense which were finally breached, enabling me to get to the actual movements of being strangled by the cord. I have yet to experience that in anything like its full intensity.

"I've also always tended to be unassertive and rather easily manipulated (a tendency of which my mother took full advantage). This tendency toward helplessness, which comes from my helplessness while being strangled, and which I also have repressed and acted against, takes as one of its forms a tendency to be quiet, particularly when I'm somewhat fearful. I think the difficulty I've experienced in getting my mouth open in postgroup and elsewhere goes back to my difficulty—probably my incapacity—in getting my mouth open to scream while being strangled.

"There has also been an underlying inertness, a lack of emotional responsiveness, which stems from the repression of feeling to which I was forced by the birth trauma. The first three weeks of individual Primal Therapy relaxed my defenses as never before, and consequently my deadness then manifested itself more nakedly than it ever had before.

"In fact, almost anything sick in my behavior can be traced back in considerable part to my birth trauma. Thus, my overintellectual approach to life, formerly much more pronounced than at present, was due to my having been emotionally turned off in the womb. My difficulties in relating to people also initially stem from that turn-off. So does my superficial and promiscuous sexual behavior.

"I've always been frightened of swimming under water, and several years ago had so much anxiety when I tried scuba diving that I had to abandon it. This obviously comes from my experience of being entrapped and suffocated. So does my fear of going too far into caves, particularly when there is little light. I've also been afraid of close relationships because I was afraid I'd be trapped and controlled. This comes in part from my mother's manipulating and controlling me, but what happened in the womb would be an earlier prototype.

"Another insight I've recently had while arcing my back in a Primal is that the weakness I've had in the small of my back comes from my birth trauma. While this weakness doesn't cause me any trouble ordinarily, it does show up when I have to bend my body forward at the waist for any period of time. For example, when I played ice hockey in high school, which requires a lot of leaning forward to handle the stick on the ice, my back gave me so much trouble that I had to wear a corset-type brace to give it additional

strength. Also, I've always had poor posture, with the small of my
back too far forward and the buttocks sticking out too far. This
distortion is intensified during my back-arcing Primal and evidently
comes from that movement in the womb.

"I might also mention that I think even my poor teeth were probably caused by my birth trauma, since that caused the muscles in
my jaws to become rigid, thus preventing normal pulsation and
functioning in the jaw and mouth."

Birth, for some patients, can be the original "separation anxiety"
situation (à la Otto Rank). What makes it a separation trauma is
when the child is not held closely and kept warm right after he is
born; it is traumatic to be thrust into the world all alone, afraid, and
not comforted. Then later separations from loved ones can produce
the classical separation anxiety—the original one.

One of the reasons that so many neurotics cannot be alone is that
their initial entry into this world was marked by that catastrophic
aloneness right after birth, when they were taken away from
mother and placed in a container alone and uncomforted. Any
situation of being alone thereafter could conceivably reactivate that
prototypic Pain.

Some patients have noted that they are easily awakened at night
by noise; still others by light. Some complain that they are most
susceptible to temperature changes and others believe they wake up
most readily when the carbon dioxide levels change due to closed
windows. What we are finding out is that these responses may be
prototypic results. That is, if a newborn could not catch his breath
at birth, a nonventilated room later may wake him up quickly. He
would wake up as a survival mechanism (to go and open the window) sooner than others might because the slight changes in CO_2
levels rewaken the prototypic threat to his life. If the initial birth
shock was strong light, the person may be more vulnerable later to
light entering the room while he sleeps. What is significant is that
these are largely *unconscious* reactions. Being particularly susceptible to room temperature change while asleep results from a stored
history which has shaped one's constitution and metabolism. This is
no different than being unconsciously susceptible to certain things
which trigger off old hurts while awake.

One patient, born Caesarean, had the feeling after a birth Primal that he could not start anything because he did not participate in starting his life. He spent his life waiting to have things done for (or to) him.

Compression at birth is the first "physical" handling by the mother of her child. If birth contractions are weak due to "twilight sleep," there is an insufficient "prime" of the body's processes so that energetic, deep respiration which aids in galvanizing the system does not take place. If we couple this with a later lack of physical stimulation of the child by the mother, we have the elements of a possible predisposition toward respiratory difficulties. I view the body's systems as analogous to the muscles—without proper and full use they weaken.

As we can see, traumas have differing effects depending on the organism and how it handles it. One last example to indicate the power of prototypic traumas on later behavior: A homosexual patient who had months of Primals continued to have homosexual impulses. He then had a birth Primal, feeling the tremendous effort it took for him to get out. The residual feeling he was left with was "Momma wasn't there for me. She wasn't going to help me." That inchoate feeling was later articulated when, indeed, his mother, continuing her neurotic pattern, was never there for him. He had a passive father, which left him some vain hope of getting something out of him. He then directed his hopes toward men and acted this out homosexually.

This is not to say that birth traumas *produce* homosexuality. But this man's birth trauma added tremendous impact to the later fact that his mother was not there for him and would not help him even to get born. He had to do it all himself. The extent of that impact can be measured in two ways—objectively and subjectively. Objectively, after birth Primals we find significant lowering of body temperature—a sign that enormous tension has been resolved. Subjectively, the patient may finally feel no impulse to act out homosexually. So, we may conclude that part of the great force driving this man to act out was the birth trauma which contributed heavily to the residual load of tension. A lesbian Primal patient had a similar experience. She felt coming out in a rather normal birth but then being left untouched and terrified for hours. In her homosexual activity she always wanted to curl up and snuggle against a woman. In her Primal she felt the basis for that—the need to curl up and crawl back inside mother; the last safe place she had in her life. These examples, I'm sure, seem a bit far out. But it must be remembered that they come from patients who have relived the experiences and are not interpretations based on the fantasies of some therapist. What all this means really is that giving a child a good start in life helps him withstand almost any later trauma. Whereas a bad start makes him terribly sensitive and susceptible to what might ordinarily be minor events later on. Without prototypic traumas, a child can have a rejecting mother and still not have so much residual tension as to drive him toward homosexuality.

To underscore what I have just discussed, I want to point out a remarkable study done by Sarnoff A. Mednick, Director of the Institute of Psychology in Copenhagen. Writing in *Psychology Today*, he told about a massive research study of 2,000 Danish males born in Copenhagen in 1936. Of sixteen men who committed violent crimes, "fifteen of them had the most horrible possible conditions at birth . . . and the sixteenth had an epileptic mother."* Dr. Mednick concludes with: "It is very possible that we are on the track of conditions that make some contribution to impulsive criminality." I by no means wish to de-emphasize the enormous contribution of the interpersonal relationships between parents and children in producing neurotic behavior. I simply want to indicate factors we may have overlooked.

Dr. Mednick's research team also did an extensive study of schizophrenic children. He indicated, again, that pregnancy and birth complications can contribute heavily toward mental illness. He studied both normals and schizophrenics. Many physiologic tests were given to the two groups, including heart rate, muscle tension, respiration, and galvanic skin response. In addition, for each child there was a midwife report on the birth—legally required in Denmark. Seventy percent of the disturbed children in the study suffered one or more serious complications of birth or pregnancy, including anoxia, prematurity, prolonged labor, strangulation by the

---

* *Psychology Today* 4, no. 11 (April 1971): 49.

cord, breech birth, etc. Dr. Mednick concludes: "[This] suggests to us that pregnancy or birth complications damage the body's ability to regulate stress-response mechanisms."* One of the brain structures most vulnerable to oxygen deficiency at birth appears to be the hippocampus. It may be that oxygen deficiency at birth affects the ability of the hippocampus to shut off Pain†; the result may be that the child is flooded with Pain, both physical and psychological, early in life and cannot adequately repress it. This is a terribly important point, for it may be that brain structures that aid in repression are particularly susceptible to oxygen deprivation at birth and are permanently impaired when such deprivation occurs. This means that thereafter the young child is constantly overloaded by traumas which other children can repress . . . the autistic child is a case in point.

A slightly defective hippocampus can leave the child confused, easily upset and overwhelmed, and mentally distractible because he cannot focus on any one thing long. That is, he cannot shut out irrelevant stimuli and attend to one essential matter.‡

The hallmark of neurosis is overreaction. One may overreact to a situation by underreacting; that is, one may freeze in a situation which should not provoke such an extreme response. Or one may overreact and become hysterical. But frequently, overreactions, whether physical or emotional, can be attributed to Primal Pains. Thus, a person may overreact to a cold room and be attacked by an allergy because of the early shock of being expelled at birth into an air-conditioned delivery room. Or he may anxiously respond to an examination, feeling overwhelmed and helpless, because that stress has activated the original helpless feeling during a long labor.

---

* *Op. cit.*, p. 49.
† Again, see *The Anatomy of Mental Illness* for the crucial role of the hippocampus in the repression of pain.
‡ This is also the point made by Lowell Storms (as reported in *Psychology Today*, October 1972, page 72): "Storms suggests that a defect in the ability to dampen nerve response produces an overgeneralization of thought and perception that leads to characteristic thought disorder of schizophrenia." The theory propounded by Mandell, et al., indicates that excitation of the nervous impulses cannot be suppressed due to a defect in the adaptive capacity of nerve cells.

The overreaction is the result of reacting to the current *stress* plus reacting to the past one. Combined, they cause what appears to be exaggerated, unrealistic reactions. The Primal overlay patterns responses, directs ideas, and helps determine symptoms. That is why it is so important to understand those very early determinants of our behavior. "How to" books avoid these complexities, tell us how to deal with the *results* of those determinants, and thus keep us operating on the surface of what are most profound phenomena.

The following is a rather detailed account of the myriad ramifications of birth trauma. It shows how inordinately complex social behavior is, and how early trauma becomes so intricately interwoven into personality as to be indistinguishable from it. That is why we have heretofore had such trouble trying to isolate specific factors in our maturation that shape personality development. The problem was that experts were doing the isolation and study instead of the patient. I wouldn't dare make half of the statements about the effects of the birth trauma that this patient made; but because he felt them and was not just intellectualizing about possibilities, he could make some rather astounding extrapolations from his Primals. Further, none of these connections or insights were "suggested" to him; he didn't learn them in some classroom. He discovered them out of his own body. The life-and-death struggle was imprinted, as it were, on a naive, inexperienced organism, whose first social event was to be strangled, hammered into oblivion, suffocated, and so on.

One patient had an unusually long labor. He sensed impending death (though such a terror was not conceptualized) because he was being oxygen-starved. He "worked" to get out so he could breathe. Finally he was out and his efforts were rewarded; there was air. But the notion of "work" became stamped in so that it became his life style and his philosophy. ("You have to work hard for what you get in life".) After a Primal, he realized that not to work for him meant death. The anxiety he felt when he momentarily had nothing to do was the old Primal anxiety where not struggling every minute would mean death. He greeted everyone with "Working hard? Keeping busy?" without ever really knowing what he was saying.

Kenneth

Oct 28, 1972

About a month ago, I noticed your request for observations from your patients about their birth feelings and their effects on the patients' lives, etc. Although, even after having been in Primal Therapy for some time, I'm not out of my mother yet (the story of my life), it seems important to me to tell you something about myself. During one or two occasions I have asked my mother to relate to me, to the best of her memory, what happened with her (and me) during my birth cycle; it seemed important to me to find out as much as I could while she was still alive and could tell me.

First of all, it seems that what had happened to me inside my mother has shaped my entire life, a life that could best be described as one that, given the chance (I always used to say), I'd never want to live any of it over again.

From a Primal last night, I now realize that the reason I don't have any friends (I have lost my neurotic friends, and I don't have any Primal friends—or even acquaintances) is that I can't find anyone who needs me; the only way I can relate to "friends" is for *them* to need *me*. I could never ask anybody for help, and the only way I could ever get help was to be in deep trouble; then, if it wasn't obvious to others that I needed help (and often it wasn't), I would be forced to ask for help. But at this stage of my need, the result was often unsettling. Like all the times I would end up "hitting people between the eyes with a club" to get them to see that I was in trouble and needed help. Like the times when, as a little boy, I had to startle my mom with my demands to such an extent that I'd get a beating from the old man; like the first (of two) times I went to my parents' home in the Midwest, Primaling, crying, and screaming all over the place, scaring the hell out of everybody; like the times I devastated my wife with the sudden knowledge of advanced deterioration of various states of affairs; like the time I called Arthur Janov at three or four o'clock in the morning, scared to death, with fluid running from my eyes, nose, and mouth; and like the time I had to blast my mom from the inside, this was when I woke her up from her sleep in the wee A.M. to get her to go to the hospital, giving her a swordlike pain, the worst she's ever felt, she said.

Then there's the obscurity-type feeling. I've always felt that I was in this world, but that I was apart from this world—that I was really not in contact with anybody; I was lonely, obscure, invisible —I could die and nobody would really care. From the Primals and experience that I've recently had, I know that this comes from inside.

I've got to say that it's difficult to talk about these feelings as being isolated from each other; it seems that each feeling is, in some total way, intertwined with every other feeling, and that, when you're talking about one, you're talking about facets of all the others.

I feel lost right now, so I'm going to talk about the biggest feeling of all—and one that has a long way to go before it becomes relatively "emptied out." And that is the feeling of not being able to get away from my mom. All my life I have been called a "momma's boy." When I was a little boy, I spent virtually all my time (except when I was pressured into going outside) in the house with my mom. As a teenager I worked as a farmhand; the pain of leaving in the morning (or even having learned that my father had proudly (??) told a farmer that I would work for him—and I got diarrhea) was excruciating; during the day, I would think of my mom, imagine that I'd hear her calling me, and would long for the day, or the evening, when I would be back with her. I remember one day—I came home in the evening, blisters all over my hands, back hurting, depressed; she knew I felt bad, and she ran my bath water to make me feel better. Time and time again, throughout life —on Monday mornings, the first day on a new job, the first day at college, when I was in the Army—I would suffer that horrible feeling of not wanting to go, but knowing I had to (to be a man, or whatever).

After the knifelike pain that woke her in the wee morning hours, she became so cold that she shook like mad; she said that she had never experienced such a cold. The first week in therapy (for about five days) I experienced a cold such as I had never known. It was a chemical-type cold, a clinging, wet cold; and I kept smelling alcohol or ether, or whatever, all the time—at the Primal Institute and in my motel room. It was a cold that I just couldn't get away from

—I turned and rolled; I was so little that I couldn't move my arms with my arm muscles. I would turn very slowly, and if I turned enough, my arms would come on around and drop. The coldest part was on my forehead, and I tried to move my head backwards (chin up), for some reason, to get away from the stinging cold on my forehead. (It's weird—as I type this, I can feel some of that cold on my thighs.) I have always been a cold-natured person; it really can't get too hot for me. And this hasn't been resolved, because I am still this way. But back to the cold at the Institute. I wore long underwear, a shirt, sweater, sweatshirt, and my jacket under two blankets in bed, but I couldn't get away from it because it was an early feeling.

My mother shook from this cold. During the time of the cold in therapy, that first week, I shook. Twice I shook violently, and one of those times I vomited into a pillow while Paul ran to get a waste can.

My mother was hysterical, and during her hysteria at the hospital she ripped her stockings to shreds. She also said something, apparently, to evoke a reply from one of the nurses to the other: "Well, if she didn't want her baby, why did she get pregnant in the first place?" I also know that Mom was in such pain that she wished God would take her and her baby. And she was anesthetized. The doctor was late, and he said that another 15 minutes, and mother and baby would have both been dead.

Another thing that is a big factor: I am a small man (5 feet 9 inches, about 150–155 pounds), and my mother is little (5 feet, 5 feet 2?). My mother ate extra well so as to build a big, strong baby. She did. I weighed over nine pounds when I was born.

So I have never really gotten out of there. Although I've lived almost half my life away from my mother (and as always, it hurt to leave), she has still taken care of me—through letters, through my own fantasies, through my girlfriends, my wife. Recently, my wife supported us for two and a half years. I finally got a job after one year in therapy.

I can't leave my mother. She's all around me. I have practically all the possessions (and most of it is junk) that I've had all my life. I have all the letters that my mom ever sent me, and I even have most of the old furniture and dishes that my parents used to have but had to get rid of. That's how I keep my mom all around me.

There are lots of reasons I can't leave my mother (my mother lives two thousand miles away—I mean the mother in me). One reason is that I'll hurt her. During birth not only did I give her excruciating pain, but I also ripped some of her tissue—I ripped her insides. This is one of the first things I can remember being told by my mom. So, throughout life, whenever I tear myself out of the arms of a crying wife, or leave a sad mom I experience the pain of hurting and tearing up someone whom I really don't want to leave.

Why did I have feelings of not wanting to leave the sac? I don't know; perhaps something about staying in there seemed easier—a lot easier. But it just can't be done. I have to get out, and I don't really want to go because it's so hard—and it's so painful.

As I have said, I have never gotten out. I have never succeeded at anything in my life. I've been good at doing a fantastic repertoire of things, and I've fought and worked like hell. But I have never gotten past that barrier. And often it is a thin barrier ("if I can just manage to get a little further"), but it may as well be ten thousand miles thick, because until I get past it, I can't get past it. I have never succeeded in anything in my life (careers, money, college, a good build—and most of all, the thing that originally was extremely important to me—the success of finding that Kenneth who I know exists around here somewhere. I started this quest when I was fifteen—twenty-two years ago). I was really afraid that I wouldn't even succeed in getting to the Primal Institute—because it was so goddamned important to me.

My wife is living in the Midwest for an indefinite period of time. So not having that momma here to take care of me, I've come face to face with myself in a new way. Previously she took care of me in various ways, including doing therapy with me. Although she's broken down now, she's not a therapist; but I still used her to listen to all my shit. And I could "reciprocate" (the need to help others) and help her get her shit out. But a month or so ago, I felt the need for some professional help—somebody who really knows what he's doing—to help Kenneth. So I came to the Primal Institute three sessions in a row. I felt the crushing need to "blast through." And I busted my ass Primaling—trying, trying, crying, body stuff, keeping all kinds of crap going for one or two solid weeks. Finally, using money as an excuse, I let up. The urge was gone, and I was temporarily satisfied. But I knew that my head was up against a brick wall—I was crashing against a barrier that I have never experienced breaking through. I have something to add to this at the end of this report.

Music has always been one of the biggest things in my life. Music has been my mommy and daddy, and my guitar has been my mate (my mommy). The guitar was never compatible with any of my real-life mates, as far as I was concerned. Music has been a therapist for me. It's almost like I play back all the music that has been stored within me all my life, and as I play it back, I play lots of my feelings back. But during two periods of therapy I have experienced a weird phenomenon. And it wasn't until the second time this happened that I realized that certain music sent me right into birth feelings. The second time was during this period of trying to "blast through." Different types of music give me different types of feelings. This particular music had a heavy throbbing bass beat to it (some of Quincy Jones' music). This music gave me some sort of "hope"-type (we're gonna *make* it, baby!) feelings—when you hope, your head sort of looks up—well, mine did, anyway; and I was feeling that throbbing beat, my head went up (my chin went up), back against my neck, and within seconds I was on the bed, fetal, rhythmically blasting (working) my way to where I wanted to go. I guess some of the music we create, like the language we create, is symbolically descriptive of our birth feelings. (Head up against a brick wall; can't make a breakthrough; in a jam; in a tight squeeze; *down* to the nitty gritty; see daylight; I can't get started; can't find my way out of this mess; don't know which way to turn; on and on ad infinitum.)

I've had some feelings lately about going through all this shit (pain, Primals, etc.) and nobody really knowing about it. (If they only knew what all I'm going through.) And all my life I've gone through a lot of shit (pain, hard work, suffering, narrow escapes, etc., loneliness, etc., etc., etc.), and nobody really knew or could know what I've gone through. In therapy, I feel that Art Janov doesn't really know how much this therapy means to me and how hard I work at it—and what I go through. That's a bad feeling, and the feeling is MOMMY, YOU DON'T KNOW HOW MUCH I'M FIGHTING IN HERE; YOU DON'T SEE MY SIDE OF IT, HOW HARD I'M WORKING, HOW HARD I'M TRYING, HOW HARD I'M FIGHTING (to get out)—and HOW MUCH I'M HURTING—AND HOW MUCH I'M REALLY WORTH! All my life, I've had trouble working hard for someone if they couldn't see how hard I was working, or if they didn't acknowledge my efforts. I could work my ass off if someone was looking at me; but if they weren't, what was the use?

During that intensive week (three sessions) in therapy last month, I got into a feeling that describes my life. I felt pressured by the therapist, at a time when I had to do something but didn't know what. I went into my feeling I CAN'T DO ANYTHING, I CAN'T DO ANYTHING, and at the same time, I was fighting like a son of a bitch. One glance at me would tell someone that I was doing a lot. And that's been my life: fighting like hell, but never believing that I could really do anything. Inside my momma, fighting like hell, but not feeling that I'm doing anything (doing any good).

There was another reason why it was hard to leave my mom's insides; I was leaving with an unwanted feeling. As long as I could stay, there was a chance for mom to indicate that she wanted me. Once I was gone, it was too late. This feeling was acted out all my life: the difficulty in leaving Mom and momma surrogates; the lonely hours and days and weekends that I would confine myself to my dark, lonely apartment, not coming to the door when friends would (seldom) call. I had to stay in there (with us), because that's where something was at. And that's when the feeling of loneliness and obscurity would come. I would stay there not eating all weekend, falling asleep on the couch with my clothes on. Just me and my music. It would be like dying.

Part of this fear during birth was that Mom didn't want me to be me (born) because I was a bad boy; I was a shitty person; I was a fighting little son of a bitch. And every time I would assert or express ME, she'd tighten up and stifle me. Hence the me that I'm afraid to come out with because nobody will like me, and I'll be in trouble. And there's a lot of me. Just like there was inside.

Now the thing I said I was going to add later. After about one year in therapy here, I experienced a feeling that was finally recognized as I FEEL GOOD. Simply that. I'm finding out that this is really a big thing with me. Two or three weeks ago, Helen said something nice to me, and it brought up a lot of stuff. Last night she was helping me, and as I sat there crying, I said, "It's very uncomfortable, your being with me here." "Why?" she asked. "Because you're making me feel good." And that, too, is the story of my life. I would make some progress in life—socially or otherwise; and I would start to feel good. As a result, I would tense up, panic—really panicky—and super-tense; and I would end up blowing the whole thing. Last night, after Helen left, I went from the feeling-good feeling—or a continuation of this feeling—into a birth feeling. And for a split second, a flash, I felt an "opening up." And I also felt that there were good feelings in my future—good feelings ahead. For the first time, I felt that I was going to "make it" (in therapy) and that I was going to make it through my barrier. And that these good feelings were not all going to come at once, but that they would be negotiated one at a time—sort of going from one rib to another in a cone.

As I say, I'm not out yet. I have a long way to go to get out; and I guess I have a longer way to go to get well. It's beautiful in that when good feelings come along, I can just feel them. They won't be barriers; they won't stand in my way. After they're felt, I'll again be relaxed, ready to accept the next feeling, good or otherwise. (Actually, even the bad feelings feel good.)

In one way, I could be summed up like this: I failed to get out of my mother's sac under my own steam; and I fought like hell. And I have been failing in life ever since; and I have been fighting like hell.

It must be a beautiful feeling for a baby to be helped through the canal by his mother's rhythmic "wanting." I was denied those feelings. All I ended up with was a life of nothingness, wasting away, a vacuum. In trying to get through on my journey to born-ness, I must have experienced a beginning of pleasure—just a little. But the pleasure ended abruptly with my mother's pain (my guilt), and I was destined to spend my life, not with any good feelings, but with loneliness and the pursuit of that good feeling. My hope.

In life, whenever I'd begin to get a sense of enjoyment (pleasure, feeling good), the guilt would come between us (me and the good feeling). For instance, I'd start to get some sexual pleasure with my wife; suddenly I'd think of a Kenneth-rejected, Kenneth-wanting, sad, lonely, exgirlfriend in her apartment all by herself feeling unloved. I could never enjoy myself, because there was always someone else who was suffering.

And enjoy was something I *tried* to do; I would *try* to enjoy things—struggling hard to get the essence of supposedly pleasurable things, trying to take it all in, trying to capture it. But in the struggle it always seemed to slip away; and at some later time it would be desperately wished for with nostalgia, another very bad feeling for me (I WANT IT BACK).

So pleasure was always bad; the good was the bad. Like in the womb, I would feel the hurt and make my move; and when I would begin to move I would start to get a good feeling. But then I would feel my resisting mother's hurt, and my guilt would prevent me from ever experiencing the feeling of feeling good. My mother's impenetrable body, her torn tissue, her pain, MY GUILT—that was my barrier.

I don't want Mom to close up and shut me off (a horrible feeling); and I don't want to hurt her because it hurts me.

But now that I'm busting out, the feelings are less and less guilt —and more and more good (that's the only way I can describe that good feeling—good). Love,

Kenneth

CONCLUSIONS

Doctors must remember that they are delivering a live, sensitive human being, not a blob of protoplasm. They should know that their actions during delivery may have something to do with the later neurosis of the child. Gentle handling is a *sine qua non*. Retarding labor until the doctor arrives is harmful. Allowing too long a labor is inimical to the child's best interests. Overly drugging the mother may have an effect on the fetus. Natural childbirth should be encouraged, perhaps with supplemental local anesthesia where absolutely necessary. Perhaps added oxygen should be given to certain mothers who are having difficult labors to insure that the baby is not being oxygen-starved. Mothers need to be active participants in the birth process, not merely taking orders from the doctor. They need to "help" the baby out into the world and they cannot do that when they are half-conscious. Of course, the best insurance for a natural childbirth, one in which the mother can tolerate whatever pain there is during the process without clamping down systemically, is to have her drained of other early Pains with Primals. This means that the Pain of childbirth won't be added to many others, making the whole experience so painful as to be intolerable.

The rearing of children begins in the womb, when life begins. In a verbally oriented society we have had a difficult time understanding that idea, because these are experiences that cannot be remembered in a verbal way nor can they be explained. They only can be experienced. The conventional therapeutic forms have neglected this very early aspect of life just because they are verbal forms. Until the advent of birth Primals, we had no way to document this evidence. All some could do was theorize about it. Certainly, before now we had no way to measure the weight of those experiences in terms of their effects on later behavior. Now we can do before-and-after studies of tension levels, brainwaves, etc., and see what the effects of resolving those situations are. We can observe changes in behavior (the cessation of epileptic seizures, for example) after birth Primals and infer what great pressure early traumas exerted on the system. We can see how early trauma has affected hormone imbalance when after birth Primals those balances change. We finally have a tool for calibrating what effect one's early experience has on later problems, such as learning difficulties. We know at last that being a good parent is not what you do but what you are.

V

Postnatal

Social life begins from the time we enter the world. What happens at that moment may have lifelong consequences, particularly when we consider that the newborn is a wide-open, sensing organism, completely responsive to all stimuli. He is unable to intellectualize his hurts; he can either feel them or repress them. First of all, he is born into a room. Is that room womb temperature? Or is it air-conditioned for the convenience of the doctor? Is that room lit with blinding fluorescents? Or is the light diffused and focused away from the neonate's eyes? In the words of a patient, let us see what effect these two factors have:

"After my third birth Primal, I came into therapy one day and felt extremely sensitive to the light in the room. Something I'd never noticed before. It really hurt and I began squinting. Suddenly, I am back into the birth sequence again, only this time I'm coming out into a strong light and it hurts. There's nothing I can do to stop it. At the same time, I feel cold—cold as hell. I'm freezing, and again there's nothing I can do to stop it."*

We have observed this phenomenon dozens of times, enough times to know that the delivery room must be carefully lit and

---

* The average delivery room temperature is about 72 degrees. Womb temperature is approximately 98 degrees. The infant being born is subject to the shock of an almost 20-degree drop in temperature. One of the effects of birth is the stimulation of temperature-control mechanisms in the brain. It may well be that difficult birth, plus the shock of the temperature drop at birth, may permanently impair the proper functioning of temperature-control mechanisms so that the person is thereafter too hot or too cold.

much warmer than we thought. Many "light-sensitive" patients, patients who hurt a great deal when they go outside into the sunlight, have traced their reaction to the delivery room. An equal number of patients have reported being colder than others all their lives, needing to bundle up even when those around them were fairly comfortable. They, too, have traced their reactions to the catastrophic experience of a cold delivery room. One patient who relived the cold shock of the delivery room came out of his Primal with the following insight: "I have had an allergy to changes in temperature all my life, and now I feel that it all began with the shock of being delivered from a warm womb into a cold room. My body never got over that shock." After the Primal, he found that his nose no longer ran when he went from a hot to a cold room, as it had for most of his life.

The next problem is where is the newborn placed. Is he put on his mother's warm, pulsating body; or is he placed in a sterile, cold container? Obviously, he should be put with his mother immediately. To be handled by strangers in a rough manner and then isolated in a plastic box must be traumatic. What happens with that containerized child is that he is then put into a nursery with other screaming infants. He has no way of understanding what is going on except that he hears the most primitive distress signal of all—the cry. A dozen or more crying babies must be upsetting to the infant and so he, too, cries (out of fear). It is a common experience to visit a nursery and see not one or two babies crying, but a whole chorus of them going off at once. Perhaps the first two cried out of hunger. But the noise itself becomes a threat to the other babies. This is not so difficult to understand; crying babies upset adults, who become tense and irritable at their unceasing wails.

A recent report shows what happens to infants when they are either with or without their mothers right after birth. Dr. A. W. Liley of the University of Auckland stated that his country's hospitals recently switched from keeping all newborn infants in a nursery to allowing them to "room-in" with their mothers.

The rooming-in babies gained weight better, cried less, and were more apt to be breast-fed. He said, "We used to take the babies to their mothers for feeding five times a day, but we find it's better to let them feed on demand than try to put them all on the same sched-ule." Dr. Liley reported on his recent visit to a hospital in Bangkok where four hundred mothers were in large rooms beside their babies: "It's the only hospital I have ever been in with four hundred babies in which I didn't hear a single baby cry."*

Obviously, there are more factors than the parent-child relation-ship which go into making neurosis. Hospital policy can help force us to begin life in Pain. The reason for the Pain, of course, is that the policy interferes with a natural parent-child relationship. The simple act of removing a newborn from its mother can be one de-terminant in the development of neurosis.

What else can go wrong and produce residual tension in the in-fant? Most of what I shall discuss will not be speculative. It will be information gathered from the observation of many hundreds of infantile Primals.

Somewhere soon after birth the young male is often circumcised. I believe routine circumcision should cease. It is traumatic. Instead, I suggest waiting until the boy is old enough to decide and then make it elective surgery. Certainly, it would be less traumatic if someone decides to do it and understands fully what is happening to him. Imagine a young infant with pain around his penis that exists for no reason that he can comprehend.

Noisy rooms, sounds of vacuum machines, and people with stri-dent, harsh voices should be kept away. Excessive noise traumatizes the infant. Particularly in those first days when he cannot see, only hear. The infant should not be startled. Nor, obviously, should he be handled roughly. One patient had a Primal in which she felt be-ing jostled roughly by a nurse who was carrying her to the nurs-ery soon after birth. Another had a Primal over having inadequate support for her head during the first days of life.

Tension in the mother's body will soon get transmitted to her in-fant, who is little more than a giant sensing machine. It is difficult for us (repressed adults) to understand the full meaning of being wide open and totally vulnerable to stimuli. Only advanced Primal patients can begin to comprehend what an infant goes through, be-cause in a literal way he has returned to that state and left himself

* Los Angeles *Times*, 22 February 1971.

open again to those traumas which caused him slowly to shut down. A mother whose movements are jerky and uncoordinated will convey a feeling of insecurity to her child. No matter how much she knows about the "book" on child care, it will help little if she isn't relaxed physically with her baby, or if she speaks too rapidly and too loudly.

Another practice that I cannot understand is that of putting on pajamas with sleeves which drape over the hands, and which are tied so that the hands are inside the sleeves. The rationale is that the baby will be prevented from scratching himself. But the inordinate trauma of being left so helpless makes this practice barbaric.

The infant can be traumatized when not changed often enough, so that he is constantly chafed. Another frequent source of Primals is when infants are too tightly bound by the crib blankets. The idea of tight binding is for the security of the infant. The effect, however, is to make him feel helpless and insecure. Temperature of the room is yet another factor. We are not yet sure what temperature babies need, but it seems to be warmer than what adults require. Not necessarily because of some constitutional difference between infants and adults, but because closed-off adults often cannot feel the coldness that exists in a room. Perhaps their "motors" are running so fast that they cannot imagine that the baby isn't hot as well.

Babies should be picked up when they cry. Crying is a signal of distress. Sometimes we cannot pinpoint that distress, but we should know that they need help. They should be fed on demand and not on some arbitrary schedule, and should be breast-fed. For how long? Listen to nature. Until they develop teeth or prefer not to breast feed. The development of teeth is nature's way of telling us something; in the same way that multiple births are freak occurrences, indicating that we really only can take care of one child at a time.

Generally, infants will not develop several teeth until the ninth or tenth month. This is usually an adequate period of breast feeding. However, some infants will want more and some will want less. What we must be careful about is foisting the mother's needs on the child, so that breast feeding goes on too long and actually reinforces the sucking reflex, producing lifelong oral fixations in the same way that inadequate breast feeding does. We have seen mothers who in their attempts to appear "hip" and liberated have gone on breast feeding long after the child really wanted to.

It is difficult to pick up babies whenever they cry and feed them on demand instead of a more convenient schedule, but rearing infants is a herculean task, and should not be undertaken by adults who are babies themselves. The parent must be prepared for the constant need that is a baby. So much parental irritability is caused by parents who did not foresee what a task rearing a child is.

The following three case histories are presented to indicate how subtle is the process of neurosis. The home life of the two young men and the young woman was nothing overtly sick. There was no drunken father who came home to beat the children, no divorce, no violence, no constant criticism and ridicule—just day-in and day-out subtleties that robbed them of themselves. Their neuroses are the most difficult to treat in Primal Therapy because the defense system is so intricate—there is nothing obvious that they can point to and focus on as the source of their sickness. They were robbed of themselves so subtly that they scarcely knew they were suffering. We can see how useless advice would have been to their parents, who were also unconscious of what they were doing to their children and who were simply acting out their own Pain against their children. What they looked like they were doing could have been taken out of a book on child-rearing—it seemed all right; all that was missing was some human feeling.

Fred

My parents were adept at the subtle screw. An example of a dialogue:

ME: Mom, I feel bad.

MOM: (anxiously and very quickly) Have you thought about playing ball?

ME: Yes, but . . .

MOM: Did you talk to your friends?

ME: No, I don't really . . .

MOM: Do you want to write something?

It always appeared to me that she was so helpful. But I still felt bad and never had a chance to find out why. The realization that she was making all those suggestions for herself, because she couldn't stand to see me in any kind of pain, to feel that she was being good—this realization was far too painful to feel. So I had to see her as helpful and me as somehow deficient, because no matter what she suggested, I always felt bad. In my adult life, I've always hated people asking me lots of questions, because I begin to feel that they care and then bitterly realize from the speed and cadence of the questions that they're asking for something—indirectly. Also, my mother's fear of pain was so great that I ended up watching myself constantly to make sure I didn't say something wrong. I was never overtly punished for putting her in pain, but the look on her face was enough. And it gave me the sickening feeling that I had erred and it could never be taken back because we could never talk about it. It was never acknowledged, so I felt sick and also helpless to rectify it in any way. A further result of this is that I started doubting my own feelings. Finally, from age six on, I internalized her in the form of an entity I called "conscience," which talked to me inside my head and which automatically pushed the buttons: It took me away from crying, from caring, from everything. My mom could then say that I didn't need to do anything for her, i.e., go to college. I was doing it for "myself." This has been the most confusing screw of all—to become aware that she is literally part of me and to get in touch with feeling that. My defense system became my mother: It took me away from myself the same way she did.

My father is much more feeling than my mother, but he did a lot too. He would never tell me how he felt, even when he was feeling really horrible. To protect me. So I ended up thinking that all his hurt and aching expressions were my fault. He never gave me the reality of his own feelings. He wanted me to be myself, so consequently he tried not to tell me anything, he was so afraid to "mold me." The result is that now I yell "Daddy, tell me what to do." He is proud of our "man-to-man" talks when I was four years old. Both of them combined to cut off my feelings in the following way: my mother's great fear of pain; my father's idiotic stoicism when he got sick made me feel that anything short of dying wasn't worth mentioning. My mother worked so hard to protect me against hurt, but when I got physically sick, I had no choice. I had to feel bad and that brought up all the pain all at once. So I became terrified of being sick to my stomach. So much so that I just somehow avoided getting sick. And when I did, I was like my father: I couldn't call for help. So I would lie in bed, nauseated for hours, in utter black terror, and just hold on. Once I was in the hospital for four days with a nausea attack following a car crash in which I badly mangled my hand. I did everything but Primal. I started hyperventilating, felt my chest being crushed, and so on. But the crucial point of this is the gap between what I normally experience as feeling and this incalculable horror. It's made it hard for me to believe that other feelings, other pain, "counts." Part of my doubting myself.

My parents are considered incredibly warm, gentle, considerate, etc. They didn't beat me, force me, or do anything out front. But that's the whole problem. They were perfect in their neuroses: never fought, never gave me anything I could hold on to. They took me away from myself in the quietest possible way. I always felt this on some level: I found myself fascinated with hypnotism, with post-hypnotic suggestions in which the person never realizes that he has slipped away. Subtlety is almost the perfect crime.

Ronald

For as long as I can remember, it always seemed that my parents and family were something fine and special. We had everything and we had each other. We were bright, healthy, athletic, talented, good looking, successful, diverse, and "close." As far as I could know, this was all there was, which is why what they did to fuck me up was so subtle. I could never pin anything down and say "Wait a minute, this is all a lie." You see, appearances were so strong it was nearly impossible, especially for a little boy, to counter them with reality. It was as if they were reading a script and doing and saying all the things that good, loving parents would do and say, but they were never behind it at all and I was merely a mirror upon which they could reflect on their act. My daddy is granite and simply doesn't feel. My mommy plays at feelings and uses them as levers. Both of them are dead. Here is some of their work:

The first thing I knew at a very tender age was that I had to prove I was sick (fever, or throw up, or just look horrible enough with the proper symptoms and explanations) in order to be cared for or, later, to stay home from school. Once I was believed, my mommy would take care of me like she cared, but as I've seen her face in Primals, she really hated it and me and underneath it all was saying "*Die*." Even then I knew what was happening—that it hurt more to ask her to care than to be sick—so I stopped getting sick. In six years of junior high and high school, I missed four days of school. So I became injury-prone. I had a long history of body injuries, mostly self-inflicted in one way or another, and with each one I felt a moment of hope that maybe this time they'd love me. Each time I found out almost immediately that it wouldn't work, and so I belittled the injury and hurt alone, until finally I still got hurt out of the need and hope, but then couldn't even tell them out of the fear and pain.

When I was young, I had trouble breathing through my nose, so I used my mouth, which required that it be open. I must have looked "bad," so as soon as I could understand the words, I remember being told to keep my mouth closed. They told me if I didn't, a bird would fly in and peck my throat, which scared the shit out of me. So I closed it and tried to sleep with it closed and had all kinds of trouble breathing. The feeling was "they don't want me to breathe," i.e., "live." Eating was another thing. I naturally did many things left-handed. When I was twelve, one day they told me they had decided I was going to eat from then on with my right hand because everyone else did and it would be better for me. I couldn't understand and said I didn't want to. They told me I would eat with my right hand or not eat. So for a few days I didn't eat. Eventually, a compromise. I was also taught how to swallow without making any noise, how to chew without seeming to be chewing— how to eat without being there. Die. I was forbidden to belch or fart or spit—even when alone—and I was taught to flush the toilet while pissing so the sound wouldn't carry. Wipe well, wash well, and kill the body! And at the same time it was acclaimed how physical (athletic) a family we were—pride in the body and all that. But never touch it or feel it—especially your own.

A million times I heard "Do what you want to do" or "We're not putting any pressure on you," and every time it was not only a lie but a cue that soon I was going to hear what it was I was going to be pressured to do for them, ass backwards. My daddy would come to me and tell me he wanted to talk to me, and it would make me shake invisibly because I knew I was about to be given some subtle directive—that something was going to change for me, but not because of a change in me. He would start our talks by saying something to reassure me, to the effect of "Do what you want . . ." and then with the same tone of voice for praise or disappointment (which was frequent), we would begin. It really didn't matter what it was, it would change me. Do more or less of something for him. Another separation between me and me-plus-them.

We were taught values—or the appearance of values. Being honest means if you're twelve, you don't go for under twelve to the movies. But values were never connected to feelings. I went through my whole childhood being honest and never feeling honest down deep. My life was a lie, and I was honest and I had no way of knowing how that came to be. Another way that there was a constant split between what seemed to be real and what was real inside. And because of unmet needs, I had to live what seemed to be real and hold on secretly or kill what was real inside.

There is more, of course; I feel I could write indefinitely. It also feels that the pain in me has been distilled and diluted in the writing. The pain fills me up and takes hours and months of Primals to feel and connect, and the writing looks so neat and definitive. Like it's unfair to write about it like this. But one of the basic over-all effects of what they did was a nearly total doubt of my perceptions, feelings, intuitions, sensations. Being split meant living for me last. I can't be me, me can't be real. Like when my daddy would come home from road trips and, as a little boy, I would stay awake late so I could sit at the top of the stairs and hear the greeting sounds with my mommy, and then run to bed before he came up out of fear of being caught. When he would come into my room, pretending to be asleep; instead of joy at his return and warmth and hug and love, there was fear and lie and hold on. Being neurotic meant being put in impossible situations and having to make them right. It meant balancing feelings with craziness and living in the deadly tension that comes of that, and it pisses me off and hurts even saying that. Damn this typewriter. The print doesn't change with my feelings.

I have a son who will be seven this May. While I have not fouled him up as a daddy living with him (he was adopted at birth), I was part of a bad start which I now know will be part of him even in my absence. I didn't love his mother; he was conceived in sloppy carelessness. A summer sex affair born out of my (and her) neurotic needs with no real feelings exchanged, only parts of absent bodies and a little tension. That summer was the last time we saw each other, and I was 20. I found out through her lawyer by mail. My father called it a "mistake" and told me he wouldn't tell my mother because it would kill her. But then he did and it didn't. They forbade me to see her or speak to her. I kept getting letters from Mary telling me she just wanted to talk to me, that her family had totally rejected her, and she didn't want me to be afraid, etc. But I needed Mommy and Daddy more than I needed her, so I was a good boy. So I've never seen Mary since that night. I've never seen my son, but he was never wanted from the beginning, and his mother was feeling no love or support, and somewhere he is walking around with that pain and any other that has been piled on since. His first feelings are of rejection and pain. He was "disposed of" as cleanly and economically and in the name of "doing what's best" as parents and lawyers could contrive.

Louise

A lot of people in this therapy were grossly deprived, with physically and mentally cruel and sadistic parents, or no parents, etc., but I'm one of those who got the subtle fuck-up. To begin with, I was an "accident," along with some very bad circumstances: born during the depression, a father out of work, and a mother thirty-seven years old with her planned family half-grown (two sisters, eleven and thirteen, and a brother twelve). Mother had to support the family with her sewing for several years after I was born, so she sewed all day and fitted the customers at night after supper. She nursed me inbetween times until I was eight months old, and was always there to feed and clothe me, but the bulk of my care was left to my sisters when they weren't at school. When they were at school, I cared for myself a lot because Mommy just wasn't "there."

With my sisters, they played with me like a toy when they felt like it, but then they had to take me with them (often taking turns) when they went to play with their friends. I would be left to sit in a stroller and watch, feeling incredibly lonely, just wanting to go home, and scared they would forget about me and I'd never get home. Even when I did get home, it was no good because my mother wasn't there for me—she was involved with her sewing and the other kids and scarcely noticed my needs. My father felt help-less around a very small child, so for me there was really no one who cared about what I wanted or needed, and I shut down early so I wouldn't even let myself know I wanted something. I "took care of myself."

Until Primal Therapy, when I began to feel all this, I never knew why I hurt, because on the surface I could never see anything wrong with my family. Now that I know what *my* pain is about, I'm also beginning to see what I have done and am sometimes still doing to my daughter, Lisa. Lisa is two now and was just eight months old when we started therapy. Most of the time she seems pretty real. But a lot of times I feel that she's being "too good." If it weren't for what I know about feeling, I'd feel really lucky, be-cause she never seems to get all that upset about anything. It's been bothering me, and in the past two months I've begun to realize that one big reason why she seems to have so few painful feelings is that as soon as she starts to cry over some small thing (like changing a TV channel when the program is over), all my pain of never hav-ing been given what I needed comes up and I give her what she seems to want and then I'll manage to change the channel when her attention is elsewhere. I think these are times when she could feel some old feelings if I would go ahead and do what I want and let her cry. I'm finding that the more I feel of that feeling of never having gotten, the easier it is for me to let her cry at those times.

Another thing I do that doesn't cause a problem now, but that I feel is bad for Lisa, is to try to be there for her at times when I'm so deep in my own pain that it's just not possible. I go through the motions anyway, telling myself that if the only time I act like I'm there for her is when I really am, she'd seldom have a mommy. There is a real conflict here for me, but I also know that a lot of my trying comes out of my own pain of no one being there for me. What I feel at those times is that I just can't let her feel that same aloneness, but I'm sure that's my own pain, and besides, I'm not being a real mommy when I do this. Another reason I try is that Lisa is often my own mommy for me, and I feel the need for her to love me. I'm afraid then that if I'm a bad mommy, she won't love me as much as she loves her daddy, who seems to be there for her more often than I am. Now that I'm thinking about it, I realize I've used lots of things to keep her from feeling her hurts. For example, if we're in the car heading for home and she wants a bottle and I didn't bring one, I have often become what Vivian [Janov] calls a "super-explainer," telling her how I didn't bring a bottle, but we're so many blocks from home and when we get there, etc., etc.—all designed to stop her crying, and the worst part is that it works. The reason again, of course, is that her crying brings up my own pain.

Although the specific circumstances are very different from my own, I find myself giving Lisa the same kind of subtle fuck-up as I got.

ME AND THEM

You're Roger for your life they said
Make sure it's all the same
And walk and talk and wash yourself
And always play our game
    I'm me, my name is Roger
    I said to selfish eyes
    I need your love for what I am
    And hold me when I cry
Be sure to tell the truth they said
And do the best you can
The world is full of freeloaders
But you must be a man

Let me be a child first
I said while losing hope
Don't take me where I cannot be
And force me then to cope
It's time to go to school they said
To learn the whys of how
Your talent's great, your future bright
You cannot fail us *now*
I'll do the best I can I said
And closed the door on me
The unreal struggle had begun
To get what cannot be
We think you're doing fine they said
Someday you'll be content
Be sure you do just what you want
That's what we've always meant
But it was all an awful lie
And I was feeling pain
And life began to flow away
Like clay in heavy rain
You're off the beaten path they said
Take hold and set your sights
A man must work to fill his time
And put down inner fight
It's too late, I cannot hear you
I said and turned away
And lived my numb tomorrows
In the pain of yesterday
You make it hard on us they said
We loved you once you know
And now it seems you've gone away
But you've no place to go
I've found a way to get me back
I said to covered ears
By feeling anger, fear, and pain
The death of many years
Go do it by yourself they said
It's time you're on your own
We've taken what we needed
And delivered you full grown

You gave me as you knew to give
I said and tried to cry
Now I'm alone and finding out
To live is not to die
We're gone from one another now
We've nothing left to say
I bought from them a life of lies
And hope that wouldn't pray
I took from them a chance to live
And feel a newborn day.

VI

Breast Feeding

One of the early traumas is nursing the infant when there is inadequate milk so that the baby is being starved. Or having an inadequate breast so that his need for perioral stimulation (around the mouth) is unfulfilled. The amount of breast milk available is intimately associated with the "emotional" center—the hypothalamus. And the size of the breast, as well, may depend on proper hormone balance. An important function of breast feeding is the perioral stimulation it provides. A scrawny, fairly flat-chested mother can't provide the feel of softness and warmth a full-breasted one can. The cutaneous sensation, in short, is different for the infant. We often see people rubbing the area around the mouth when preoccupied or thinking through a task, and I can't help wondering if these people were not left to stimulate the perioral region for a lifetime for themselves because of poor breast feeding or perhaps exclusive bottle feeding. Stimulation is the key term, for, as we shall see in a moment, the brain depends on stimulation for its physical development.

I have noted elsewhere (*The Primal Scream*) that the breasts of some female Primal patients have grown after therapy. The patients became different people in a most literal way, which had nothing to do with how they performed in the world. This difference will affect their newborn babies in terms of how much stimulation the mothers' bodies will provide, and this stimulation will help in the development of the brains of the offspring—all because of a change in body structure.

Breast feeding is crucial because of the sucking, the warmth, the physical contact and the rocking. Experiments in the feeding of monkeys have shown that the rocking motion is an added benefit in keeping them satisfied and relaxed. Too often, bottle feeding is simply a process in which a bottle is stuck in the baby's mouth while he is lying in the crib and he is left to fend for himself. This eliminates the warmth, physical contact, rocking and just about every necessary ingredient in making a child relaxed and satisfied. Bottle feeding, at best, is artificial and can never be a real substitute for the natural breast-feeding process.

A neurotic mother who has trouble producing milk may also handle her newborn in a jerky, hurried, harsh manner so that breast feeding is not always a pleasant experience for the infant. Children, especially infants, who have an acute sense of touch, can sense the pain and tension in a parent while breast feeding and respond to *this* sensation first, so that instead of being relaxed while feeding, they are tense. Obviously, one bit of rough, hurried handling is not going to produce a neurosis. But months and years of it, together with other traumatic factors, add up to overbearing pressure. I shall discuss handling and touching in greater detail later on, calling on animal research when relevant.

There is a good deal of research on the importance of breast feeding. Ashley Montagu cites much of this research.[*] Breast-fed babies have better immune reactions because the rich colostrum which is secreted by the mother in the first days of the child's life is rich in antibodies which help the infant combat infection. The nutritional benefits of breast milk have been documented by Montagu. Nonbreast-fed babies are much more likely to suffer respiratory ailments, diarrhea, eczema, and asthma. Breast feeding is crucial for the proper development of the facial and dental structures. And, finally, adequate sucking at the breast is intimately associated with deep breathing. That is, the greater the time the baby sucks, the more likely he is to have a full and deep breathing pattern. The more deeply he breathes, by and large, the less likely he will be to hold down feelings. To put it another way: In neurotics everything is part of the defense system, including the musculature and the

[*] Ashley Montagu, *Touching* (New York: Columbia University Press, 1971).

breathing patterns. Breathing patterns *are* behavior, and when children need to hold feelings inside, breathing is likely to be shallow and constricted.

One of the most important factors about breast feeding is the physical contact with the mother. Physical contact tends to increase the oxygen content of the blood, and, as Barron has shown with animals, "[There is a] rise in the excitability of the respiratory center [which] in turn increases the depth of the respiratory effort, increases the level of oxygenation of the blood, and so enhances the capacity for further muscular movement and strength."*

Then, of course, I have cited elsewhere the importance of the heartbeat, indicating that the reassurance provided by the steady beat may be imprinted in the womb on the infant.

To summarize thus far, any number of factors can produce tension in an infant. Mostly this tension is imperceptible. But each factor becomes a tributary adding to the underlying stream of tension, which finally erupts into symptoms such as colic, eczema, diarrhea, or simply continuous, inexplicable crying which is the infant's first-line defense to signal that he is in trouble. The choice of the symptom is not something "thought out" by the infant. Rather, it is the result of many tension-inducing experiences and occurs at the focus of the deprivation. For example, a child insufficiently touched or harshly handled may have skin disorders. One inadequately nursed may be constantly putting objects in his mouth or babbling. A child who is prohibited from, and punished for, crying may develop a running nose.

By and large, the focus of the symptom is the area of need. It is the area which requires special "treatment." It is the area of *overload*. Thus, a child forced to toilet train before he is ready may become a bed-wetter and later sexually promiscuous. He will use his penis, in short, to relieve tension in the exact area where the trauma originally occurred. This, of course, becomes complex because the overload may not be a single stressor. A child may be weaned improperly, forced to train too early, or fed on a schedule not of his making. His choice of relief area will depend on his life circum-

---

* Ibid., p. 61.

stance, his cultural milieu, and what his parents allow. In a religious household, masturbation (to relieve too early toilet training) may be out of the question because the child is so riddled with fear. So his oulet will be something else—constant praying, for example. Once a relief area is set up, it will be the focus for relief of *all* the generalized tension.* Thus, a facial or mouth tic will occur regularly and for a lifetime as the spillway for the tension that results from a variety of sources.

The body does not differentiate. It only responds to the overload in its habitual "grooved" way. What happens as we grow up is that the need-Pain remains as pristine as the day it began because that need-Pain is our physiologic truth, and truth knows no time boundaries. What does happen is that the defense or outlet changes. It becomes more sophisticated—from thumb-sucking to smoking, from bed-wetting to masturbation, from boyish fist-fighting to sophisticated tongue-lashing. Sometimes the defense remains unaltered for a lifetime. Recurrent dreams are one good example. Tics, asthma, ulcers, and poor skin are others. In any case, symptoms are the indication of the split. The beginning of a symptom, say allergies or stuttering, is the beginning of the split. Sometimes the split does not occur with a dramatic symptom; the personality just becomes "fixed." This simply indicates that the child, split away from his Pain, has found a set way to handle the overload. It may be the male child delighting in wearing his mother's clothes or a daughter who becomes pale and sickly, quiet and polite.

Even though Primal Pains have different origins, some physical (circumcision) and some psychological (rejection), the bodily processes involved in handling the Pain are the same. That is be-

---

* H. B. Miller reports in *Science Digest* (July 1970): "[I] suspect that malignancy [cancer] is really a generalized disturbance, with the tumor itself being a local manifestation of the over-all process." He discusses how tension affects the pituitary and hypothalamus, which then produce secretions which eventually affect the cells of the body. He attributes the possibility of tumor development to metabolic disturbances (emotionally caused) which excessively stimulate tissue and cells until there is structural disorganization. He discusses reversal of tumor growth with emotional procedures. I have often thought that cancer is the "insanity of the cell"; of cells gone wild and uncontrolled due to primal pressure. That pressure must ultimately affect us on a cellular level.

cause psychologically induced Pain is still processed by the physical system; neurosis is physical. Children in unloving institutional settings can die from the so-called psychological stress.

Because symptoms are extensions of need, being the funnel through which need-Pain is poured, we can learn a lot about a child and his underlying problems through observation of his symptoms. Indeed, in Primal Therapy, daily scrutiny of the patient's changing symptoms tells us about which Pains are close. For example, if a child invents a friend who sits with him, talks with him, plays with him, etc., and this delusion goes on for months, he may be having the equivalent of an adult delusion of being the "child of God," a God who is ever-present and watchful. Both of these unreal ideas may be symptoms resulting from the blockage of feeling alone and abandoned. They are the misconnections caused by an overload of feeling, and their content indicates to us the kind of feeling being diverted. The amount of overload is indicated by the bizarre quality of the idea. The further an idea is from reality the more bizarre its nature. It is the level of Pain which causes this generalization. Pain is the force which drives ideas away from their reference points. So a child may not only invent a fantasy companion because he is rejected by his family, but eventually may become convinced that the companion talks to him and directs his movements. This later may become solidified into a delusion that a hidden force (now external) is behind his actions, and of course there is a hidden force behind what he does—Primal Pain. Because we can see the unity of symptoms and their causes, we must take care not to study symptoms as discrete and viable entities.

When a child is taken to a doctor for the treatment of symptoms, the doctor is treating the *result* of all the forces that I have mentioned up to now—birth trauma, circumcision, crib noise, inadequate breast milk, insufficient nursing time, etc. It does not matter whether it is a "head" doctor treating stealing or phobias, or a "body" doctor treating allergies and colitis. They are dealing with the end point of a historic process. There usually is no single factor which could be pointed to as "causing" the symptom he sees. Unless the doctor is ready to delve into the underlying stream of tension and root out the various contributing causes of the symptom, the best that he can do is handle the "head of the monster" and hope for the best. His treatment can never cure.

The following is a good example of what I mean when I say that a Primal is a compacted experience—pain after pain laminated together, symbolized in a single event. The patient isn't screaming in terror from that one event he is reliving; rather, that event sums up and represents hundreds of similar events, all producing the same kind of hurt.

Evelyn

In my sixth week of therapy, I got really overloaded for about two days, mostly with terror. In group, even after sobbing and screaming for forty minutes like a possessed person, my body was still traumatized. Even when I was feeling and letting go totally, it still felt as though the individual cells in my body were being seared and ripped apart. Finally, I asked for some tranquilizers; my body was like a limp rag after two and one-half days of this, and still the terror kept coming.

That night, just as I was about to take a thorazine, a friend came in. We talked a little, he gave me a wonderful head massage which acted as a natural tranquilizer, and I was able to sleep for six hours without interruption. He slept on my floor that night.

In the morning, somewhat rested, I lay on my back on the floor while my friend made some breakfast. I still felt weak, a little dizzy. When I stood upright, my head would begin to swim, and I would have to lean on something and lower my head. With my head lowered it was a little better. I noticed that the lower I could get my head, the more the "sickness" subsided; thus, lying on my back was the most comfortable.

Then breakfast was ready and I sat down to eat. I looked at the food. I became agitated, the thought of eating the food made me sick. My friend said, "What's the matter?" and my right arm suddenly flew up above my head in defense, totally involuntarily, and I looked up, horrified, as if something were about to hit me. The plate of peas! It was the plate of peas my mother broke over my head because I wouldn't eat!

I became extremely disoriented, backed away from the plate of food in horror, could barely speak to my friend. I finally asked him to put the plate of food in a paper bag and carry it to the Institute for me. He had said he would sit with me. Walking to the Institute, I was feverish, disoriented, sick with fear and anxiety. I only made it because I had his support.

We got a room, went in, and for one hour I was totally immersed in that incident from eighteen years ago, coming out of it only seconds at a time. As soon as I got in the room, I threw myself on the floor, both arms clasped over my head, screaming, "My head, my head, my head, my head . . ." It seems odd to say "I" threw myself because it *felt* as if something else had thrown me on the floor—some inner force had taken over. There was no conscious volition, no decision, no control, yet "I" was doing it.

How can I possibly describe the chasm I fell into that day? I screamed in sheer terror for about twenty minutes, throwing myself into various primitive defensive positions—on my back, my arms up, screaming "No, no, no, no . . ."; crouched in the corner, screaming; rolled up in a ball, my head tucked to my chest, arms covering my head, still screaming. Then a new, stranger horror overcame me, and I became completely silent, my eyes wide open. I looked to my right—it was my father, my wonderful, kind, but also scared father, sitting to my right at the dinner table, after the plate broke.

I knew that I wanted to call him to help me, but no words came. I reached out my right hand toward him. I felt him sitting there, my lips silently formed the syllable "Da—." It felt as if I was calling him from across a desert, as if his name had been barely formed in an incredibly deep cavern inside me at the time of the incident, and now that barely formed name was moving up slowly from the bottom of that pit, and my lips formed again "Da—." Still no words.

There were no words for ten minutes, only that silent syllable and my arm stretching, reaching out to him. Finally I made the sound "Da—" in a wooden way. Then again "Da—," and finally "Da-ddy . . . Da-ddy." I just kept repeating "Da-ddy," wooden and stiff; "my Daddy, my daddy, my daddy, my daddy . . ."—

screams and screams and screams and screams as I moved from my place at the ghost-dinner table over toward him. I looked at his face and screamed-sobbed, "Daddy—tell her—tell her—tell her (screams) —I can't—I can't—eat it, I can't—eat it, I can't eat it."

Then screams and sobs for another fifteen to twenty minutes, but the peak had been reached when I uttered the syllable "Da—," and although the crying now was still from pain, the fear was marginal. I was now crying in relief, and mostly for my father whom I had just remet after an estrangement of twenty years. What can I say about finding my own father? There are no words for it.

I was terrorized throughout my childhood by my mother; she hit me nearly every day, never hurting me much physically, but the look on her face said "I hate you and I'm going to kill you." Then she would chase me.

Also, the process of being emotionally cut off from my father took place largely over about two years for me, between five and seven.

But although both of these traumas occurred over time, my immersion in this horror from the past somehow broke the back of both of these pains: Much of the terror I experienced at the hands of my mother seemed somehow gathered into that one china plate shattered over my head; likewise, the pain of the slow emotional disengagement from my father, whom I loved and adored, coalesced into that one time when I hadn't been able to call out to him. So that when I felt the plate break and when I choked out "Da—," some kind of spell was broken.

Incidentally, when this actually happened in my childhood, I was completely silent, I didn't cry, I didn't look at either of my parents. As soon as I realized what had happened (she came from behind me and the plate was smashed on my head without warning), I became oddly calm, finished eating in silence, and went to my room. I was seven.

VII

The Needs

ORALITY

Freud believed that there were stages in early life which were the central focus of the child's existence. Thus, the child first passed through the oral stage, moved to the anal, and finally developed to the mature, genital stage. Fixations during these stages were supposed to determine the kind of personality the person would have later—oral-dependent, anal-sadistic, etc. Lack of satisfaction at any stage would keep the child stuck in that stage forevermore.

In one sense, Freud was right. Lack of satisfaction does cause fixation—continuous attempts to fulfill that lack later in life. But there is no "stage" of fixation. There are so many early needs which coexist and are coterminous that one could not characterize those periods in terms of a single need. For example, an infant who is not allowed sufficient movement, who is swaddled or otherwise continuously restricted, is being traumatized or "fixated." This may well occur in Freud's oral stage. Or if the child is not held during this same time, he is again being hurt. He will have to go around touching things thereafter, perhaps. There is no way to compartmentalize development because we develop as whole human beings with a variety of needs, *all* of which must be satisfied at each step of the way. In Freud's time, eating was important. Little was known about the need for touch; and particularly in Vienna, the show of physical affection was not something practiced broadly, so it is no wonder that the need for touch was minimized in deference to oral needs.

Let us look at some of the needs of infants and children and see how crucial they are. I shall call upon many of the research studies in a recent volume by Newton and Levine to corroborate my observations.*

Seitz studied cats who were weaned early, normally, and late. Here are his findings: 1. Early-weaned cats are persistent but disorganized in attempts to get food; 2. They are the least goal-directed, least apt to share food, and are more suspicious, fearful, and aggressive with other cats; 3. They are the most anxious in novel situations.† All of this can be attributed to a single traumatic focus. What is clear is that early deprivation in a specific area produces *generalized* neurotic behavior because that specific deprivation produces generalized tension—not just tension around the mouth. And it is the organism, not just the oral cavity, that is deprived of need fulfillment. We can understand this better, perhaps, if we think of how tense we can become when deprived of sex for a length of time. It isn't merely that the sex impulse is left unfulfilled and the genitalia unstimulated, but that the organism itself is deprived of the release. The skin may break out, headaches may occur, or irritability ensue. The sexual deprivation creates generalized tension. We can see the dialectic at work here: specific deficits produce generalized behavior and generalized tension produces specific neurotic acts. The specific is always part of the general so that generalized behavior always contains the specific. To solve the specific is to change the general. This is more than semantics, for resolving specific origins of amorphous neurotic tension eliminates that tension, and it is the *only* way that tension can be eliminated. Dealing with the general behavior, the overt neurotic behavior, then always leaves the specific origins intact. The importance of the cat research is twofold: 1. It shows that specific deprivation can produce generalized behavior; and 2. it indicates that early deprivation has long-lasting effects.

Here is what Newton and Levine have to say about animals de-

* Grant Newton, and Seymour Levine, *Early Experience and Behavior* (Springfield, Illinois: Charles Thomas, 1969).
† P. F. D. Seitz, "Infantile Experience and Adult Behavior in Animal Subjects," *Psychosomatic Medicine* 21 (1959) pp. 353–378.

prived of normal sucking: "[They] have the same forms of stereo-typed acts, regardless of large differences in other aspects of their social experience. Thus, home-reared animals, animals reared indi-vidually in open cages or in complete isolation, may all develop thumbsucking and engage in repetitive movements."* We must not automatically conclude from this, however, that a child sucks con-stantly because he was weaned too early. Sucking is one of the few ways an infant can relieve tension from *any* source—it is an instinc-tual pacifier.

In Primal Therapy, we frequently see Primals in which the pa-tient will suck his thumb with enormous suction, an involuntary act which may go on for one or two hours. The patient will usually report later that it seemed as if months were compacted into that two-hour sucking Primal and they often state that afterward all need to smoke is gone. The relived sequence involved the entire need, compacted into the history of the organism, coded into the patient's physiology in a most literal way. Thus, a homosexual may go around sucking penises for a lifetime and never resolve that sucking need, yet have a two-hour Primal where he relives the need *in context as an infant* and resolves it. This is to say that the need is felt for what it always was; it can never go away until that happens, no matter how long it is acted out symbolically. Of course, in humans the sucking need is overlaid by many other needs, so that a person turns to sucking penises, not only because of a need to suck, but also because there is a need for human warmth.

It is important to understand, therefore, that a parent's one mis-take does not irreversibly harm his child. It is not that on one spe-cific day the baby was left to cry too long or that he wasn't changed when he should have been. "It's as though," said one pa-tient, "my system has been trying to make up for some *develop-mental* need. It was like my body was and is crying out for a breast that was never there when I needed it. Nothing I could do then would shut off that need, so I did the next best thing—I became a head-banger and I suppose that it is not unrelated to the fact that I have so many masochistic fantasies today."

The complexity of the neurotic symptom is illustrated in the case

* Op. cit., p. 448.

of a patient who stuttered. His first Primals were about being made to say things before he could even form the words—for example, "Say Grandma!" After he came close to pronouncing the words with an almighty struggle, there would be loud applause by his "audience." He was being traumatized, and the area of trauma was the mouth; but why stuttering? Aside from a possible neurological predisposition, what else could cause it? In this case, a Primal about having to speak before he was ready led to reliving a vague anxiety in his crib, heretofore completely forgotten. All he knew was that he had fear, the same kind of fear he experienced when unable to say the words that his grandmother insisted upon. In the darkness in his crib, he remembered being afraid and crying; suddenly something was thrust into his mouth, a bottle, and he was truly terrified. There was no caressing and holding, no soft words of comfort, just a thrust of a bottle into his mouth by a hurried and impatient mother. Not only didn't the bottle pacify him, it also traumatized his oral area, another factor in the origins of his stuttering. The bottle-thrusting routine was not an isolated incident. It happened again and again until finally the boy stopped his crying in order to *avoid* it. Yet his fear remained. Not only did he stutter, but he had a lifelong fear of the dark, a fear that began with an incident or set of incidents which predated his memory.

Two more examples may help clarify the point. Overeating and alcoholism are considered by analytic theorists as oral-dependent neurotic habits. Children may have a good day, yet when left alone, their thoughts will turn immediately to food. Putting them on diets hardly changes anything, because when they are alone, what is often reactivated is the early time in life when they were schedule-fed, often starving between feedings and having no mental capacity to understand that mother would be around in an hour or two. All they could feel was abandonment and terror. Indeed, so many of us were brought up on scheduled feeding that overeating has become a national syndrome, and dieting a national fixation. The problem with dieting is that in a sense it is the child who is being starved again, producing that original anxiety (and desperation for food) over being hungry.

If we could only put ourselves in the infant's place, we could understand these traumas better. Infants cannot rationalize. They cannot think in terms of hourly spans. Being starved and being alone in the dark in Pain means death. They have no conception when Pain will end, so they cannot defend against it in a cerebral way. We recently saw an alcoholic who had been drinking for twenty years. He was using liquid as a pacifier. Obviously, that liquid was being poured through the oral cavity. But the Primal he had was of being so catastrophically thirsty that his tongue hung far out of his mouth for over two hours during the Primal. He came out of it feeling unbelievably parched. He was not orally fixated, as his previous analyst had told him; he was traumatized by thirst in the first weeks of his life, and that plus having cold, unyielding parents combined to produce alcoholism. Using liquid to pacify was the prototypic defense against a prototypic trauma.

If the prototypic trauma were around food, then *any* later uneasiness might cause the child to snack, because that uneasiness reawakens the original one.

It is important to understand that it is not necessary to relive each trauma in order to reverse the neurosis. Each trauma is connected to a central, overriding feeling, say of being helpless, and when that feeling is relived it brings with it a plethora of painful memories clustered around it. Thus, a single Primal may relieve the pain of a traumatic experience that has occurred several times. We can begin to appreciate the complexity of the many incidents and traumas that go into the making of a neurotic symptom, and how useless it is to treat the symptom as an independent entity.

In conclusion, we must take care to avoid categories of development because humans do not develop in categories. A child restricted and prohibited from moving might well be "fixated" in terms of that trauma. He might feel anxious whenever confined and need to keep free and on the move. But we certainly would not have to call that period of his life the "kinesthetic stage."

MOVEMENT—MENTAL AND PHYSICAL

We might not think of movement as a basic need but, like not getting love, it only hurts when it isn't possible. The need to move and explore isn't simply a psychological one but is necessary for the stimulation of brain growth. It is through movement that we learn proper visual perception, balance and coordination, and get a feel of ourselves in motion. Perhaps the need to be rocked early in life is the inchoate need for movement, something a newborn cannot do for himself. In any case, I see it as part of the need for stimulation. Burlington found that "the well-known rhythmic movements such as rocking . . . are known to increase where the children are confined too much in their prams or cribs."* Other investigators have noted rocking and head-banging in infants who were not allowed sufficient movement. Kulka indicates that this may derive from "an attempt to gratify . . . kinesthetic needs."†

There are many explanations for why children head-bang or rock compulsively. The selection of symptoms and the notion of prototypic anxieties and defenses are discussed in detail in the section on birth. One reason why something such as head-banging comes about is that the earliest area of trauma may have been the banging of the head against the pubic arch during the birth process. Any later stress may reactivate that original trauma and produce head-banging. The symptom is a reminder of stored trauma in the child's system.

A child may rock compulsively in his crib because of excessive physical restriction much earlier in his life—too tight a blanket, for example. Or he may rock compulsively because of inadequate rocking by his parents during the first weeks of life. The traumatized child is trying to "make up" for his early trauma. This is the Primal "rebound effect." A child who had to wear corrective braces in his earliest months when restriction had a profound effect on the development of the brain, may be someone who must compulsively move and be hyperactive later. Thus, any situation of confinement (confinement in a classroom, for example) will reactivate the early situation of restriction in the braces and produce anxiety and the need to move.

* Dorothy Burlingham, "Notes on Problems of Motor Restraint During Illness," in *Drives, Affects, Behavior*, R. M. Lowenstein, (New York: International University Press, 1953) vol. I, pp. 169–75.

† A. Kulka, et al., "Kinesthetic Needs in Infancy," *American Journal of Orthopsychiatry* 30 (1960): 306–314.

There is research to indicate that a number of visual disturbances are associated with children who were not permitted to crawl sufficiently. (See Carl Delacato's work in regard to this.) The rebound effect seems to be lifelong—the child graduates from rocking to hyperactivity on the playground and in the classroom, to having to keep on the go as an adult. Later, any restrictive situation, such as having to sit still in a lecture hall, may trigger the early trauma and produce anxiety and a vague need to "get out." Foot-tapping or finger-drumming are other manifestations of this physical rebound effect. One may only wonder at what deleterious effects result from the Oriental practice of swaddling infants.

Confinement is not only physical. It is more often mental. The child is only permitted to express "allowable" thoughts. He is put into a mental strait jacket almost from the day he can utter words. He will have to be religious and think religious thoughts if that is his parents' desire, or he will be allowed to say only what is good about people and can never be critical. This kind of confinement may produce a different kind of defense—mental running, otherwise known as fantasy and daydreaming. Confined in a boring classroom, this person may find himself lost in fantasy; he has fled with his head. Having been strait jacketed mentally, the rebound became mental.

Of course, the idea of a purely "mental" strait jacket is erroneous. To suppress a feeling and its thought counterpart is to produce a physical pressure; thus one may fantasize and tap his foot at the same time. It is important to remember that thoughts are not viable entities floating in the space of the mind. They are inseparably tied to, and are part of, our bodies and our feelings, so that suppressed thoughts mean suppression of parts of our neurophysiology. This means that in some ways you grow up distorted when you do not grow up "you." The face, mouth, and body, in a literal way, twists to become "them." In many purely physical Primals patients will find themselves involuntarily twisting and unwinding, while in tremendous Pain, feeling how they were literally twisted by the idealogical strait jacket of their parents. Additionally, patients have felt how their fear hunched over their shoulders, caved in their chests, and so on.

How many times have we heard parents say "Now you sit there and keep still"? Too many parents forget that children are naturally active and exuberant. Parents who have turned themselves into robots attempt to mold their children into their own "dead" image. They do not understand that to restrict children's bodies is to restrict their experience. There are sensory receptors all over our muscle systems which feed information to the brain. By exercising our muscles spontaneously, we are also in a sense exercising our brains. Movement *is* an experience. Through it we learn spontaneity of feeling. Deprivation of movement is a deprivation of experience, and that experience in turn affects the growth of the brain, especially early in life. Allowing children freedom shouldn't be seen as a "nice" thing for an "enlightened" parent to do. Freedom is a biologic necessity!

Children who are constantly reprimanded for darting about and exploring soon automatically check their movements so that they move in cautious, circumscribed ways. Children who cannot say "I think my teacher is terrible—I can't stand her or school," soon learn to examine each thought just as they examine each movement. The cautiousness becomes automatic and the spontaneity of *any* feeling or movement is lost. Later in life there may be frigidity, not because of poor sexual training, but because the child was never allowed to show and feel his excitement. One patient relived a scene where he got very excited about something at the age of six. He looked into his parents' eyes and realized in a flash that they were both lifeless. He knew then that he had to be "dead" to get by. He squashed his exuberance and became like them. Later counseling to encourage him to act more alive would obviously be useless.

When a child has his thoughts restricted, those thoughts and their bodily counterparts simply don't vanish. They remain sequestered, exerting a pressure. That pressure pushes the mind into derivative channels so that the person will have "neurotic," non-straight thoughts about almost anything because he cannot be straight without Pain and fear; being straight, in itself, becomes a danger. That is why unstraight people are so consistently unreal about so many diverse aspects of life.

The same pressure from the real feelings creates the daydreams which are again derivatives from the real feelings. They are mental stories, bizarre ideation created by submerged thoughts and feelings. Why is this bizarre ideation unreal? Because if it were real, the person would simply be feeling his feelings. Clearly, if underlying feelings can produce unreal ideation such as daydreams, they can also produce other forms of unrealistic thinking.

One example of the subterranean pressure of denied movement is seen in a recent Primal in which a patient relived being held down in a wrestling match with his brother. His brother kept him pinned down for fifteen minutes until the patient was in a panic state. That experience lingered on and was left unresolved. And later, whenever he felt fearful, he had an inexplicable aching and tingling in his arms. Reliving that feeling *in context* resolved that.

An almost universally sanctioned method of "pinning down" infants is the use of the playpen. This literally constricts the field of movement of the child. Few mothers understand that this is a form of jail for their young ones. Somehow infants are supposed to take confinement gladly. "Well," the mother can answer, "I can't be with my baby every minute and if he isn't kept in his playpen, he could wander around and hurt himself." Playpens are a convenience, there is no doubt of that. But we must find ways of constructing rooms and backyards so that the child may crawl around freely without danger of hurting himself.* What it also means is that mothers are going to have to be mothers, spending much more time with their children rather than penning them up so that they can get their important housework done. This applies equally to the father if he is home while the mother works. After weaning, it doesn't matter who stays home, mother or father; what matters is that the parents be a parent and not make the child an afterthought who is taken in and out of "jail" when it is convenient.

---

* Lining the child's room with old mattresses so that he can be free to crawl around wherever he wants is an example of what I mean. We have a fully padded "freak-out" room at the Primal Institute, which is about seven by ten feet. Its popularity, according to patients, is due in part to the fact that they can relive early times in playpens or confining rooms where they could not move around freely. Now they can crawl, thrash, and throw themselves about without worrying about being stopped or being hurt.

A woman anthropologist who has been studying chimpanzees in Africa has reared her child like the chimps, without playpens, given him a free environment, and has reported on how content he is. Generations of us have grown up in the infant jail and we have seen the results of this in Primal Therapy. Patients have spent their adult lives acting out trying to feel free by constant traveling, keeping on the move with many appointments, and having so-called "free" sex lives. Some have gone to weekend growth centers and engaged in games where they literally "break free" by breaking out of a group of people who surround them. But, of course, acting out being free only insures continued internal restriction, while feeling those early constrictions, such as in the playpen, finally produces real inner freedom.

Not permitting a child full movement is a form of sensory deprivation. That is, the child is being inadequately stimulated from inside. His brain has insufficient internal input. And we know from our previous discussion what the effects of sensory deprivation are. One of the key brain structures involved in discrimination of movement is the cerebellum. It is very immature at birth and would be vulnerable to lack of stimulation. So again, we see how the brain's literal development depends on freedom (in this case, the freedom to move). The hyperactive child may, in his own way, be responding to a need to make up for the lack of freedom and stimulation very early in life. That is, he has adopted a defense that might have been life-saving. His system recognizes his need for stimulation and movement, but his parents continue to punish him for it, and take him to doctors who try to slow him down with drugs.

The need to be free, in body and mind, is psychophysiologically essential. We see evidence for this need in animal research. Bernhaut found that restricted animals became dull and apathetic.* He maintains that early restriction dampens the alerting center of the brain, the reticular activating system, so that it is deficient in its output. The result is a general slowness and dullness. This research would lead to the conclusion that there is an optimum level of

* M. Bernhaut, E. Gellhorn, and A. T. Rasmussen, "Experimental Contributions to Problems of Consciousness," *Journal of Neurophysiology* 16 (1953): 21–35.

stimulation (and movement is self-stimulation) that is necessary very early in life to set the reticular system on its proper course.

Research by Carpenter found that total physical restriction in young rats, even for one day, resulted in later disruption of behavior—a greater disruption than when rats were deprived of light and sound for the same length of time.* More importantly, work carried out at USC indicates that physically restricted animals are more tumor-prone. We might find out one day that freedom is literally a matter of life and death in terms of the possible catastrophic diseases which result when it is absent.

It is becoming evident that being moved very early in life is a basic need. Monkeys reared with only a moving pendulum (which they could cling to) in their cages developed faster, gained more weight, and were far more socially adept than monkeys reared with a stationary pendulum. Infant monkeys who could not swing on a pendulum were terrified of humans, seemed less explorative, and were generally maladaptive. The question is "Why?" We see that just being allowed movement during infancy is not sufficient; there must be *rhythmical* movement. In other words, the basic needs which are evident immediately after birth are to have those conditions which most closely parallel life in the womb . . . a steady noise like a heartbeat, movement, warmth, and much physical contact. To the extent that each ingredient is missing, the lack of rocking, or rhythmical movement, for example, there will be damage of some kind to the infant's development. One of the ways that research with monkeys and other primates is helpful is in defining some basic needs which we have not considered up to the present. Of course, we do have some research now on humans as well, which helps. Premature infants developed better both physically and psychologically when they were in incubators which moved and rocked. Again, incubators which mirror intrauterine conditions will offer the infant the best chance of survival. What this means is that life after birth is a developmental extension of life before birth, and the less it deviates in a basic way from those prebirth conditions, the better for the infant.

* P. B. Carpenter, "The Effect of Sensory Deprivation on Behavior in the White Rat" (Doctoral Diss., Florida State University, 1959).

Being real means to be able to move freely. It does not mean being constantly on the move, propelled by tension. It does not mean acting free by dancing and running around the room acting like a gorilla. It means to have a fluid, nontense body which responds as a whole in a coordinated way so that one can be good in most sports naturally; so that one can dance with the full use of his body. I am convinced that normal children are naturally good in athletics. This does not mean that athletes are not neurotic. A good runner may still not have *integrated* use of his body so that he can respond and dance to feelingful stimuli such as music. Or, someone who has good use of his body may show his neurosis mentally. There is nothing absolute about it, but all things being equal, a person who throws awkwardly, who cannot learn to swim, etc., is showing signs of neurosis.

I am not at all sure that Primals can completely undo the lack of physical coordination in a previous neurotic. Once the neurosis has "set" into the body, producing lack of coordination which lasts for years, a lot of the damage is done. The neurotic can never be what he would have been had he grown up straight in the first place with years of practice in athletics. Nevertheless, we have seen remarkable changes in coordination as a result of Primals.

THE NEED FOR STIMULATION

There is an optimum level of stimulation based on a child's need. Primal Pain can exist when a child is overstimulated just as easily as when understimulated. A child handled too much out of the anxiety of the parents may well suffer, because his feeling is "Leave me alone!" and he is powerless to stop it, especially during infancy. Several patients have had Primals about being constantly tweaked, tossed in the air, made to do this or that and never allowed sufficient respite. This is because what the parents or grandparents or friends were doing had no relation to the child's needs. Again, neurotics cannot see beyond their own needs. Overstimulation takes many forms. A parent who constantly discharges tension through incessant talking can do it. He will leave the child no time to think his own thoughts; no time to reflect and feel. A parent who constantly fondles his child can do it. A parent with too loud a voice can do it because excessive sensory input literally causes Pain. How does one know when it is too much or too little stimulation? It depends on the need of the child, and a straight child makes his needs known. And a straight parent with no tension to push him will not overstimulate his child.

Overstimulation is usually the lesser problem, however. More often, it is understimulation—another word for it is rejection. We know that the cortex of the brain actually grows and becomes more dense when stimulated, so that there is a need for experience as such. Since experience is first and always of the self, the greater the openness to oneself, the greater the experience of life. Or, to put it differently, the greater the experience of the living processes of the body, the more one experiences life. Newton and Levine point out that "restriction of experience impairs the social development of both monkeys and chimpanzees.* Lack of stimulation made them more excitable in a diffuse way and also more fearful. Further, their social responses became fixated on inappropriate objects, so that they were sexual toward these objects instead of toward their mates. In humans we call this a "fetish." The implication of primate research is that early restrictive environments can produce organisms more attached to things than to people. It is a variation of imprinting; instead of a child being given human warmth, he gets an object such as a bottle or a toy and he fixates on objects perhaps for a lifetime.

TOUCH

It would seem that one index of how much of what kind of stimulation we need would be determined by the amount of brain area involved. The area of touch, for example, has a very large area of representation in the brain. I think that this neurologic fact is an evolutionary testament to just how important touch really is. An infant who is frequently touched is not in Pain from lack of it.

* Op. cit., p. 468.

Thus, he can fully experience the touch of others because he can fully experience himself. A child rarely touched hurts from its lack, whether he knows it or not, because his physiologic need—a need as important as eating—is neglected. Pain seals the touch experience so that later he is blocked against the reception of touch and caressing and can feel "nothing." Too much touch can be just as painful as not enough, for excessive handling can overstimulate a child to the point of shut-down. Overstimulation is not meeting a need, since it is based not on the need of the child but upon the need of the parent.

At birth, touch is one of the few sensory areas fully developed. In fact, after just twenty weeks of fetal development, cutaneous sensation can be experienced. This is reasonable in that the skin constitutes the largest sense organ; it represents a great needing area. It would seem that those areas of the infant's brain which develop sooner correspond to man's ontologic development. So, myelinization of the somesthetic (touch) area would come before myelinization of the areas concerned with meaning. Meaning is a late evolutionary development, so it has a later ontologic development in man. In terms of the development of the brain, the more "animalistic" needs—the needs we share in common with animals—take precedence. It is for this reason, perhaps, that animal research dealing with touch deprivation has particular relevance to human behavior. But animal research cannot do justice to our understanding of neurosis in humans, which is so inextricably tied up with language, thought, and meaning.

Spitz studied institutional children who were seldom held and found a higher incidence of eczema.* Others have found that the same neglect resulted in atopic dermatitis. Bakwin found that artificially fed babies had a higher incidence of both eczema and respiratory illness.†

Ashley Montague reports on a case of a girl with acne treated at the Temple University Medical Center who "was cured by treat-

* R. A. Spitz, *The First Year of Infancy* (Paris: University Press of France, 1958).
† H. Bakwin, "Feeding Programs for Infants," *Federation Proceedings* 23, pp. 66–68.

ment involving tactile stimulation in a beauty parlor to which she was sent by a perceptive physician when every other form of orthodox medical treatment had failed."* This physician was treating the area of trauma. Touch is the tranquilizer of the skin.

The obvious conclusion is that the body becomes sick when deprived; what is not so obvious is that it gets sick in specific ways. Why is it that nonheld infants develop eczema? I think it is because the skin is the area of need and of deprivation and therefore the focus of the hurt. Of course, we shall have to include hereditary predispositions as a factor in the formation of symptoms also.

To be deprived of enough touch is not to be loved, no matter how loudly parents protest to the contrary. Deprivation of love is not just something psychologic; it is psychophysiologic. This is true despite any statements about how "they really loved me only they just couldn't be affectionate."

Harlow is one of the pioneers in research on touch-deprived primates.† He found lasting effects on monkeys who were raised without real mothers. Those who had "mothers" made out of cloth fared better than those whose "mothers" were made out of wire and spikes with no opportunity for touch. The "touchless" monkeys were later more fearful and less exploratory. Later, Harlow added warmth to the cloth mother by heating an athletic sock.‡ Warmth made a significant difference. Those monkeys who could have an "athletic sock" mother without the warmth added did less well. Warmth-reared monkeys were more apt to cling to their "mothers" when afraid. Too much time with a cold "mother" produced everlasting effects; the infant would be shy of any contact, even when a "warm mother" was introduced. Harlow says: "Apparently, being raised with a cold mother had chilled him [the monkey] to mothers, in general, even those beaming with warmth and comfort."§ To extrapolate from Harlow's research, we can say that a warm environment later in one's life does not eradicate

---

* Ashley Montagu, *Touching* (New York: Columbia University Press, 1971), p. 207.

† Discussed at length in chapter on "Love" in *The Primal Scream*, A. Janov (New York: G. P. Putnam's Sons, 1970).

‡ H. Harlow, *American Psychologist*, February 1970.

§ Ibid., p. 167.

early traumas; it only attenuates them. A cold mother early in life leaves the infant everlastingly fearful because there was no one he could run to to ameliorate his apprehensions. Thus, a child adopted at eight months is going to have problems later if his first eight months were spent in a relatively cold institutional environment.

Not having a warm mother early in life produces an overload of fear which lingers in the form of vague anxiety. If someone were later to ask the child, "What are you afraid of?" he wouldn't have the slightest idea, because: 1. there was no one specific early fear which stood out; and 2. fears occurred long before the infant could conceptualize what he was afraid of, or even that he was afraid. It would be a mistake to say to that child, now afraid of "neutral" objects such as dogs, heights, or elevators, "There is nothing to be afraid of." He is reacting now in terms of a forgotten, but still alive, early history. Early touching, preferably warm touching, would have gone a long way toward easing his generally fearful state.

Human behavior provides ample evidence for Harlow's conclusions. Those mothers who are said to be "cold" are women who are so constricted by their own Pain that they are, indeed, cold to the touch. The bloodstream itself is narrowed against Pain, causing poor circulation, and thus coldness. No number of rational lectures or articles about warmth in motherhood will alter this kind of woman's coldness. Her coldness is not simply an attitude; it is systemic.

CRITICAL PERIODS

Not only must infants be touched very often, but for it to be effective there are critical times when it must take place. An institutional child adopted at eighteen months into a warm family may have already been traumatized for a lifetime. No touch during the first eight months of life when the nervous system is most receptive and when other sensory modalities are as yet not completely developed may cause lifelong damage. Critical periods when stimulation does the most good are known as imprinting periods. Ducks with a brief exposure to a moving object at about fifteen hours after hatching will become imprinted to that object and may follow it (a human, for instance) for a lifetime. Placing an object near an infant duck after four days may not affect it at all. In a study by Denenberg, it was found that rats who were handled in the first five days of life survived stress longer than rats not handled until the sixth day.* The behavior we observe in adolescents and adults may be more directly related to what transpired in the earliest months of life than to any deleterious parent-child relationship that occurred later. A "proper" early infancy may be critical in coping with later adversity; this may explain why one child can "make it" later and another cannot.

Tapp and Markowitz have found that physical handling early in life has a direct effect on the actual growth of the brain.† The more enriched the experience, the heavier the brain. They also noted that there were particular developmental periods when this was so. There is also a direct relationship between the area stimulated and the growth of the corresponding area in the brain. Blinded rats have a poorly developed visual cortex. If an infant is not touched sufficiently or nursed sufficiently very early in life, this may have a much more profound effect on his later intelligence than any formalized education. Educators should note that it isn't how we fill children's heads that counts, but how we fulfill their needs.

There are now literally thousands of research studies concerning touch. It has been found that rats who were "gentled" were later more relaxed and not as excitable.‡ In another instance, isolated, untouched rats were terribly excitable when first introduced into "so-

---

* V. H. Denenberg, "An Attempt to Isolate Critical Periods of Development in the Rat," *Journal of Comparative and Physiological Psychology* 55 (1962): 813–815.

† J. T. Tapp, and H. Markowitz, "Infant handling: Effects on Avoidance, Learning, Brain Weight and Cholinesterase Activity," *Science* 140 (May 1963): 486–487.

‡ Lindsley suggests that early deprivation changes the balance in the arousal center of the brain which organizes the cortex toward specific activity. So, with less cortical organization there is more diffused, random excitability. In humans we call it "free-floating" anxiety. What Lindsley is suggesting is that a less ramified and organized brain is more prone to overload, even with what would usually be nonnoxious stimuli. (See the work of Donald Lindsley on the functions of the reticular activating system of the brain—Neuropsychiatric Institute, UCLA.)

ciety" again. When given chlorpromazine, they were more trac-table.*

I want to cite just a few other studies to indicate how important touch is. In 1965, Casler took a group of institutional babies and gave them an extra twenty minutes of handling each day for ten weeks.† Testing revealed that these babies were better socially adjusted than those babies not handled. Also, handled babies were far less likely to show regurgitative behavior. Another crucial study, in Primal terms, was done by Melzack and Scott.‡ Isolated dogs failed later to respond normally to Pain. This same apathy is what Bowlby described in his classic studies of institutional children.§ My hypothesis about this is that it is extremely painful when early needs are unfulfilled or unattended for inordinate lengths of time, and that for self-protection the system automatically dulls the organism against this Pain. Thus it takes a good deal of stimulation later on to penetrate the protective barrier.¶ While early traumas may dull sensitivity to Pain, they also produce a kind of agitated behavior that makes the organism unable to attend to Pain very long.

The neurotic needs to dull more and more of himself as a barrier

* David Symmes of the National Institute of Mental Health did, indeed, find that in isolation-reared mokeys there was a defect in the reticular activating system—that it was chronically set too high. One indication of this was the lack of slow-wave deep (and we might add "restful") sleep.

† L. Casler, "The Effects of Extra Tactile Stimulation on a Group of Institutionalized Infants," *Genetic Psychology Monograph* 71 (1965): 137–175.

‡ R. Melzack, and W. R. Thompson, "The Effects of Early Experience on the Response to Pain, *Journal of Comparative and Physiological Psychology* 50 (1957): 155–161.

§ J. Bowlby, *Maternal Care and Mental Health*, World Health Organization Monograph Series #2, 1951.

¶ Here is what Newton and Levine say about this dullness: "Since pathways from the skin to the central nervous system appear to be operative earlier than other sensory pathways, skin stimulation activates the reticular formation sooner than other forms of stimulation do." The implications are that reduced stimulation reduces arousal centers in their activity. I wonder if it isn't the opposite; namely, that insufficient stimulation causes overreaction of the arousal center in order to *blunt* the pain of the neglected need. The brain is alerted to danger because when need is neglected, life is literally in danger. See also J. C. Lilly, "Mental Effects of Reduction of Ordinary Levels of Physical Stimuli on Intact, Healthy Persons," *Psychiatric Research Reports* 5 (1956): 1–9, for a full discussion of this.

against Pain. It is no wonder that institutional children seem "dead." In the final analysis, it is the constant accretion of Pain which results in most of the later symptoms of mental illness—manic excitement, catatonic states (dulled in paralysis), and random flights of ideas resulting from the pressure of the body's Pain. This same pressure results in delusions and hallucinations—the expansion of the mind produced by a system overflowing with hurt.

After assessing the great bulk of research on need deprivation, Newton and Levine conclude: "The higher the species on the evolutionary ladder, the greater the confounding effects of stimulus deprivation."* This means that humans suffer most from early deprivation.

* Op. cit., p. 710.

VIII

The Inner Environment

This chapter may be difficult to understand. If you find it so, move on to the following section. Essentially, my point is that the inside of our bodies forms a milieu and this "environment" affects our mind just as our external surroundings do. There is a very delicate chemical balance in our bodies that depends on proper mental integration for its balance; and in turn this balance affects our mind-set and our attitudes. In a real sense there is no independent field of psychology. It is psychophysiology that we must understand in examining individual behavior. Physical and psychological traumas during our lives upset the inner chemical balance, which in turn alters mental balance. The earlier the trauma the more likely there is to be lifelong chemical imbalances.

We don't usually think of the inside of our bodies as an "environment," yet the processes going on internally send messages to the brain just as outside events do. There are sensory receptors inside of us which feed information to brain centers informing it of our balance, position, and the amount and location of inner Pain. The body and brain are an inextricably interrelated unit. The brain relies on proper information and the proper functioning of the body in order to maintain its integrity. Changes which occur in the inner environment early in our lives can have lasting effects on the system, just as outside early traumas can.

The early introduction of sex hormones into animals can hurry the later onset of puberty. Administration of thyroid hormone to newborn rats will permanently suppress thyroid function.

Psychological or physical trauma very early in our lives can upset and distort the inner environment, rendering, for example, the thyroid functions inadequate. The slightly hypothyroid child may then meet the world in a passive, apathetic, and lethargic manner, suppressing himself. This in turn may again affect and suppress thyroid function so that a vicious cycle is created where neither is cause or effect and both are cause and effect. Personality and bodily function mesh, become one, and continue in this way perhaps for a lifetime. The brain depends on hormonal output for its function. Infant rats given thyroid hormone early had an advanced development of their brains (earlier myelinization). Their eyes opened sooner than would be expected and they were far more alert to their surroundings than other rats their age. The significance of this research is that early experiences (and inner alterations *are* experiences) have profoundly enduring sequels. Changes in later intelligence and maturation can result from unobservable, subclinical distortions in hormone output very early in our lives. Some of our patients did not menstruate until very late in their teens and others of the males did not develop beards or pubic hair until their twenties. The full growth potential of many of our patients has not been achieved because of various Primal traumas which imperceptibly affected the growth hormones. (I will discuss this in detail later.)

Here is what Levine says about hormones and intelligence: "In view of these findings it was hypothesized that infantile stimulation endows the organism with the capacity to make finer discriminations of the relevant aspects of the environment, including making appropriate responses to stress."* In a word, more "real." What Levine indicates is that circulating hormone levels have a direct effect on the development of the brain itself. Levine believes that the adrenal steroids are central to all of this: "We propose that this difference [the difference in behavior between handled and non-handled animals] is a function of some action of the adrenal steroids during sensitive periods which *permanently modify* [my emphasis] the organization of the central nervous system."†

It is my assumption that any continuous Primal traumas which

* Op. cit., p. 49.
† Op. cit., p. 51.

cause suppression of feeling will affect hormone balance because hormones are the biochemical mediators of feelings. If the traumas are severe, we may well expect later hormone-related disease, often called "psychosomatic disease." This is especially true where there are hereditary predispositions to these afflictions.

Newton and Levine discuss the experiments where the inner environment has been changed: "These events and their effects, initiated by sensory input during such critical periods, may structure neuronal development into connecting patterns which, after being established, become relatively difficult to redirect."* In short, once the die is cast, it is very difficult to change. They indicate that alterations in the system affect the brain, producing new kinds of connecting brain patterns called "misconnections" in the Primal context. These new grooves cause the brain to bypass correct mental connections, especially under stress, so that there is misperception, neurotic distortion, and inability to comprehend or discriminate properly. These misconnections do more than affect thinking and perception. They also distort hormone production so that either too much or too little hormone is called for. By suppressing thyroid, for example, both thinking and action are simultaneously affected. The child may decide "There's no use in trying" when he meets a frustrating situation or an overly aggressive and competitive playmate. He won't compete, feels defeated, and eventually comes to feel inferior because "everyone can do things better than me."

As brain pathways become rerouted due to trauma, a "groove" develops, making the diverted pathway more likely to be used again; so misconceptions and misperceptions will tend to become reified. What this means is that there is a less ramified brain structure to cope with stress. There will be narrow "fixed" responses to events. The person will become rigid and stimulus bound, responding in the same way over and over again to similar situations. He will have less of a repertoire of response alternatives. In a physical way this child will have less of himself to call on. This is particularly evident in learning disorders where the child will not be able to see things from differing perspectives, and where broad areas of thinking are interfered with because of the high residual tension

* Op. cit., p. 266.

levels produced by early trauma. This level of tension prevents calm
and reflective thought, so that perhaps the child will be more hy-
perkinetic, in constant motion, rather than being introspective. It
may not be subtle brain damage that is causing this hyperkinesis.
Rather, it may derive from the early trauma which leaves him with
chronic tension.

The point I am making was shown in Diamond's research. He
took two groups of rats and gave one group an enriched environment while depriving the other group of stimulation. The experi-
ence-enriched rats had an increased cortical (brain cortex) blood
flow.* The enhanced flow insures that all the necessary nutrients
for proper functioning will reach the cortex. Conversely, we might
assume that when proper stimulation is absent, brain functioning
may be impaired. Animals with an early enriched environment have
a quicker hormonal response to stress. They can react to danger in
a more organized and instantaneous way. If we are ever to talk
about "ego strength," we should realize that it means the ability of
the *total* organism to handle stress and survive; "ego strength"
should not be some vague notion about "strength of the mind."

The interaction of the glands and early stimulation is pointed up
in a study by Hamnett.† He operated on two groups of rats and
removed the thyroid and parathyroid glands. One group had been
gentled and handled frequently; the other group had not. Within
two days, almost 80 percent of the nonpetted rats died. Only 13
percent of the gentled rats succumbed. One conclusion of this experiment is that proper stimulation at the proper time can produce
a resistance to the malfunctions of the glandular system. The body,
it seems, can withstand almost any assault if its needs are met. What
seems clear is that hormone disruptions do not occur in a vacuum.
Not only may they be due to psychological trauma, but how far-
reaching their effects are may be determined by one's psychological state. Primal fulfillment may be an important countervailing
force against even congenital hormone deviations.

* M. C. Diamond, D. Krech, and M. R. Rosenzweig, "The Effects of an
Enriched Environment on the Histology of the Rat Cerebral Cortex," *Journal of Comparative Neurology* 123 (1964): 111–19.

† F. S. Hamnett, "Studies in the Thyroid Apparatus," *Endocrinology* 6
(1922): pp. 222–29.

There have been a number of studies on early deprivation and trauma and lack of proper growth. In 1947 there was a review of one hundred children who were abnormally short for their age. In half the cases there was no obvious physical reason for this. Many of these children, however, had highly disturbed early lives, being overtly rejected by one or both parents. The conclusion was that the children suffered from emotionally induced pituitary deficiency. There is a study of German orphanages which found similar results.* Children who had a pleasant housemother grew better than those with one who was a strict disciplinarian. We may find that the pituitary is a key organ in emotional disturbance and that many of us have not grown to our full potential because of trauma-laden childhoods. Primal patients in their twenties do report growth of up to one and one-half inches. This has been documented in about a dozen cases. Robert Blizzard, in his research, found the same things.†

The effects of painful events stored in the brain eventually produce effects on the growth center in the brain. I again wish to stress that being flat-chested or short may not be serious events in and of themselves, but may indicate serious blockages in the endocrine system leading to other catastrophic disease later on.

Recently, a connection has been found between release of growth hormone and the manner of our sleep. Research at the University of Edinburgh found that the total amount of growth hormone secreted by children during the night was much greater than during the day. Growth hormone release in adults occurs predominantly in the first two hours of sleep. If the person remains awake,

---

* L. I. Gardner, "Deprivation Dwarfism," *Scientific American*, July 1972.
† Robert Blizzard, as reported in *The Primal Scream*, p. 126. Patton and Gardner have postulated the physiologic pathways whereby emotional disturbance affects the endocrine system: "Impulses from the higher brain centers travel along neural pathways to the hypothalamus and thence, by neuro-humoral mechanisms, exert influence on the pituitary gland. Research on 'releasing factors' secreted by the hypothalamus, which in turn are responsible for the secretion of various trophic hormones by the anterior pituitary, has shown that hypothalamic centers exercise a major influence over this neighboring gland." (*Scientific American*, op. cit., p. 79). They point out that almost all the blood reaching the pituitary has first bathed the hypothalamic median eminence.

growth hormone is not secreted. Honda and his associates believe
that the activity of the cerebral cortex somehow inhibits the secretion of growth hormone. Conversely, deep restful sleep seems to
induce growth hormone release.*

We are not certain at this point whether an overactive mind in a
child, a mind that permits only poor sleep, will eventually help
make that child short, but it is not an impossibility. Again, it is not
simply that tension keeps the mind going so that sleep is impossible;
rather, that same tension that drives the mind is also affecting the
endocrine system. Moreover, the active mind also complicates the
situation by further stimulating or suppressing hormone release.
And so a birth trauma may accomplish several things: It leaves the
child with a high residue of tension which keeps his mind going;
and it changes the proper functioning of the endocrine system. The
original trauma alone may not accomplish changes in growth, but
that trauma plus severe Primal deprivation (lack of caressing, understanding, and kindness) may well do it.

I have indicated that stress and tension interfere with the diurnal
rhythm of hormone secretion. A neurotic who might ordinarily
have a high steroid output in the morning to help him meet the day
and a drop at night might have a continuously high steroid output
into the night. This alteration alone can stunt growth; physicians
have long observed that children who have had to be on steroids for
prolonged periods do not grow properly. In addition to this stunt-
ing process, the immunity system is affected so that the child is
more susceptible to certain kinds of diseases.

One can see how complicated the notion of "personality" becomes. An infant who starts out in life with higher steroid levels
may be more subject to infections and may, therefore, become a
"sickly" child. This child demands more, is more of a drain on the
parents, and may be seen as that rather than an object of love. The
child now feels rejected, is under more stress, becomes more sickly
and subject to infections, and so it goes.

There is more evidence to show how bodily systems affect and
are affected by Primal stimulation or its lack. Early handling is
beneficial to the immunity system. Rats who had been handled had

* *Scientific American,* op. cit., p. 81.

a higher serum antibody count after immunization than those who had not.

What is becoming clear is that the nervous system is an organized, integrated *system*. When there is trauma, there is interference with the smooth integration of the system and this interference can have lasting effects resulting in, among other things, disorganized behavior (lack of coordination) and thinking. Slight distortions in hormone output associated with trauma very early in life may not show their effects for years. They do produce a vulnerability, so that after years of stress we see breakdowns of organs and the hormone-related diseases.

It is crucial, in my opinion, that all traumas such as circumcision, which can be avoided during the first six to nine months when so much of the brain is being developed, should be eliminated. Too many functions are just getting organized in the first few months of life for there to be sudden switches in houses, in rooms, changes in cribs, etc. Some Pains, such as minor surgery, can better be integrated later when there is the ability to understand what is going on. We know what a severe impact even minor trauma can have in the first fragile months by comparing slight brain injury at birth with that in adolescence. The amount of injury which might slightly impair thinking in the teens can have a disastrous effect if it occurs very early in life when the brain is becoming integrated.

The sudden death of infants (crib death) with no apparent cause may be in part due to the terror an infant feels about being left with a total stranger very early in his life or being moved to a strange room. I think it is traumatic for an infant to be fed a bottle by a sitter while the parents take a vacation. The mother must be prepared to be with her infant constantly during the first crucial eight or nine months. This is the meaning of motherhood, and women should think twice before assuming that role.

Information sent to me by a coroner's office read as follows: "I am sure you are aware that these [infant] deaths occur in apparently normal, healthy infants from every socioeconomic class. Autopsies reveal no pathology in the tissues of these infants. One of the facts surrounding these deaths is that *they occur only when the infant is alone* [my emphasis], either for a nap or for the night.

To our knowledge no crib death has occurred in the presence of a parent."

It seems clear to me that the child is overwhelmed by terror; there is not one thing he can do about it except experience it, there is a failure to shut down against the onslaught and death is the result. Even if the child does not die, it should be clear what a trauma being left alone is to an infant.

Why does one infant die and another not? It may be that a certain vulnerability is set up by trauma at birth. As I have previously noted, the lack of oxygen at birth has a primary effect on the cells of the hippocampus in the brain. The hippocampus is the agency of the brain responsible for shutting down against Pain. So a slight damage to these nerve cells may not show up until there is an overload of terror and then we find a failure to function adequately.

THE HORMONOSTAT

It is believed by some investigators that there is a "hormonostat" in the brain which keeps hormones circulating at a certain set point.* Stress alters this set point and causes either too much or too little hormone output on a continuous basis. The hormonostat, for example, sees if current steroid levels, say at the age of six, are commensurate with the set-point level established at birth. If it is too high, then ACTH secretion will automatically be lessened, very much like your thermostat at home regulates heat against the set point previously selected. If the set point of steroid levels is too high and later stress reactions have no proper set point to refer to, then there will be a chronic oversecretion of ACTH. (ACTH is a stress hormone which aids the body to mobilize in order to defend itself against threat.) On an over-all basis the person may appear to be "high-strung." We may attribute this to a genetic factor when it is the result of early trauma.

There is a good deal of animal experimentation to indicate that such a hormonostat exists. Rats who were not handled sufficiently early in life showed a small range of ACTH output. Those who

* Seymour Levine, "An Endocrine Theory of Infantile Stimulation," in *Stimulation in Early Infancy*, A. Ambrose (New York: Academic Press, 1969).

were handled a lot had a larger range. Flattened affect (found in seriously disturbed humans) seems to be mediated in an almost literal way by a "flattened" hormone output. This does not necessarily mean that the general output is low; rather, that the organism cannot seem to respond in any labile way to emotional situations because it is *already* overresponsive (still responding to the early unresolved trauma).

The hormonostat can produce other results. If it is set too low, there may be insufficient energy in the organism. The general drive level may be low, producing a so-called "passive" personality. This is the kind of person who cannot get himself to do anything. He cannot get organized and moving. His general sex drive may be low, not only because of sexual inhibition but because the sex drive depends in some way on the general energy level. It is not something which exists apart from the general systemic functioning. It is not unrealistic to think that one's later sexual functioning is very much affected by what happens around birth.

I have talked about the hormonostat in general terms. To be more specific, the evidence we now have indicates that there is a specific brain structure known as the hypothalamus which may well be that hormonostat. It is situated down low in the brain, almost encased by the limbic system. The limbic system is a ring of nerve structures which store and modulate Primal Pain, among other things. So a stored Pain has almost immediate access to the hypothalamus, which is the key hormone-regulating brain structure. A reverberating Primal circuit directly and continuously affects hormone output, either overstimulating it or producing an insufficiency. There is some evidence that there are small sections of the hypothalamus that can be constantly stimulated without entering a refractory phase (that is, no longer susceptible to stimulation) as is the case with most other brain structures. Thus, there can be a continuous stimulation of certain stomach acids leading to stomach problems, for example. Severe stomach problems such as ulcers may not show up for three or four decades of life, because it sometimes takes that much constant assault before an organ will finally fail.

What is interesting about the hypothalamus is that it has few solid direct neural connections to the cortex. Rather, its messages are intercepted by the limbic system. What this means is that there can be constant stimulation of the system hormonally, and the thinking part of the brain, the cortex, is not only unaware of that situation but even when it is aware, is powerless to stop the hormone flood.

The hypothalamus is the central area where feelings become translated into physical realities. It is the transducer of the mind and body. It regulates many vital life systems including core body temperature. So far as we know, it is the only part of the nervous system which secretes hormones. It secretes hormones called "releasing factors." These control the hormonostasis (the equilibrium) of the body and hence can properly be called the hormonostat. Because the hormonostat is situated so delicately within the feeling circuits of the brain, I believe that childhood trauma can alter its set point permanently. The reduction we see so consistently in core body temperature in post-Primal patients is but one indication of the correction of that set point in one key area after childhood traumas are relived and resolved. Conversely, it would seem that Primal Pain permanently raises body temperature in neurotics, producing more demand on the system.

We now have ample evidence to assume that the growth hormones secreted by the pituitary (a small offshoot below the hypothalamus) are controlled primarily by the hypothalamus. So here again we can understand how easily it is that growth can be stunted by alterations of the set point early in life. And we do see soft tissue growth in post-Primal patients.

One of the key target organs affected by hypothalamic secretions is the thyroid gland, part of the general hormonal system. Thyroid dysfunctions are quite prevalent in the population, contributing to the lowered energy levels of which I spoke, dryness of skin, changes in hair texture, alterations in the general body configuration, and, when severe enough, brain impairment. Again, many Primal patients on four and five grains of thyroid a day to correct severe hypothyroidism find that after therapy there is no need for any; and medical tests indicate that the output of thyroid has changed. I again assume that this is due to a correction in the set point.*

* For an excellent discussion of all this see "The Hormones of the Hypothalamus" by Roger Guillemin and Roger Burgus, *Scientific American*, November 1972.

The releasing factors also affect both the gonads and the adrenal glands. What this means is that limbically stored Primal Pain, converted into tension because it does not have proper access to its connections in the cortex, is rerouted through the hypothalamus and then perhaps on to the gonads, causing continuous sexual stimulation. The neurotic is then constantly feeling "horny," engaging possibly in either compulsive masturbation or sexual activity. What he is releasing is the Pain-tension converted into sexual feeling. Conversely, alterations in the releasing factor can inhibit sexual feeling. It may be that the Pain-energy has access to appetite centers, and so when tension rises the person compulsively eats rather than has sex. Once the set point is altered permanently, the person will always be hungry when tense, and usually not know why.

When the adrenal cortex is affected, the steroid hormones are released (or inhibited). The steroids are the stress hormones, lucidly discussed in a number of books by Hans Selye. The output of steroids ultimately affects growth. But it also affects the bone structure (making it porous and subject to fractures), fat deposits producing "moonface" and a shoulder hump, alters white cells which leaves the person more susceptible to both allergies and infections, causes changes in male-female hormone balance producing such phenomena as excess hairiness in women; its lack can contribute to Addison's disease often associated with depression, just as too much is associated with Cushing's disease and frequently associated manic states. Imagine the magnitude of the effects of changes in the hormonostat. It is a wonder that the body takes all those years to break down into such afflictions as hypoglycemia and diabetes. So Primal Pains not only cause the changes in body build and body structure, but they also produce the psychological effects. In other words, when you look "out of whack" or warped, you are also likely to be so psychologically. As if all that weren't enough, the hypothalamus also determines the kind of mother you are. It sets the amount of milk a mother produces for her baby, and the kind of menstrual periods she will have. It also plays a role in whether a woman gets pregnant in the first place.

A high set point usually means that the person will be "high strung." And, when his life circumstances (such as having a seductive mother—as against one who urges food on the child) channel that high drive into the sexual arena, then the person will be hyper-sexed. This is because sexual functioning is part of the general emotional reactivity of the organism, and it is the hormonostat which helps determine how emotional we can become. We can see that hypersexuality isn't due to a pure sex drive; rather, tension is re-routed via the hypothalamus into sexual channels. Sex is the outlet for tension. Trying to treat such things as nymphomania and satyriasis as sexual maladies alone is doomed to failure because only the outlets are dealt with instead of the causes.

When an early home environment allows for few outlets (because it is a religious and rigid household, for example), the person with a high set point simply stays "high-strung" and becomes chronically anxious. He is the one more likely to crack psychologically from the strain in his teens or early twenties.

People with high set points seem very energetic, and they are. That energy comes from a system continuously galvanized to ward off Pain. Some pour it into sex, others into business. The "hyper" will usually find some avenue to funnel his energies. It is only when outlets are blocked that the tension becomes retranslated into the real Pain that it is. So long as the outlets are there, the person will have no idea that he is in Pain or, often, that he is tense . . . he just feels energetic.

The notion of Prototypic Trauma and Prototypic Defense is instructive with regard to energy levels. One patient recently underwent a birth trauma and found tremendous energy finally released. Afterward, he became energetic. The feeling during the Primal Trauma, which he acted out from then on, was "All those things are happening to me and I can't move—I can't do anything about it." Because he was stuck in the birth canal for almost an entire day, he finally "gave up," became resigned, and no longer tried to fight it. He had a resigned, lethargic personality thereafter. Under any stress he felt immobilized. That is, under stress the original and real immobilization which depleted his energies was reactivated and he felt unable to get himself together to do anything. When a term paper was due for two courses, he could not sit down to write anything. Later, when his rent and car payments were due, he could not go out and find a job and do something about them. He couldn't "make a move." The point of this is that the early trauma may have seriously affected the hormonostat and depleted him. Under stress he developed a rationale of "What's the use, anyway?" He developed a "passive" personality based in part on depleted energy levels. Or he met the world passively and the world helped reinforce the passivity. He found people to lead him and tell him what to do; people to offer advice and dominate him. In a gross way, it seems that life is but a rationale for our constitution. The very ideas this man developed in life depended very much, it seems, on events that occurred when his life began. Ideas and concepts are very much an outgrowth of one's total physiology, and it does no good to try to change someone's mind about things unless you are prepared to change his physiology.*

Let us examine how a specific hormone change under stress affects and is affected by the passivity of which I speak. The brain hormone, norepinephrine, seems to play a key role in active, assertive responses. Depletion of that hormone (called a "neurotransmitter") can lead to passivity, and in severe situations, to depression.

Animals rendered helpless and then shocked during research studies showed a decrease in norepinephrine levels. If they were allowed to be active on the shocking grid, it increased. What I believe is that the nature of the trauma at birth sets the stage for either increased or decreased norepinephrine levels, and thereby dictates either passivity or activity as a characteristic mode of response later on. If the fetus is immobilized by being stuck tight in the canal for many hours with no opportunity to move, or if he is being strangled by the cord so that movement means death, then he is more likely to have a decrease in the neurotransmitter and a lower set point. If he continuously struggles to get out, there will be a higher output of another catecholamine—epinephrine. This neurotransmitter acts as a balance to norepinephrine and is chiefly responsible for energizing the system for flight or fight. A rigid person paralyzed by fear would be higher in norepinephrine. I am assuming, however, that rigidity as a personality trait had its beginnings at the start of

---

* This is precisely why the conditioning techniques and therapeutic methods, such as Reality Therapy, dealing with "changing the mind" do not work. The coded past still exists in the nerve cells of the brain.

life where being rigid and immobile (in the birth canal) was life-saving. Thus rigidity which becomes neurotic later on is an early adaptive prototypic response. In that sense, each of our personality styles was at some early time very important for sustaining life and the integrity of our bodies. An example of a rigid response was illus-trated to me by a patient who was giving a lecture and realized that he was going overtime. Even though there were comments from the audience that he should speed up his lecture and perhaps skip a few parts, he found himself unable to do so. Once set on his course he could not deviate, particularly under a stress situation such as a lec-ture before a large audience. The reason that he reacted in a rigid way was, he discovered, due to a birth trauma in which he "could not make a move." There were simply no alternatives for him at birth, and this became a fixated unconscious mode of response in all later stress situations. The prototypic defense is crucial because all other defenses lie on top of it. It fixates "personality." There can be no profound personality change therefore until the *prototypic* trauma and its defense are experienced and resolved. When we talk about personality change, we must understand this point. It is pos-sible to make major inroads into personality, but profound change depends upon prototypic resolutions. This means that to *completely* cure homosexuality, asthma, or general rigidity, we have to get to the original fixating trauma, which may not be birth; it can well be something which occurs later on in life—in the crib for example.

A struggler at birth, a fetus fighting to get out, may well have his set point of epinephrine set too high. He will be chronically "souped-up." He will tend to be a doer, particularly under later stress, rather than a contemplator. His characteristic approach to problems will be to attack rather than to contemplate and reflect. He may not feel his anxieties so much because he is always working them off. His early trauma (plus crucial life events) may point him in the direction of a football player rather than a poet. All this because on an unconscious level attack means life and passive contemplation means death. His system, in short, is constantly being galvanized (on many levels including the biochemical) to fight off the original Primal trauma. If he was active at birth, he will be a "hyper," and if he was immobilized at birth, he will be a passive-depressive. Any later stress, say a wife leaving a husband, will set off the characteristic response—either "What's the use?" or "I'll make you stay, I'm not going to let you leave." The vicious circle is that once set up, the hormonostat produces a personality which then reinforces the hormone problem. They feed back upon each other. What I believe breaks this closed system is Primals because the trauma is relived and resolved.

We need research on the relationship between types of birth traumas and later personality types. Such research should go beyond personality types, however, in order to discover which later disease is associated with specific hormone alterations at birth. For example, is the hyper more likely to become a hyper-secretor developing ulcers? I have noted elsewhere that immobilized stressed animals are more tumor-prone, and we will want to know how this fact relates to human tumor development. In other words, is tumor proneness set up by the birth trauma? That is, are certain specific, enduring endocrine changes associated with later tumor disease? I would speculate that this is very much the case, particularly since there are some kinds of tumors which, when opened, are found to be loaded with norepinephrine—far out of keeping with the normal range. There seems to be a "pile-up" of it, and for some reason it cannot be released and properly utilized by the system.*

Norepinephrine is chiefly a vasoconstrictor. It causes a buildup of blood pressure by constricting the blood vessels. Why are the blood vessels chronically constricted? One reason is that we withdraw or constrict away from threat. Primal Pain is a constant source of threat and must be dealt with continuously. The release of norepinephrine constricts the general supply of blood so that most of it can be preserved for use by the brain—the brain that must think its way out of problems and find solutions. It also keeps the body from going into shock, which would be a certainty if all the Primal Pains were suddenly released into the system. This is particularly true in a traumatic birth where the child is being strangled and has no opportunity for

---

* For a technical discussion of this, see Stanley Gitlow et al., "Diagnosis of Neuroblastoma by Qualitative and Quantitative Determination of Catecholamine Metabolites in Urine," *Cancer,* Vol. 25, No. 6, June 1970.

flight or fight. Something must happen to keep him alive and functioning, and one important item is norepinephrine.

Once the norepinephrine levels are set too high so that blood supply is restricted, we can see how it is that later hypertension is produced. Of course, later stress plays its part as well toward the formation of that affliction. If the child lives in a ghetto, if he is black and poor, attends a rough school where threats and fights are the order of the day, then the added stress will make him break down earlier with hypertension. If he has a serene atmosphere he will hold out longer, maybe four decades or more.* I submit that one reason that causes of malignant tumors have evaded research investigators all this time is the neglect of key psychological factors (hence biochemical factors).

It is no accident that early-isolated rats (and although it is never mentioned "isolation" means "no mommy") are more prone to hypertension, and what's more have a much greater buildup of norepinephrine in the limbic system (where I believe the Primal Pains are stored). The point is that it isn't a buildup of norepinephrine which *causes* all those diseases; it is a buildup of unresolved *feelings* which are mediated by certain chemicals. Those feelings are the subject for study, not just the chemical changes which take place. After all, those chemical changes do take place inside of human beings.

What I am indicating is that it isn't a "personality type" that determines whether a person will be ulcerated or asthmatic, but rather specific alterations in the biochemistry occasioned by early trauma which produce *both* a specific personality type and a related hormone disease.

It is clear, therefore, that for any psychotherapy to achieve profound personality change, the basic endocrine system must be altered. Otherwise we simply have a "hyper" redirecting his energies into behavior considered appropriate by a psychologist or psychiatrist. He would still be a hyperactive, "on the go" personality.

Clearly, it isn't just the brain which is affected by early traumatic events; changes in hormone levels affect the rate and nature of

---

* For technical discussion of this, see M. Mendlowitz et al., "Catecholamine Metabolism in Essential Hypertension," *American Heart Journal*, Vol. 79, No. 3, pp. 401–407; March 1970.

physical development. Neurotics often "look" neurotic. In one way or another one part is either overdeveloped or underdeveloped. So we find too small a torso, too short legs, a puffy face, stunted growth, etc. Conversely, well children look well. Their physical development is integrated and their bodies appear that way—in harmony. We don't have a lot of data on this as yet, but of the Primal female children who have reached puberty we find shapely appearances and full breasts. They do not appear dessicated, withered, and sticklike.

It should come as no surprise that neurotics can appear neurotic physically. Body shape continues to change for many years. Some parts of us develop sooner than others. The legs and arms develop sooner than the trunk; the head develops sooner, along with the hands and feet. These bodily changes are mediated by a genetically coded hormone-release system. If key traumas, both physical and psychological, occur at the critical times when specific hormones controlling aspects of physical growth are released, then bodily integration is going to be affected. It may be in the subtle way that calf development is retarded or trunk development is distorted. The end result is that the person does not appear physically integrated. His body may remain small and may start to grow far too late in adolescence to ever catch up to what would have been his real growth potential. When psychologists speak about "personal growth," they need to remember that growth is not just something the mind does.*

I have indicated elsewhere (*The Primal Scream*) that neurosis is like having your motor turned on for the rest of your life and not ever being able to turn it off. We are beginning to see some biochemical evidence for this analogy in terms of having one's hormonostat set too high and not being able to lower it by any act of will. What does seem to lower it, however, is Primals, which finally resolve the trauma that caused the system to continuously overreact in the first place. That is, I think the hormonostat gets set too high because it must continuously respond to an *unresolved* threat or

---

* For an excellent and detailed description of all the growth processes, see M. Tanner, "Physical Growth," in *Manual of Child Psychology*, 3rd ed., ed. Paul Mussen (New York: Wiley and Sons, 1970).

event. The system has been chronically galvanized against the Pain and so has been in a constant state of overreaction. One can "condition" the *behavior* based on the drive level set at birth (through Behavior Modification Therapy), but one cannot condition the *brain* and the drive level itself. That is, one can redirect a delinquent, acting-out, hyperactive child so that he behaves better and channels his drive into schoolwork, but one cannot alter the drive level set point. So there will be a price for better behavior; it could be bed-wetting, nightmares, or whatever.

One of the key points about Levine's research is that he has shown that female animal organisms with a poor early history, in terms of satisfaction of need, have an altered hormone situation so that they become "bad" mothers—neurotic, indifferent, with poor milk output for the infant, etc. There is evidence now to indicate that, contrary to Freud, it isn't the first six years of life that are crucial; it is the *first six months*. Primal deprivation during this period sets a course—behaviorally, physiologically, and biochemically. This is the most crucial period of our lives and great attention must be paid to the infant during this period if harm is to be avoided. This means that no mother should return to work right after her baby is born. If she has a child, she should be prepared to be a *mother*, not a worker somewhere.

What is necessary to be normal, or oneself, is a free brain, one not clogged by interfering cortical censoring which suppresses feelings. A free brain is one that has been allowed its maximum physical growth. And, as Krech has shown, this leads to better and faster learning.* Real learning, then, is the freedom to grow and develop at one's own pace; rote and drills only stunt that freedom. An enriched and free early environment seems to help elaborate brain connections in a literal way so that the person can understand more. I may add that comprehension of oneself, known as insight, is included in this, so that being insightful is literally derived from a well-developed, liberated brain. It used to seem to me to be merci-

* D. Krech, M. R. Rosenzweig, and E. L. Bennett, "Relation between Brain Chemistry and Problem Solving, among Rats Raised in Enriched and Impoverished Environments," *Journal of Comparative and Physiological Psychology* 55 (1962): 801–807.

ful that those in horrible environments were often too "dumb" to know what was going on, but now it seems that "dumbness" is a literal neurologic result of such an environment. Nature mercifully dulls the brain when the Pain is too great.

If we want our children to be truly bright, perceptive, and insightful about themselves and others so that they won't be easily manipulated by the world, then we must produce conscious children; Primally conscious children. Their consciousness will come from having a brain where there is a fluid access between all areas. Faulty consciousness comes about because the brain is not working as a harmonious unit; instead, one section is busily repressing another. This is why insight and perceptiveness cannot be taught in any significant way. They are functions of a normal brain.

IX

Long-Range Effects
of Early Experience

There are many experiments to indicate the long-range effects of early trauma. Melzack and Thompson, for example, found that early-restricted dogs could not compete later with other dogs for bones. They were "losers." These dogs seemed continuously confused and suffered "diffuse emotional excitement."* They were nervous. Other research in the physiologic area with regard to restriction (it is often called "sensory deprivation") showed that when an area was deprived there was a corresponding effect on the development of the brain in those areas. For example, deprivation of light and sound impaired the development of the visual and aural areas.† Not only was the brain affected, but the sensory organ itself. Riessen, in his work with monkeys, discovered effects on the tissue of the eye itself in visually deprived animals.

I do not want to give the impression that symptoms can always be understood in terms of a direct line, say from toilet training to bed-wetting. So much happens to us in growing up that it is difficult to point to one episode as a major factor. The only way we can understand the linkages between symptoms and origins is through feeling. For it is feeling which links even the most widely disparate human events. For example, one patient could not concen-

---

* R. Melzack, and W. R. Thompson, "Effects of Early Experience on Social Behavior," *Canadian Journal of Psychology* 10 (1956): 82–90.

† E. Gauron, and W. C. Becker, "The Effects of Early Sensory Deprivation on Adult Rat Behavior Under Competition Stress," *Journal of Comparative Physiological Psychology* 52 (1959): 689–93.

trate on his studies in school. He had a Primal about "Mommy, let me go out and play like the other boys." This solved his reading problem without any discussion of the problem itself. How? This boy always had to do his chores before he could relax and play. His whole system developed a block against having to do anything *first*. Reading was just one more chore to be resisted. It was not a conscious process; rather, each time he sat down to read he found that his mind "wandered." It was saying, "I want to be free." Once he relived the early, continuous trauma of being constantly restricted to his house, he could really be free mentally. He could study in a relaxed way without that gnawing agitated sensation inside which caused him to fantasize after reading about two paragraphs of a book. No amount of special tutoring, cajoling, or threats could alter that reading block until the feeling dynamic underneath was resolved. The linkage between reading that book and going out to play was indeed circuitous; only the feeling helped make sense out of it.

What we need to understand is that life in the uterus begins our orientation to the world. We are already receptive-perceptive beings in the womb and if it is a comfortable place, then our initial life orientation after birth may be a positive one. If it is uncomfortable, if the mother is chronically tense, has a fast or irregular heartbeat, jerky movements, and smokes and drinks and takes drugs, then the fetus has an unconscious orientation that the world and life is unsafe and not to be trusted. This *in utero* experience, plus a harsh birth process and lack of proper handling in the first few months, solidifies an inchoate orientation that began in the womb. It will be conceptualized later when the child can form concepts, and his ideas will be "No one can be trusted. The world is a rotten place," etc. All these so-called paranoid ideas have real roots—in the real experiences of the child dating back to his uterine life.

In the womb, the fetus "scans" his world not by eyes and ears, but by his tactile sense. Later on, he will scan with his other senses. He does not differentiate as yet among the senses. The point is that the fetus is an indiscriminate sensing organism on which traumas can produce the same kind of sensory overload which might occur after birth with the same result; namely, a dulling of sensory perception. We might speculate that the fetus is much more susceptible to sensory overload because of its inadequately developed neurologic apparatus.

The result of sensory overload during the period before and just after birth may change the brain so that specific abilities are affected. Later the child may have inadequate mechanical abilities. He may not be able to see how things fit together; he might not be able to visualize the relationships of furniture in a room; and he may not be able to understand how certain gears fit together. These deficiencies may be a result of very early experiences predating birth, rather than inherited difficulties, as we have believed in the past. Of course, we should not ignore the tremendous impact of post-birth experiences. For example, if parents refuse to let a child explore and touch things, his mechanical abilities may be diminished. That is, he will not be able to physically experience his environment, an essential for a mechanical ability. Being kept passive in a baby buggy dulls perceptions in the same way, simply because there is inadequate physical exploration of the child's universe. He becomes less perceptive in a total way. It is this exploratory behavior very early in life that helps produce a child who has proper spatial concepts.

Not allowing a child full play of his physical senses may force him to become abstract—to become a conceptual rather than a mechanical person. He may turn out to be an intellectual with excellent abstract thought and poor mechanical ability. One reason being an intellectual is often neurotic is that the intellectual has been abstracted from himself. The point is, however, that deprivation of the full play of the senses early in life may force a child into a style of thinking and being that will direct him for the rest of his life.

It would seem that given a good start in life, almost any kind of stress can be withstood later on. Given a poor start just insures more problems later. More importantly, a good start can mean a good ending, or at least an end which does not come prematurely. William Berkowitz reported in his work with animals that properly stimulated ones lived longer than those who were not. Their offspring lived longer if the mother had a "good" early life.* So those

* As reported at the American Psychological Association meetings in Washington, D.C., September 1971.

early months may well be a matter of life and death. Those are the times when the father must be around to help out with the chores so that the lactating mother is rested and in good health. Those are the times when parents need to produce a relaxed, nonargumentative environment for the newborn, to insure that the baby is not bombarded with loud noises or restricted too tightly by a blanket, or is not left wet, or hungry, or thirsty too long. In short, the first months mean constant attention by parents, and when thinking about having a child, a parent must understand those facts.

Society ought to recognize this as well. For, if it were possible, both the mother and father should not have to go to work for months after the child is born. The father should get some kind of leave to attend to the most important job in the world . . . helping a new human being get the best chance possible in life.

X

Psychologic vs. Physiologic Needs

Although it should be obvious that there is no such thing as a psychologic need, one that exists in the mind alone, numerous books have been written about just such a thing—the need for prestige, power, self-esteem, and so on. One of Freud's colleagues, Alfred Adler, based his entire theoretical system on the need for power and wrote volumes on it. But a need isn't a state of mind. It is a total, systematic state. There is no need that isn't an expression of our whole system. That is why deprivation in any single area has generalized effects. Institutional children deprived of warm touch in their first six months were later found to be *generally* "restless, depressed, and unable to concentrate."*

Psychologic needs are only physical needs symbolized. They are always one step away from reality. Because they are derivative rather than real needs, one could have all his neurotic, symbolic needs satisfied and not be changed at all. One could give a child everything and still he would be sick. We have gone astray in our treatment because we have failed to make the proper distinction between real and unreal needs, and have therefore attempted to treat systemic problems cerebrally. What we have accomplished is to change the mind of the person to think new thoughts while the bodily needs remain unchanged; and profound "personality" change cannot take place without access to underlying needs.

I raise this point because books have been written about the special needs of children, which I doubt exist. For example, the "need

* M. Pringle, and V. Bossion, "A Study of Deprived Children," *Vita Humana* 1 (Basel, 1958): 65–92, 142–70.

to belong." In the psychologic literature this is variously known as the need for affiliation or the need to socialize. It should be apparent that there is no way we can belong to anything but ourselves. When parents do not give us ourselves, then we must struggle to feel "part of." The struggle is to live through a group, a team, a "family" of friends. When allowed to live through ourselves, there is no need to belong to anything. We can participate in activities and enjoy ourselves, but the motivating force is not neurotic. This can best be understood in terms of a simple dialectic. When parents let us be ourselves, we feel part of ourselves; when they don't let us be ourselves, we feel apart from ourselves. Then we begin to struggle to be "part of" anything. Thus, when someone complains "I just don't feel like myself today," he is talking about something deeper than just a temporary malady.

Not belonging to oneself results in various consequences. Awkwardness and lack of coordination are two examples. Where the body does not belong to the child, he may have a hard time mastering it. That is, he may not be agile and graceful, and may be unable to learn sports well or be able to dance—this despite years of dance lessons. Another patient explained her awkwardness: "It's not my body. It's theirs. I just carry it around but it does what *they* want." Another expressed it in terms of his body being something alien that his head just carted around. Another patient was learning how to play tennis, and was having a particularly poor day. He became so agitated by his clumsiness and "stupidity" that he sat down in the middle of the court and had a Primal. Afterward, he told his partner (also a Primal patient) that the feeling of "not feeling like myself made me irritable and intolerant of myself. As soon as I began crying, I felt the old hurt of never being allowed to do the wrong thing or to do a thing badly. I began to dislike in myself what was only natural—lack of skill, not knowing an answer—which my father made me feel was dumb and wrong. I never had the freedom to feel that I could do something wrong or poorly. So, any time something like that would happen I would feel not like 'myself.' " When this patient felt that it was perfectly natural and all right for him not to be perfect all the time, he began to play better tennis, unafraid to make errors.

Something else that we are not born with is the need for attention. Attention means satisfying children. A child doesn't come into
the world with a need for someone "out there" to listen to him. He
has an inner need to express himself and what is required is a listening person. Needs flow from inside out and not the reverse. Thus,
this so-called psychologic need for attention or interest from others
is really a physiologic need to feel safe and protected in the world.
Once a child can feel this he is unafraid to venture out and can
more freely express his other needs. This fulfilled need means that
the child can feel free to run and play, assured that he is being
watched over by a protective parent.

One of the more common so-called psychologic needs is to feel
"important." Again, it is a spurious need. If a child is important to
his parents, he won't have to struggle for a lifetime in order to feel
important. That is, if they listen to the child, speak to him, ask his
opinions, look at him, call his name, acknowledge his existence, they
are, by these simple human acts, telling the child that he is important to them. If they do none of these, the child will be left feeling
unimportant and will try to do those things in life which will make
him important. Whether he becomes a movie star or a professor
won't change the feeling. What makes that spurious need to be important evaporate is to feel the "unimportance." It is a dialectic
affair; feeling unimportant drives away the push to be important.
Becoming "important" in the world keeps the underlying feeling
there. No matter what importance is attained, the person will be
driven on because the worthless feeling is always there waiting. The
person will think that everyone has a need to be important, but if
he didn't feel unimportant he wouldn't have that "psychologic"
need.

If we understand that personal needs are really personal and do
not involve others, then we can understand that there can be no
needs for superiority, for dominance, power, submission, prestige,
or esteem. The central Primal need is to be oneself, an individual,
and we need parents early in life to help us do that.

Neurotics are interested in what satisfies their need. Interest in
children is no different. The parent is going to try to convert his
child into someone he can be interested in. And the child will try to

be that. He will be the top athlete, the perfect gentleman, or the neighborhood's reigning pugilist, if that is what is called for.

One of the more significant findings about Harlow's monkeys who were touch-deprived was that they made poor mothers. They showed no interest in their offspring, and paid no attention to them. What does not being touched early in life have to do with interest and attention? Translated into human terms, to be "interested" in an infant is to touch him. The infant has no psychologic need for someone to "take an interest." He has a physical need for touch—and interested parents do that. Harlow's touch-deprived monkeys could not love because their needs were not fulfilled. They could not be mothers because they were, in Primal terms, in Pain. Cold mothers are ones who were treated coldly. To encourage a cold mother to "take an interest" in her offspring is usually a vain exercise because her "interest" is a function of her own early childhood. To be more precise, the "interest" of her system is on herself and her deprivation, which is why there is a lack of interest in her child. If parents don't pay attention to a child, he may get sick so he can pay attention to himself; in effect, he becomes his own parent. One could try mentally to take an interest in one's child but the body (the repository of the true feeling) would prevent real interest, and the child would sense that the concern was faked. What would come through, instead, would be a remoteness, an emotional aloofness. Obviously, the parent would not be "all there" with his child because part of him would be "back there."

There are many parents who, with the best of intentions, want to give their children "everything I didn't have." What their children will get, however, will be based on the unfulfilled need of the parent, and their interest in the child will be on how he fulfills their need. So they may get too much of what the parent lacked (higher education, for example). In this sense, the child never gets to sort out what he really wants from life because he is busy living out the life of his parent. An old need in the parent will work adversely on the child. Thus, suppressed anger may later be unleashed on a child who is defenseless. If the parent has an unconscious hate for his mother, he may generalize this hate to women, and his female child will assuredly suffer just because she is female. The male children may be unconsciously favored, so that the girl becomes neurotic in order to be loved and then is punished for being neurotic. In a self-fulfilling prophecy, she becomes perhaps, a hateful or obnoxious, demanding child, justifying the parent's anger. Because she lost with her parents, she will lose for a lifetime, and will become someone unable to get love. The tragedy of her life was that she had the misfortune to be born a female to a parent who hated women. Even if the child were to change and become different, the parent would not see it because of his need to keep her a symbol of his repressed feeling.

For straight, feeling people, parenthood is quite simple. They don't try to give something of themselves, because there is nothing of oneself to give. But *being* oneself as a parent is what does the giving.

XI

Human Implications
of the Research

A good deal of research has been cited, and now it is time to indicate what it all means in human terms. Early hurt has a lifelong effect. Later behavior can be stabilized around hurts that occurred in the first months or even hours of life. A child can become an exile from himself in his earliest years. Proper stimulation is absolutely essential for a developing organism, and without it serious lifelong damage can occur.

In the first months of life a baby needs his mother. He needs her milk, warmth, softness, and gentleness. I have observed from Primals of patients that an infant can distinguish the body of a mother from a father very early in life; he needs his mother at first, usually until weaned, and then either parent can provide the caressing and physical care he requires. This does not mean that the father plays no role in the earliest months; rather, in terms of physical contact his role is not primary.

If an infant's need is not fulfilled, then soon in life he will seek substitutes and fulfill real needs symbolically—symbolically because those others are not his parents and were not present at the time of great need. A man may come along in the boy's teens and provide the warmth he never got from either parent. The boy may become fixated on men and during his time of sexuality may become sexually fixated. More often, first true warmth is found in the dating stage of adolescence. Youngsters become fixated sexually because it was with sex that they felt their first hugging, caressing and kissing.

But all the sex in the world cannot make up for the early denial of the pure asexual need. The point I have made throughout is that one cannot "make up" for his past, one can only experience it fully. Neither can trying to forget the past and concentrating on the present help, because below the level of consciousness the entire system is constantly and automatically reacting to the past.

The fulfillment of natural need does not spoil a child. A straight child cannot be overindulged because *he* won't allow it. "Spoiled" children are neurotic children who are missing something. They usually demand the wrong things, but that is because they do not know what is missing. To fulfill each and every need makes a child whole, not spoiled. The fulfillment of need and the attendant wholeness is what gives the child the naturalness of being himself and enables him to move on through maturation as he feels it. The father who vows to "make a man" out of his young son is only guaranteeing that his son will grow up neurotically trying to be the boy he never was. Letting a baby be a baby for as long as he has need to is what guarantees his natural growth into later adulthood.

A normal child does not whine and cry endlessly. Whining is the child's way of signaling that he is dissatisfied and uncomfortable. Parents tend to get exasperated with a whiny child because nothing seems to please him. But that is because the child's dissatisfaction stems from not being *properly* satisfied earlier, leaving him with vague dissatisfactions which become focused on one thing or another. It is much the same as being overloaded with fear early in life, say, of being left alone in the dark in the crib, blocking that fear because it was too much to integrate, and then displacing it later onto things that are not inherently fearful.

If we understand Primal Theory, we know that a child who chronically misbehaves in school is under pressure from the past. If he is a daydreamer, if his mind wanders and he cannot pay attention in his classes, it is because Pain is driving his mind away from the present. His daydreams are all-consuming because his Pain is. This is not a matter for ridicule or punishment. It is a matter of understanding. Once there is this understanding, then acting-out children will be treated as human beings in Pain rather than people who have to be "whipped into shape."

In regard to punishment: Children do not have to be punished, because punishment teaches nothing. One may ask, "What about when my infant runs into the street. Shouldn't he be punished for that?" To call a sharp "No!" a punishment is stretching the meaning of the term. But in any case, spanking a very young child who runs into the street or yelling "no" at him is not the most efficacious way to teach him. Before it ever happens, it can be explained that he can be hurt if he runs into the street. If he is old enough to run, he can usually understand simple explanations. If he has fallen down, the parent can tell him that running in the street can bring a worse hurt than that. If the parent has great residual fears, then the lecture will probably instill terror into the child instead of a lesson. If parental fears are absent, the child can be effectively educated.

But parents do punish their children out of some mistaken notion that it builds character; so those parents should know that after any punishment there must be immediate love and affection. That will not negate the "lesson," but it will keep the child from feeling overwhelmed by an "unloved" feeling. Chimps hold their offspring after they slap them, and that affection never dilutes what momma chimps are trying to get over to their young. We must understand that it is terrifying for young children to have their parents angry at them. They have no place to go with their feelings except to shut off. So telling children you're angry or disappointed in them, ignoring them, etc., all take a terrible toll.

Chimpanzees and primitive men can teach us a lot about child rearing. I will discuss chimp life later. There is an Eskimo tribe on King William Island in the Arctic untouched by white civilization. The baby in this group is a tyrant. He can wake up in the middle of the night howling for tea and the parents get up and make it for him; no complaints or grumpiness. It is expected that the baby demands and that they will fulfill. They laugh and play with the baby for hours until the little one decides he has had enough . . . a switch from our society where the parents decide when the child has had enough. It is really quite confusing for a child in civilized societies to feel he hasn't had enough play and just goofing around with his parents, and to be told, "There, there, you've had enough now," and the child is supposed to say, "Okay, Mommy." Much straighter for a parent to say, "I've had enough. I'm tired. I know you want more, but I can't do it."

The Eskimo baby is totally indulged, yet he grows up as hardy as any human alive. Maybe our problems began when we left the so-called "primitive" life and began to educate people about how to rear children. Now we have to de-educate them so that they can come close to being something natural with their children.

While we are on the subject of primitive tribes and so-called "primitive emotions," there is a tribe still living in the Stone Age in the caves of the Philippines: the Tasadai. Until recently they had no contact with the outside world. They do not hunt or kill animals; rather, they are food gatherers, eating mostly fruit. To me, they are the Primal People. They have no weapons, no aggression, and no punishment. They cooperate in all efforts without anyone giving orders to anyone else. They have great respect for their children, touching and hugging a great deal. These children are neither aggressive nor are they "spoiled." They are not whiners. They have no religion or religious rituals. They do not even have words for anger, hate, and hostility. They are "beautiful people" in the real sense of the word, inside and out. Their total lack of outside contact shows us what human beings really are naturally when left alone. Their style of life says all that needs to be said about child rearing. The family is nearly always together. The father takes little children into the streams with him to help catch fish. There is no yelling, criticism, or ordering the children where to stand, how much noise they can make, etc. All is live and let live. I suppose we think of them as naive and childish because they are so trusting. They don't have the sophisticated paranoia as yet, trusting no one. After they have been exploited for a time by "civilized" society, which has now discovered them, they will be much more "grown-up" and distrusting, we can be sure of that.

We can learn from "primitive" societies. One good example is the "papoose carrier." I believe that whenever possible, infants should be carried on the mother's back (or in front) in a papoose carrier. Use of the baby buggy should be limited. As soon as the infant can sit up, the papoose carrier is preferred because it offers constant stimulation by the mother's or father's body in terms of warmth and touch. It offers the great security of being attached in a literal way to mother or father. It allows the infant the opportunity to see and hear everything the mother or father does so that he has maximum stimulation rather than lying passively in a buggy. It fosters a more active rather than passive approach to life, and, importantly, it produces the rocking, rhythmical motion which primate research indicates as important for the young.

The rocking that occurs when the parent walks may in some way parallel the rocking that occurs during the time when the fetus is carried in the womb. There is little question that there is a rhythm to life, and it would appear that the infant comes closer to that natural rhythm on the back of his parent than in a buggy.

I think that we have used the buggy for decades out of the old mistaken notion that the infant is just a "thing," not a needing organism that requires constant stimulation.

Perhaps the greatest harm a parent can do to a child is to put him in boarding school. Boarding schools, no matter what the rationale, are usually dumping grounds for unwanted children. They are the graveyards of childhood because there is rarely a time when a child can be truly little in them. Instead, children are taught self-reliance, discipline, and how to hide their feelings. Children must have a mommy and daddy to run to—impossible in a boarding school. Among our most disturbed patients, are those who were sent away to school.

The discipline children learn in these schools usually means doing what you don't want to do without complaint. That is the virtue in neurotic situations—doing what someone else wants you to do without any fuss. Discipline results when people do not have faith in children. They think they have to be trained to do things, otherwise they won't do them. They have to be trained to do neurotic things, it is true. But to do what they want is the best discipline of all; for a feeling child helps others, is considerate, and can do what is best for a group. A neurotic child needs too much to do that. That is why he must be disciplined away from his needs; why he needs external control.

Children are often sent to boarding school because of the separa-

tion or divorce of the parents. At the very time when the child
needs support, he is sent away to handle all his disturbing feelings
by himself. Instead of feeling his littleness, he must act grown-up
and self-reliant.

I can't think of a greater tragedy for a child than divorce by the
parents. That is why people should get to know each other for
years before considering having a child. It isn't the divorce as such
that is so damaging. It is all the events surrounding it . . . having
a new "daddy" who gives him orders; or watching many "daddies"
come and go so that he can never get involved in a feeling way
with any male adult without the gnawing sensation that it will all
come to naught. Divorce means that mothers often have to go to
work and leave the child with a stranger or in a strange school. It
means having a mother who is tense and irritable and worried over
finances. It means losing the real father in many cases—the father
who has decided to start life over with another woman and another
"new" family. The child is just the helpless victim of all this tur-
moil. He can stand almost any kind of social stress, such as moving
from one place to another as the father is transferred from job to
job, when he has his parents. But without the warm support of two
parents, these new traumas just deepen his problem.

I believe that there are stabilizing forces that help a child withstand the battering that comes from divorce. One important one is
living in the same house and neighborhood. Here he is in familiar
surrounding with his old friends with whom he can talk. Sending
him away to school or camp wrenches him away from the kind of
social roots that might help maintain his mental balance.

It is terribly important during a divorce for the child to be main-
tained in his home surroundings; and, if he cannot have two parents, the most important way the events of the divorce can be
ameliorated is to have one loving parent with whom the child can
feel. If he can talk and cry with the remaining parent about how
he feels about the whole mess, about losing his other parent, then
the damage will not be as great.

Too often what happens is that the child is pulled apart by the
now-feuding couple. He becomes an "ally" for one or the other.
He must choose between them. He must listen to their complaints

about each other and, in general, act as their marital counselor instead of their little boy or girl. He becomes the parent. Having heard the Primals of my patients about the divorces of their parents, I can only reiterate that couples must make very sure of each other before thinking about children.

Why is it always the parents? one might ask. Why doesn't a bad teacher or being poor produce neurosis? I can only reply that we have observed thousands of Primals about the deep hurts of childhood and they are nearly always about the harm the parents did. Being poor added to the problem but was not paramount. If a child was made to feel inferior because he was rejected by his parents, then being poor compounded the situation because in this society the poor are looked at as inferior. A child who grows up with children who have better clothes, money to entertain themselves, sports cars, etc., is bound to feel that he is not as good as they are. But if he feels important to his parents, if they value him and respect him, then the experience with richer children will not have a devastating effect. Certainly it is aggravating to be involved with a critical, cold, harsh teacher for six months. But this cannot be compared with living year in and year out with that kind of person. When the parents are cruel and unfeeling, the child has no place to go with his feelings but "in."

In unreal families, being a child *is* the tragedy. The child will predictably suffer. He is helpless before the whims, needs, and anger of his parents. Almost any child we see today is a walking tragedy. Some hide it better than others. Some "fit in." They can produce a socially approved front and get by. Others are just sullen and depressed. The sicker of the two groups are the children who "make it" in an unreal society. They have been wiped out so subtly that they are not aware of their Pain. They just join the sickness, merge into it without a flicker of awareness that they have been destroyed. Children who do not fit in have the best chance at health if we learn what to do with them.

A mother transmits her feelings in every word and every touch with her infant. It isn't how much she says or necessarily how much she touches; it is the feeling behind her acts which the child picks up and responds to. She (and he, the father) *is* the message. Telling her "how to" is but a very weak message which gets lost in the Primal needs of the mother.

Beth

I have three children. Beverly, seven and one-half; Tom, six, and Don, almost two. I have much to write about with all three, but I'm using Beverly because I feel her hang-ups are more similar to mine. I always know how Beverly "feels" about things. I just have to look into her brown eyes, and I know what she is feeling. Since I have been in therapy I ask her how she feels and I'm usually right on. My mother is cold, mean, and I feel that I look just like her. When I get angry at Beverly, I "feel" like I look like my mother. I can't remember my mother telling me not to call her Mommy, but I can remember feeling that I had outgrown the word. Beverly calls me "Mom" and I can also remember feeling funny when she used to call me "Mommy." I asked her the other day why she didn't call me Mommy and she said she didn't know. I said I'd like her to call me Mommy and she replied it made her feel funny. I know just how she feels because I can't say "Mommy."

My mother was constantly after me to stay clean. I could never go into a sand box because I would get sand in my shoes. A mud puddle was death to me. I just never went near them. To this day I can't enjoy the feel of mud on my feet.

I have a picture of Beverly taken when she was three. She was sitting in a mud puddle, but the look on her face was "What do I do here?" The only reason she got that close was because I was busy sun bathing and couldn't be bothered. It is so sad to see that picture: a three-year-old baby who didn't know how to play in the mud.

Beverly tells me she doesn't need or want any friends. The reason is because I will never let her bring other kids into the house. They annoy me and kids can tell that. The reason they annoy me is because my friends were afraid of my mother; she let them know they were not welcome and so I in turn do the same thing. If my mother had been nice to my friends, it wouldn't be a constant reminder to me that she wasn't every time Beverly brings someone into the house. I really want to be a nice, warm mommy, but every time I get close to Beverly I feel like I'm pretending and that is the same feeling I get from my mother. My mother will start talking very fast and that is what I do, not just with Beverly but also with my husband. If he tries to hold me, I will blabber about anything. If I try to hold her, she will say, "Hey, Mom, do you remember . . . ?" I have never held Beverly very much. It seemed like when I wanted to hold her, she would squirm away. I wonder why! I think of my mother holding me and I feel kind of sick and dirty. I think of touching her breast and I feel crawly. I know that Beverly "feels" that same way. When I kiss her good night, she wipes the kiss away so she won't get chapped lips. My mother would always hide her body from me, and I thought when I had kids they would see me. But they do see me, and the same feeling has come through to both Beverly and Tom. They both look very carefully, but the look of not liking what they see is there. My mother always referred to women by the kind of breasts they had and so do I; Beverly hopes she never "has to grow" boobies.

My mother was so wrapped up in worrying about my dad leaving that she didn't have time to worry about me. My dad always got the biggest piece of pie or, if there was only one piece left, he would get it. She worried about him so much that my sister and I really bothered her. She was jealous if my sister and I talked too long to him, and I am the same way. I want my husband to see me first when he comes home from work. He gets the biggest and the best and the last. Beverly looks after her daddy the same way. She worries that he'll get hurt drinking and driving. This was my biggest fear as a kid—that Daddy would get killed. When Beverly has something to say to me or to her father, she talks very rapidly so that she won't lose our attention. My husband and I need each other so much that when one of the kids intrudes, we get angry. My mother *always* got mad when I interrupted, and this is something that just came to me—I get furious with Tom when he interrupts Beverly and me.

Beverly does not like ice cream, peanut butter, or watermelon, and I know it is because she cannot taste the food. She is that shut down that food has no taste to her, but she doesn't eat like I do because she knows that I won't like her if she gets fat. I'm always dieting and so is she. My mother would feed me cookies whenever I was hurt. I can remember going home crying and she would say, "Here, have a nice cookie and it will all go away." I don't quite say that, I'm too smart (?), but the same feeling comes through to my kids. If they hurt, they eat.

I asked Beverly if she could think of any similarities between Grandma and me (she stayed with my mother for seven weeks this summer and gained twelve pounds). She said, "Yes, you both always fuss about my hair, only Grandma didn't pull it like you do." I get great satisfaction out of pulling her hair when I brush it because I know I hated my mother fussing about my hair all the time. That was the only thing that was nice about me to her. People would comment on how beautiful my ringlets were and she would feel good. Now to get back at her, I pull my kids' hair. Beverly hurts when people treat her nice. I think my mother and dad never treated me nice, and that is why I hurt.

There are two more characteristics that both my daughter and I have. If she loses anything, I go out of my mind. She gets frightened to death, and I scream and yell. I can't ever remember losing anything in my whole life, and I think that in itself is good reason to believe it was so scary to lose anything at my house. Then the last thing is that Beverly cannot look into a mirror and see Beverly. She never looks at *herself*. I asked her to do that the other day, and she said she felt funny because people would think she liked how she looked. That's how screwed up Beverly is. My mother always said, "People who look at themselves in the store windows when they walk down the street like themselves." I did a good job of not liking me and Beverly feels the same way about herself.

XII

Childhood Sexuality

Sigmund Freud believed that children have an active sex life, and that the reason that no one had discovered it before him was due to sexual repression in society. But Freud notwithstanding, there can be no sexuality in children until there is sexuality—until puberty is reached and sex glands have been activated. Until then, there is *exploration* in areas of pleasure which are "sexual" for adults. It is because adults impute sexuality to naive, childish touching games that inhibitions are imposed and guilt fostered.

We need to differentiate acts from inner experience. A child touching his genitals finds it pleasant. He will not compulsively and continuously have to touch himself to make himself feel good, unless he continuously feels bad because no loving parent made him feel good. His compulsive masturbation is not a sexual act. It is an attempt to relieve tension. Neurotic parents become anxious over such *behavior* (instead of being anxious about the child's obvious anxiety) and proscribe or circumscribe certain areas of the body, which become "demilitarized zones" where not even the child may enter. His own body becomes segmented and walled off from itself; genitals barricaded away from the hands and the mind sealed away from thoughts about certain areas. Thus, disapproval for touching himself can fragment the child and produce dissociation from the body.

When a child becomes dissociated from himself, he will have to rely on fantasy. Because he is not allowed the experience of his body (feelings are physical facts; they are the body), he will have to conjure up strange notions later on in sex in order to feel anything. Thus, the transformation from normalcy to perversion occurs because a child was diverted away from himself and forced into the world of perverted images.

What happens when touching oneself is prohibited? It depends upon other experience. A fixation may be set in motion so that the child becomes a compulsive toucher, needing to put his hands on almost everything (because he could not put it on the one thing). As he becomes sexual, he may get girls, or his siblings, to touch him, with the unconscious hope that enough touching will allow him to feel; that somehow external contact will put an end to the anesthetization of the body. Or the opposite can happen. If the child is locked into the parental approval—if they give him just enough so that he'll want to please, then he may completely internalize those early prohibitions and not even think of sex later on. He may also become quite cold and hard, afraid of touch. He would never even think of touching himself or others.

How can this be corrected? Will touching do it? If touching later on in life helped, then many promiscuous people who touch and have sex continuously in order to be touched would have their problems solved. In order to be sexually liberated, one must relive those early nonsexual scenes and resolve them by *feeling* the correct response. The reason that reliving the scene automatically provides the correct response is that the response is the real feeling which was momentarily felt back then but immediately suppressed. In one Primal, a man was back in a scene screaming out to his mother, "It's not dirty, Mama. It's all right! It's mine, Mama, mine. My body belongs to me. I have a right to feel it." At this point in his Primal he unconsciously began playing with himself. This went on for one hour. He never had an erection because he was not sexual back then. He just wanted to be able to touch himself. He assured me later that if he played with himself for one hour now without being in a Primal, he most assuredly would have an erection. Feeling the correct response brought back feeling to the area. He was no longer impotent when women wanted to touch his penis. Isn't that what most impotence is about? The inability to feel and to be stimulated in the genital area.

This is a crucial point and I shall dwell on it for a moment. The early scene at age three of Mama saying simply "No, no" to her son when he put his hand on his penis became a locked-in memory circuit, unresolved so that each touch of the penis reactivated that memory-inhibition. The only way to solve the problem is to resolve that memory circuit; that is, to activate the circuit and have a new correct response, so that the old response can be eliminated as an unconscious force.

Otherwise, when the child becomes sexual at puberty, he can never feel fully free when he masturbates. He may think he is feeling guilty, but what is happening is that the old inhibitory feelings are reactivated and play against the current attempts at sexual pleasure. Notice the progression. Inhibition of nonsexual pleasure at a very early age interferes with the experience of sexual pleasure at a later age, so that sexual problems such as frigidity and impotence have their origins in nonsexual events and times. Counseling about sexual techniques or focusing on sexual inhibitions will never deal with the real, underlying forces behind sexual malfunctions.

A patient who touches himself for an hour or more during a Primal is in much the same position as someone who sucks ferociously during an infancy Primal—they are reliving compacted, telescoped experiences which may have gone on for years. The patient isn't just touching himself over that one remembered episode. He is touching himself for all the times he wanted to and never could. Afterward, he may lose most of his drive to masturbate, just as the person who has a sucking Primal loses the drive to smoke.

The prohibition against touching one's body is not something isolated. Neurotic parents seem to spend their lives keeping young children from touching anything. They stifle and inhibit curiosity so that later the child comes to lack curiosity, and then he is punished for being an apathetic student not interested in his studies. He is simply reacting to his early life where reaching out freely, being interested and alive, were punished. One result of not being allowed to be curious and interested in one's own body early in life is that forevermore there is an inordinate curiosity in bodies . . . a neurotic reaction which keeps nude bars a thriving business.

INCEST

One of the standard notions in psychology, particularly Freudian psychology, is that at a certain age the child develops, and must suppress, incestuous feelings toward the parent of the opposite sex. I think that this is an erroneous idea. Incestuous feelings are neurotic. Jane Goodall, in her study of chimpanzees, remarked that incest rarely, if ever, occurs. She believes that the close and prolonged relationship of the young chimp with his mother establishes her role quite firmly. The young chimp simply does not see mother as a sexual object when he enters adolescence. If a mother is a *mother*, who is constantly around her baby, protective and warm, it would seem that a child would not develop incestuous feelings. It is when mothers play some other kind of role, not necessarily seductive, but rejecting and unmotherly, that incestuous feelings may occur in a youngster. If a child is neglected and needs warmth desperately, he may eroticize that need if he cannot fulfill himself in a direct and straight way with his parent. The love need and sex then become confused and incestuous feelings can arise when the need for love does. But incestuous feelings are not inevitable, in my opinion. One of the things we learn from Dr. Goodall's studies is how very long infant youngsters stay close to their mothers; how much touching and caressing goes on and how much protection they offer their young. They aren't out working and shopping. They are there for the child.

A not unimportant finding by Goodall is that rarely, if ever, is there homosexuality among chimps. I raise this point because some homosexuality we have seen has been due to seductive mothers who tantalize their children unconsciously and drive them away from all women in order that the children may avoid incestuous feelings.

One of the reasons that Primal Therapy is effective is that the patient is not simply discussing his sexual problems with the therapist, he is touching himself, feeling his body, and *doing* what he could never do. Conventional therapy usually focuses only on *saying* what one could never say. As though the problem were solely one of words and thoughts—dealing with the patient in a split way, apart from his body. For example, an exhibitionist may show his penis in group during a Primal and feel the reason behind his exhibitionism ("A big penis isn't a nasty one, Mommy"). He isn't sitting in a chair *discussing* his exhibitionism.

Sexual functioning, then, is not a matter of *sexual* education. It is a matter of education in the broadest sense—education which stresses the desirability of feeling. When a child enters puberty he will be a feeling person, and with the added sexual activation which puberty brings, he will be a sexually feeling person. Sex education means that parents will allow their children to be expressive, reactive human beings who will later be able to be expressive and reactive in sex. It means to have always allowed full physical movement to children instead of the constant "Now sit still!" so that the whole body can be involved in sex in a free physical way. Ultimately, it means not to have repressed *any* crucial feelings in a child because that much of being a feeling person has been suppressed. In the real sense of the term, there is no *sex* education. There is only letting someone be so he can become a sexual being.

Nancy

On the third day of Primal Therapy the feeling began with a scene that had flashed through my mind many times before without making any connections. My mother and I were cleaning upstairs when she called me to her. "You see this," she said, dangling a pair of my sister's bloodied underpants in front of me. "This is what's going to happen to you!" My God, that's how she told me about the mystery of life.

I got into the feeling of having such a stupid, coarse mother and then jumped immediately into a feeling of disgust about my body. That feeling was so powerful that it connected me immediately to having intercourse with my husband. Yes, the disgust was there, too. I would try to make love and there was my mother standing behind my shoulder saying, "What a degrading display of your animal nature. We shouldn't give in to those feelings; they're part of our fallen nature!" And so it was, time and again my body would become rigid and shut down into a frozen lump. Then the final connection—my father never acknowledged that my body existed. He never commented on how I looked, or how I danced, or how well-formed I became—and worst of all *he never touched me*!! That was it! *I didn't have a body*!

After that connection things happened so fast I could hardly keep up. My legs sort of popped into the air. I began to touch them and then rub them as hard as I could. THERE WAS NO PAIN! Before, the slightest bump on my skin was excruciating. Even when Dr. Michael examined me, when he pressed on my lower leg, and it was so painful (I didn't mention it to him).

Next I touched my thighs and buttocks and stomach and rib cage and then, WOW—my breasts! They felt so round and soft and warm. Then, like a shot that went through my body, I found my nipples. I immediately felt my genitals start to throb. Helen said, "Don't you think it's kind of hard to feel a new body with all those clothes on?" At first I was hesitant, but I couldn't resist the feeling. I anxiously took off my clothes and greedily felt all of me. I was playing with my toes when I noticed my hands. I stretched my fingers this way and that; they felt so nimble. Then it hit me— NO PAIN! The arthritis of my hands was gone!

I finished my discoveries back at the motel. After practically ripping my clothes off, I lay on the bed thinking that I could seduce and enjoy a hundred men! Me—frigid old Nancy! I felt my genitals. They were soft and warm, moist and slippery. I fell asleep with my body completely open—legs spread, arms flung carelessly over my head—my God! I still can't believe it. I've always had to sleep crunched up in a tight little ball.

Colors are jumping out at me now, as if a gray haze had been lifted.

My thighs are tingling as though blood were rushing in for the first time.

After one of my birth Primals, something snapped as if my legs just cut through a thousand ropes. Best of all, the excruciating pain in my ball-and-socket joints, of my legs and hips, was gone. I could actually sit in the half-lotus (a yoga position) without having my knees in the air.

XIII

Children's Fears—Night and Day

I have already shown how early trauma engenders fear. Fear is the agent of repression. When Primal traumas or buried Primal feelings threaten to break through the defenses, fear begins and signals us to defend more. The organism is afraid because its integrity and survival are threatened. Fear, then, is a survival mechanism. What happens to those catastrophic early Pains and their fears is that they become buried and stored in the brain, and the organism acts as though the early traumas were an ever-present threat. In a sense they are because when we are older they are in the brain and must be dealt with. The system does not say to itself, "Oh, I'm twenty-five years old now; I can take feeling being abandoned in the crib." Because in terms of that feeling, the person is not twenty-five. He must go back and be six months of age and feel those frozen fears as an infant. An unresolved six-month-old experience is locked in the brain and cannot be ended by "understanding" that experience from an adult point of view. That would be a split, neurotic event with the "adult" looking at the "infant" inside of him.

What happens to all those buried fears is that they form a Primal pool of latent fear which, as the person grows older, become attached to one thing or another (depending on life circumstance) and turn into phobias. Phobias are irrational fears—they have no basis in reality. They have no basis in external reality, it is true, but they certainly are a reflection of internal reality.

Let us take an example of a phobia—the fear of having one's arms pinned down or being in such close quarters that one cannot move freely. There should not be terror over being in an overly crowded elevator with little latitude to move. The terror that comes up may be due to a reactivation of early fears, such as getting stuck in the birth canal. The overreaction is due to past experience being added to a current one.

The fear of the dark is a frequent childhood fear. Children are afraid of the dark because there is nothing there. That is, lying alone in their beds, relatively undistracted and defenseless, the latent fears are nearer consciousness. These fears are then projected into the darkness where the child is afraid of robbers in the closet. The child has made up a story to fit his fears. It is very much the same process as in dreams. Feelings arise when consciousness slackens and the mind makes up stories in order to make sense out of ascending Primal feelings.

Pinpointing a robber in the closet is a way of focusing on the underlying amorphous amalgam of Primal fears ranging from birth trauma to circumcision. There is no way for a child, or anyone else, for that matter, to "understand" those early nonverbal traumas, so he is helpless against them. All he can really do is distract himself with radio or television, or repress himself further by pretending he is not afraid. He will pretend when he hears his parents saying approvingly, "There, that's the big boy. There's nothing to be afraid of." Imagine how confusing it is for a young child to be told he is not afraid when he really is. His parents, those omniscient authorities, must know more than he does; and so, subtly, his whole perceptual framework changes. He becomes disoriented because the perception of his true feelings has been changed to something else. This is how a child becomes alienated from himself, how he loses touch with reality.

I have often wondered why it is that the fear of the dark is such a universal phenomenon; I wondered until my last Primal. I am going to discuss this Primal in some detail because I think it is instructive in terms of fears of the dark. I had been swimming during the day in a very warm swimming pool. I swam under water a lot, seeing how far I could go without coming up for air. After I finally came up for air I began having an anxiety attack with the odd feeling that I was going crazy. There seemed to be a pressure in my head that was too much to withstand . . . and I could not seem to catch my breath. I rested for a few minutes, tried to talk myself out of it, and then forgot about it. That night, alone in bed, I began to have that feeling of going crazy again. I was afraid of something undefinable. I ran into the bathroom, turned on the light, and tried to get hold of myself. Having the light on calmed me down, but I didn't know why; nor was I aware at the time that turning on the light was tranquilizing.

I went back to bed and had more anxiety. I sank into the feeling, letting it sweep me away. I began having a birth Primal, choking and losing my breath until I must have been purple in the face. Once I was into the Primal, all fear left; I was simply reliving a forty-hour labor and trying to get out. As I came out of the Primal, I understood my childhood terrors of the dark. I understood why I always had to have a light on when going to sleep. There was a feeling during the Primal of being all alone in a life and death struggle with no one to help or comfort me. When I finally got out of the canal and into the light, someone did hold me and make me feel safe finally. Being in the light was a conditioned response; that is, light became associated with safety and comfort. Fighting for breath and life in that canal was associated with darkness. Later, fears of the dark came up because being all alone in bed at night reawakened my unconscious birth terror. Last night in bed, when I had my anxiety, I reflexively ran into the bathroom and turned on the light without the slightest idea of why I was doing it. It turned out to be symbolic of the calm and safety I felt when I finally made it into the light at birth.

Perhaps the universal primordial fear of the dark is in some way related to the traumas we suffer in the darkness at birth; at least it was true for me. I had "lost" my fear of the dark for decades, but obviously it had never gone away. With just the right combination of circumstances it returned. Losing air in the warm swimming pool reawakened the very early terror. Because I had no idea what was happening to me, I only felt afraid and that I was going crazy; my mind could not stand the upcoming pressure. Had I not had years of Primals it is doubtful that being in the swimming pool would have done anything. The early terror would have remained out of reach and would have been siphoned off into "acceptable" adult fears like the fear of electrical outlets or the fear of flying, or the fear of being enclosed and locked in an elevator. These adult fears are symbolic derivatives of a gigantic early one.

As a child with relatively weak defenses, the terror was more specific . . . fear of being alone in the dark. Those same wobbly defenses allowed for continual nightmares of being underground trying to get into daylight. I was much closer to myself then.

Nonverbal fears are not the only buried ones, of course. Fear of one's parents must be added to the list. Such terrors, in fact, that a fragile child dare not feel at all; dare not feel himself despised and disliked; dare not feel the murderous rage in his father or the suicidal despair in his mother. He must not even feel afraid, if he senses more disapproval for being a "sissy."

Aside from instilling fears into a child directly, fears are transmitted by what kind of people the parents are. A constantly critical, harsh, and angry parent will make a child fearful. He will be so busy mollifying the parent from his earliest days that he will never be able to sit back and feel the extent of the fears. A weak, nonprotective parent can do the same. The child will have an unconscious fear that there will be no one to protect him. He may struggle to make that parent strong (make his mother stop drinking, for example), so that he'll have someone to protect him. This struggle is nothing conscious and deliberate. It is automatically motivated by inner fears due to his parent's lack of strength. A constantly apprehensive parent will cause his child to bury his own fears because he senses that it is not safe to be fearful around a fearful parent. I remember once seeing an accident where the mother was sitting in the front seat of the car, unhurt but hysterical, while her baby was sitting in the back seat petrified. No one was there to help the child feel protected so that he could safely feel his fears. His terror, therefore, was overwhelming and repressed.

Often a child is afraid of falling asleep. There are many reasons for this, such as the fear of never waking up. But the most frequent reason is that he is afraid of the nightmares he has. A child can pretend to be unafraid all day long, but when he is asleep and defenseless, his fears will plague him. I have said before that early catastrophic events seem to fixate defenses around them. One of the ways we see this is in nightmares. The early trauma, preserved in pure form, arises during sleep, especially if something during the day triggered that memory circuit. For example, being stuck in a fence or squashed by many boys in a football game may reactivate the feeling of being squashed at birth. As I have noted elsewhere, what arises in sleep is the *exact* early sensations of being squashed, and the child then wraps his nightmare around it. Only the *sensation* arises because there is no way to correctly conceptualize it without Primal Therapy—no way to understand what it really is, since it is nonverbal. That sensation is terror. If a child could know that those sensations were from birth, assuming he were open enough, he might transmute the nightmare into the Primal it is. Nightmares, then, are inverted Primals. Primals are the antidotes for nightmares, particularly the recurrent variety.

I had a recurrent nightmare for thirty years of trying to fire a gun at an enemy, and it would never work. The gun barrel fell off, the trigger wouldn't work, and so on. The Primal was of being in pajamas with the sleeves that tie over the hands. My hands were useless in my earliest months and it showed up in my dreams. There was a lot of terror in being rendered so helpless so early in life. The feeling of helplessness meant being powerless to shut off constant frustration, Pain and terror.

Even after this Primal I still had the nightmare, only less intensely and more sporadically. Months later I had the same nightmare, only this time I let myself sink deeper into the feelings underneath it. I was gasping for breath; my face was physically warped to one side; my mouth seemed paralyzed shut, and in a flash I felt what it was . . . I was in the canal trying to get born and my hands were useless; I could not use them to help myself out into the air. This was a prototypic helplessness of the hands. On top of that lay many experiences including the tied pajamas. After that "Primal" in my sleep and its connection, I did not have the nightmare again. Not only that, but the general lack of physical ability which I had for a lifetime, in which I could not use my hands properly to construct things or fix them, changed as well. My physical helplessness was over.

An early pinched umbilical cord may result in nightmares of suffocation, while being clogged with birth fluid may give rise to nightmares of drowning. In each case the sensation comes up, and it will continue to come up and produce nightmares until it becomes a *feeling*—a Primally-connected event.

FEAR OF WANTING

One of the key fears of children, simple though it seems, is the fear of wanting. Straight wanting opens the possibility of straight rejection. When parents are obviously unreachable, obvious eccentrics, excessively harsh or totally withdrawn, the child must shut off his need for them. He must act out his need because if he does nothing about his need, he is faced with feeling catastrophic hopelessness very early in life—too early for it to be fully accepted. The child pretends not to need and becomes fearful when the need shows. The child becomes afraid to even say, "Mommy, can I have," "can I get," etc., because chances are Mother will point her finger and snap, "Now you just be quiet and stop bothering me."

Most of us block wanting so automatically that we don't even know it has happened. Not wanting is the way we keep fear at bay. Some months ago I was sitting in a restaurant next to a grandmother and her two granddaughters. The children were each given menus. One girl looked at it and said, "You know, I don't think I'll order an entree tonight; I'm just going to have all kinds of hors d'oeuvres." The grandmother, without a second's hesitation, said, "Oh! That's a grand idea. Go ahead and pick everything you want."

This child was unafraid to want. Yet how many children would even take a chance on saying something like that. Neurotic parents usually meet anything out of the ordinary rut with, "Stop the silliness and order properly!" In this small way, repeated daily in a myriad of ways, wanting means rejection. Given enough disapproving looks, a child becomes a "proper young lady" or "little gentleman" rather than a free, fun-loving, wanting child.

Parents who are in need themselves do not want their children to want them. Children are most often praised for being self-sustaining and unwanting. "If you want," explains one patient, "you'll have to be *afraid* that you'll never get what you want." The only thing safe to want in neurotic households is what parents want, and what neurotic parents want is for their children not to want directly. They must perform first and "earn" what they get. They must act out their wants. And neurotic parents don't want children to want because they can't give.

Children's fears should be indulged. If a child is really afraid of the swimming lesson or of jumping from a diving board or of getting on a horse, he should not be forced. Children will usually do things up to the point of their fears. To force a child to "overcome" his fears is to overload him so that he must sequester them into the Primal "pool."

A crying, terrified child should not be wheeled into surgery without his parents, just as a scared child should not be left at nursery school. Young children should not be abandoned to doctors and nurses in hospitals. Parents should not be cowed by physicians who ask them to leave a child to them. Children need their parents in times of stress and if a doctor doesn't realize it, at least the parent should. Whenever possible, parents should choose doctors who understand these points.

Children who are normal enjoy doing things. One can't force a child to be normal by making him do things. He will only act unafraid and then be very afraid at night when he is alone and able to feel that fear.

The reason fears, particularly night fears, should be indulged is that they are usually complex matters. One person relived being shut away hungry and thirsty in his crib in a dark room. Seeing a light when his parents opened the door was a signal of rescue. Leaving the light on in his room later was simply reassuring, though he never knew why until therapy.

No child grows out of any fear. If it is irrational, it is Primal. And Primals don't disappear. What better testimony to this than nightmares which begin at age five and continue into the sixties and seventies. We *think* children outgrow their fears because they keep changing them and making them more subtle. No bride would admit to fearing robbers in the closet, but she still may be afraid to enter her house in the dark. And, too, as a child grows older he can learn to channel his great fears. He can take up auto racing and galvanize tremendous fear and then find relief for a time after the race. So though he looks like a brave soul who "used to be afraid," he has simply found an outlet for it.

If a child needs distractions at night, if he needs to be tranquilized by having his parents near by, then by all means do it. Let a child have his fears and don't compound them by shaming him into burying them. The dialectic of fear is that the more one feels it, the more courageous or fearless one is; the more one blocks it, the greater the fear. This is another way of saying that the more one feels himself, the more one *is* himself, and the less there is to fear.

Here is an example of the fear of wanting and what it does:

"One of the reasons why I've undergone Primal Therapy is that I've always had a fear of touching people. It's not that I never had any friends, I have, but I've always been afraid to give or receive any form of physical affection. Even as a child, I could never accept any warmth from my mother. I just couldn't trust her. In her words, 'I used to call you my perpetual motion, always wiggling and wanting to go, certainly not still enough to be rocked, read to, or just plain cuddled.' Needless to say, I've been virtually impotent my entire life.

"After five months of Primal Therapy, I've actually begun to feel the cause of this: I've had a number of Primals where I lie flat on my back—I keep raising my head with my mouth stretched so far open it feels as if my lips will split at the corners—I can't get any words out nor can I move from the stomach down. It's just this agonizing feeling of want/fear.

"Late one night, when I was about fifteen months old, I was crying for "Mummie" to come pick me up. When she didn't come, I shook my crib so much that I began to walk it across the floor. My dad is a light sleeper and became very angry with me. They came and tried to tie me down in my crib.

"Describing a feeling for which our language has no vocabulary is futile. I haven't felt that horror in its entirety yet—the murder of my need for the people who were my world will take many more Primals to feel. I'm a lot freer with my affection already. When I look down at my feet now and see the enlarged veins from all those years of motion (I even hitched around the planet a few years ago), I realize that my need had to be kept down somehow."

XIV

Parental Need

I have already indicated how neurotic need often determines why children are conceived. The parent's neurosis doesn't stop when the child is born. It usually becomes more blatant as the child grows older, because there is more that the child can do for the parent. The final result of this is that when the child becomes an adult, his parent often becomes a little, needing child again, asking advice and direction. It isn't that parents deliberately ruin their children. It's that they seek the fulfillment of their own needs through them, and that ruins them.

In neurotic families everyone is a victim. The way the neurotic cycle is set up, everyone becomes the perpetrator and the victim; no one wins. Everything must be incorporated into the need structure of neurotics so that when a neurotic has children, they also are swept into the need-vortex. Neurotics cannot let people be themselves because they must make them into what they need. Need distorts reality for the neurotic because he is so busy molding his children into his need-fulfillment that they never become independent persons to him. The parent's unfulfilled Primal needs are implicit commands to the children. Look at the children closely and we often see what the parents need. Children will be made into servants for their parents to make up for their own inattentive parents. Children will be dressed and fussed over (to the point of discomfort for them) by the mother who always wanted that for herself. The father who failed as an athlete and lost his father's love to an athletic brother may try to mold his son into that image. On the other hand, the "hopeless" child is one who cannot be fitted into the parental need. A child who cannot be understood will soon be converted by parents into something they can understand—or he will be considered hopeless.

In neurotic families, a child's talents and abilities become marketable or saleable items so that the *parent* can gain wealth, prestige, importance, power, or whatever. If the parent lost out with his siblings, then his child will be the foil by which he symbolically competes with and triumphs over "them." His child is but a symbol, not a reality, used so that the parent can finally win out and feel whatever he didn't feel as a child—"important." All of this is carefully rationalized, since the parent cannot feel his feeling of unimportance and worthlessness. So he tells his child how important practicing his lessons is for him (the child), or how she must keep herself pretty and well dressed, how she should keep up with her dancing lessons, etc. The child is easily seduced, since he would like to please and tends to believe that his parents have his best interests at heart. But his feelings—"I want to play, not practice"—*are* his best interests.

Often we hear neurotic adults say, "I wish my folks had made me stay with it and practice." The reason they say this is because their tension and agitation derived from being forced to do too many things, rendering them unable to stay with anything long enough to do it well. The best discipline is the child's own desire. Wanting to do something is part of the child's natural self-paced growth and development. It is the only way that a child will learn and enjoy what he learns. No amount of regimen or cajolery can make a neurotic parent's want a legitimate want of the child.

We can see parental needs at work in simple ways. A person ignored by his parents may withdraw and feel unworthy. His feeling is that he's not important to anyone. As a parent, he can't imagine that his love is crucial to his children, so he ignores his children because he feels himself to be a nonentity. Parental inattention may also produce the opposite result—a person who talks constantly and loudly in order not to be ignored. Talking is the way this person keeps his Pain away. His children will have to listen and often be unable to express themselves because the parent must discharge tension. Because the parent is constantly yakking, the child becomes overloaded due to the fact that his senses are never allowed sufficient rest. He is so busy listening that he hasn't time to enjoy his surroundings, to be attentive to beauty around him, or to introspect. The verbose parent constantly diverts attention toward himself, and the child can never say shut up out of fear of being punished for being disrespectful. The child becomes a "listener." He is praised because he listens so well, when in actuality it is nothing more than a defense.

The child, it is clear, is the symptom of the parent, and unfulfilled need will force the parent to be sick with his children. What does being "sick" mean? It means having such needs and Pain that nearly all of reality is distorted in their service.

Children nearly always try to be what parents want. And the parental wants are like any other neurotic wants—symbolic of need. It is terrifying for a delicate young child not to strive to please, because when parents are angry, there is no one in the world a child can turn to for comfort. They steal, wet themselves, masturbate— all to soothe themselves, and then are punished for that. We can understand the childish terror when we think about being criticized or snubbed as adults. Our first impulse is to call up a friend for consolation. Children can't do that. They have to suffer it all alone.

Now we are beginning to see why it is that pure needs are never satisfied and yet persist. If a young child has to do chores and to take care of his mother to receive her love, then he will, by and large, become that helpful person. Later, he will marry a helpless person like his mother so that he can be loved in the way that he learned love was given. Still, he may act out the independent "I don't need anyone" posture because to act differently is to bring up the old Pain and the fear—fear that he will never be cared for or loved for himself. Indeed, to give in to his own need (to be cared for) is to bring up anxiety, since that need to lean on Mother brought no love.

So the recognition of need equals Pain. In order to somehow feel vaguely safe, this man will maneuver his life so as not to fulfill his need. At the same time he will struggle symbolically with his wife for her to act independently; it is a vicarious struggle to produce a real, independent, protective mother. He may rail against his wife's dependence, her indecisiveness and passivity, but his need drove him to marry her. He is dissatisfied because of his choice, yet in a real sense he had no choice. This kind of person must avoid a warm, open wife because to be given warmth openly, without having to struggle for it, is to arouse the Pain of the old want and the old deprivation. So again, in dialectic fashion, need produces Pain and warmth produces avoidance—avoidance of the *old* feeling of no warmth.

Need is unconscious both because it is painful and also because, never having had anything, there is simply no recognition of need. One patient remembers selling newspapers at the age of eight a mile from his house. There was a street meeting going on nearby and he went over to listen, getting lost among all the big adults. He just felt "funny" for a few minutes and then went on to sell his papers. He did not feel "Oh, I need a mommy to take care of me; I shouldn't be out here all alone." He had grown up neglected. He didn't know that there was another way to be. Only his body, his need told him something was wrong. He felt "funny." That need drove him to be a neurotic, independent person, and yet to try vainly in devious ways to find someone on whom he could lean. That need, recognized or not, was that boy's central truth. And it won't disappear simply because an analyst points out this need to him. This boy's neurotic behavior was a matter of course unconsciously set by his parents; their philosophy was that working hard and being industrious builds fine adults. All it builds is neurotics.

The boy in the case just cited carried his unfulfilled need around with him every minute. He was left to flounder and select his own ways to fulfill himself. Generally, it is happenstance which determines what avenues someone will choose for himself. A kindly paper-route boss who praises him for selling many papers may set him to be that industrious neurotic. Or a kindly history teacher may help him to become submerged in history. Or a gym teacher can help him enter into athletics. The slightest fulfillment of the need may determine the child's life course. This is why we can all remember so well our kindly, warm teachers. Obviously they were outstanding in our lives for the warmth they dispensed without our having to struggle for it.

If the boy becomes industrious, then making money becomes his defense and his fulfillment. Money merely quells the need; it fulfills nothing. Obviously, the need does not change, only what one does about it. What one does about the need is what we call the form of neurosis. To become homosexual or perverted or moneymaking are attempts to fill the need in some symbolic way. As an adult and a parent, the person is still driven. He is out at night drumming up business, making more money, never relaxing because relaxing and playing with his children bring up the anxiety over not being industrious, and industriousness *is* his vain search for love. Society praises his go-getterness and the man may be drunk with success. Meanwhile, his wife and children may suffer from neglect because he's bent on personal satisfaction. Any advice against overworking is meaningless because it is like saying to him "Don't eat!" when he is starving.

I call needs "Primal" because they take precedence over any other human activity, precedence even over the needs of one's children. Parents are not consciously unloving; indeed, if you asked most of them if they loved their children, they almost certainly would reply in the affirmative. Yet they make their children neurotic. They will believe that they act in the child's best interests when they demand high grades and admission to top schools. No amount of persuasion can shake them from their belief that this is done out of love. Few neurotic parents believe that what they are doing, such as making money, taking night classes, etc., is for themselves. It is rationalized as necessary for the family; sometimes, it is seen as a "sacrifice." When the children complain, the parent feels justified in yelling, "Look at what I'm doing for you, ingrate!"

Some parents are in so much Pain that they must constantly live in fantasy—that mental web they spin around their Pain. When the child asks a question, he is often not even heard; when he persists, he may be scolded for being a nuisance. If the parent does not flee inside his head, he may flee outside to parties or nightclubs. A mother who is chronically depressed may need to go dancing or be in bars to find relief. The fact that the child is suffering is of little matter to a mother who is also suffering. She is not going to help her child until she feels, rather than acts out, her misery. Once that is done she will see what she is doing to her child without any words necessary by anyone.

Neurotic parents cannot be reached because they are not themselves. The child must deal with a "front"; this is no different than the experience of therapists who have such a difficult time reaching patients who are well-defended. Anyone's front is a mask for what lies beneath. Not unexpectedly, parents force their children into becoming masked by putting demands upon them. What the child does is to develop a "personality" that insulates him from the Pain and that enables him to survive. It is not surprising that "personalities" are encouraged. For example, if the child learns to defend himself with jokes, and if his ability to evoke mirth is pleasing to his parents, he will persist in using that particular defense. Others around him may like him better for his merriment, and soon he finds himself liking what he hears—that girls like his "personality"!

The front is nothing that we put up consciously. It is woven by thousands of experiences where the real self could not simply be. That is why we are so unconscious of the front. The struggle is automatic. If a boy tries to be a "man" for his father, he may develop a low voice. His voice would be lower than normal, especially for a young boy. The low voice is the unconscious way the child tries to please his father, and the child is often not even aware that his father wants him to be tough and manly. It happens in subtle ways, such as the interest the father has in reading the sports section of the newspaper or his praising of athletes on television. If that is how to get Father's attention, then obviously the child must come to realize that he cannot be himself and be loved. So he learns to be what will get him love.

The "act" of a low voice, or being sweet and polite is the unconscious performance that will last a lifetime. The act may mean playing the loser to a father who has to be a winner, or it may involve acting dumb because one parent has to feel smart. In adulthood, it can mean being the constant helper, a role perfected by a child caring for a sick mother throughout one's childhood. A final example is the mediator act played out by someone who found himself in that role with his belligerent parents; keeping them together meant preserving a family for himself.

The parents are just as unconscious of what is happening as is the child. A parent who was required by his parents to be well-behaved may try to mold his child that way. A parent who is psychologically dead will automatically hush his child when he laughs too loudly. The parent may be acting out a "Hush, don't wake Father" dictum laid down by his own parents. When a child does not behave, when he is not smart and receives low grades, when he misses a note on the piano, he is not just making a mistake . . . it has meaning, and that meaning is "I am not loved." This is why there is such fear in children who cannot measure up. A child may overreact to a teacher's criticism because it arouses the deeper fear of no parental love. Why do parents demand such perfection? Because they need love and are acting out their need through their children. A "sassy" child is a threat to the mother who has been "sweet" all her life in order to think she is loved, just as a nonstudious, "dumb" child is a threat to an intellectual parent brought up to value academia. Thus, a child can continue his act and *think* that he is loved, but it is a far different matter to actually be loved —something requiring no act whatsoever. The purpose of this lifelong performance is to make parents into what children absolutely need—loving people.

Tragically, the front we all have is the way we preserve the past in the present. We "act" shy, belligerent, smart, or fearful in the present when it is not altogether appropriate. Normal people are not shy. If these types of behavior are not appropriate to circumstances in the present, then they must be from the past when they were appropriate. So, unconsciously, the past is brought into the present. This is done so that the feeling of unlovedness will not rise up. Primal patients are made anxious and are brought close to these real feelings because we do not allow a façade, an "act." In this regard, the therapist is the opposite of the parents.

When neurotics act in the present as if it were the past, it means that they do not experience that past, that horror, as a separate experience. They are still struggling symbolically. And children become part of our struggle. Thus, as I have already mentioned, one patient had a Primal where he first saw the deadness in his parents' eyes and realized for one horrible, epiphanic moment that he, too, would have to be "dead" in order to live. Being lifeless was the stabilized way he behaved until he relived in therapy the early terror of what it meant to be a happy-go-lucky youth—devastating rejection.

We can see why a "how-to" book on child rearing is so limited. A child who is not looked at, rarely talked to, or asked for his opinion insidiously develops an unconscious feeling of being a nobody—someone not worth anyone's attention. Every later act based on that feeling will also be unconscious. This "nobody" who becomes a parent may push his child to achieve and be a "somebody." That is, he will enlist the aid of his child in defending himself against the feeling of worthlessness. No matter how many child-guidance books he reads, he will push his child to achieve. It happens in subtle ways. He carries his five-year-old around with him and they see a sign. He asks his baby to point to the letter "A." If the child can do so successfully, the parent will then ask him to point out other letters, not allowing the child to finally feel successful until he has pointed out all the letters the parent wants him to. He is not simply "teaching" the child; he is driving him. The lesson is not for the child; rather the lesson becomes a tranquilizer for the parent who needs a smart, "somebody" child. This parent may later insist that the child do hours of homework, taking pride in his studious offspring and rationalizing that all the work is in the child's best interest. But we see that it may be something quite different.

A psychologist who writes a "how-to" book may caution parents that "children should not be pushed to achieve." But the neurotic parent doesn't even know that he is pushing his child, or, if he does, could not pinpoint the subtle ways in which he does . . . so the advice is lost. Further, the parent may well reject the psychologist's admonitions, claiming to have intellectual disagreements. He may rationalize that we were "put on this earth for a purpose" and achievement is part of that purpose. The rationale is again a defense. The psychologist is addressing himself to the parent's front—to someone who feels like a nobody. ("No body" is an accurate term for a nonfeeling person bereft of all of his body.)

If we understand that we do not *have* feelings but literally *are* our feelings, then if those feelings are unconscious, we *are* unconscious of our actions. Until we change the state of being of the parent, advice can only be of minimal value. Intellect is not a crucial factor in this regard. No matter how smart the person, he will be blind to those areas which involve his need. Neurotics cannot see beyond their needs. And even if someone were to point out to them the harm they are doing to their children, they could neither accept nor understand it. We know that some parents treat their infant sons as girls almost from birth. That is, they look at a boy and "see" a girl. Other parents look at that same infant and "see" a "dummy." No matter how the child acts, the parental perception based on the unconscious need remains the same. As the child begins to warp himself to that parental need, his own perceptions about himself change. He, too, looks at himself and sees a girl or a dummy and his actions follow accordingly. The misperception becomes a reciprocal relationship. Nothing will make either the child or the parent more perceptive in the blind areas because perception is an outgrowth of buried feelings. A parent may be quite perceptive in selected areas that do not directly touch on his need. A mother, for example, can "see" that it is not important for her son to be an athlete, but a father with special needs cannot.

These misperceptions are a special form of unconsciousness. Buried feelings continuously divert perception so as to keep the person unconscious of what is really going on. This person may be a very acute child psychologist, seeing what others do to their children, and yet be completely unaware of his own behavior. How unconscious we are in our perceptions depends on the strength of Primal Pains. The greater the strength of underlying feelings, the greater the misperception. Someone with an inordinate need for love will choose anyone who shows even the slightest interest in him, and this person will not "see" the other for what he is. The greater the Pain, then, the greater the misperception; the less the underlying Pain, the more specific and true the perceptions. And that is the real meaning of being objective about ourselves. The closer we are to ourselves, the less we will misperceive, distort, misinterpret, or be fooled.

So long as a person is not himself he is a "nobody." The only thing that will make him a somebody is feeling—feeling the "nobody." Feeling is what makes us real. So the dialectic: blocking a feeling of worthlessness makes a person act out through his children. As soon as the parent can be himself, he can stop pushing his child and allow the child to be himself without advice from experts. We rarely write books telling children how to behave toward their parents because we know that children treat parents in terms of how they feel about them. Why is it so difficult to understand that the same holds true for parental behavior toward children?

Whenever I think about parental need, I am reminded of those machines in amusement parks where there is a car and a simulated roadway that moves from side to side. The player's task is to keep the car within the proper lane. Neurosis, of course, is never so graphically delineated, yet in an unconscious way parents lay out their own neurotic boundaries within which they attempt to keep their children. The only time there is ever friction is when the child veers off course, when he doesn't line up properly. Parental need is what sets these boundaries. And there's trouble for a child who attempts to outsmart a parent who needs to feel smart. It cannot be overstated how uncontrollably unreasonable parents can become when confronted with an obstinate or "off-course" child. A lifetime of Pain can be aroused and a host of defenses can be activated by something as minor as a child not combing his hair to a parent's satisfaction.

When a woman marries a "father" who is brutal, someone she can struggle with to make gentle, her need will supersede her children's welfare. She will knowingly keep them in a household with a brutal father because she herself is a desperate child clinging to "Daddy." She may tell the children that she is staying for their sake, but it is a lie. A parent who keeps her child indentured to a cruel parent is just as unloving, and perhaps more so, than the overtly bad one.

In the children's minds, Mommy may be seen as a victim, too; there may be feelings of "She's trying her best for us, but she's helpless." The children cannot feel that Mother has betrayed them, that her need for love from her husband supersedes her children's welfare. Because Mother is also the little girl, the entire household may revolve around "Daddy's moods"; everyone treads on eggshells, and the children wonder when Mommy is going to leave Daddy and take them away from the misery. They have a long wait. They will have to wait until Mother gets over her need, which is a hopeless expectation, indeed. These children will spend years warding off their father's bad humor, hoping for a day that won't come.

It should be clear by now why counseling parents about their children's needs is of minimal value; it is a futile attempt to turn the parental head against the needs of the body. Many parents already "know" that they are doing something wrong; they also "know" that they shouldn't smoke or drink to excess.

Parental needs do not disappear with advancing age. When a parent is angry at his child because the child has been indifferent, has not answered promptly enough, etc., he is feeling a real feeling —out of context. He is really angry at his father's indifference, for example, and he will have to feel that anger in context before he can stop being furious when his son doesn't react immediately to him. Feeling the anger in its proper setting toward the proper person changes the father's behavior to his child without one word of advice, without even mentioning the child at all. What has been euphemistically called "child-guidance" work should be "adult-guidance," guiding the parent into his own feelings.

If a parent should later see the light and get straight and want to make up for what he has done to his child, a few words about being "sorry" can't undo the past. He cannot take away years of unexpressed hurt and resentment. The best he can do if he is loving is to let the child feel the hate first, the old hate. To really love a child who has been damaged means more than giving him a loving home in the present, although that helps. It means freeing him of his past.

PARENTAL ROLE

Many articles and books have been written on the parental role: how to be a good father, mother, wife, husband, etc. Yet, if we think about it, there is no such thing as a role. Roles are something neurotics latch on to. Roles such as "father" are abstract concepts.

Trying to live up to a role is living a symbolic abstraction. Neurotics get locked into roles and have no flexibility in their relationships. Thus, a father is always a father giving orders, providing for the family, etc. When things are bad he will not consider allowing his wife to work because he is "the provider."

People are just people who have relationships in which sometimes they take care of others (wife, children) and other times are taken care of. Advice on "how to be a good mother" is meaningless. How to be anything but yourself is, indeed, meaningless, and there can be no advice on how to be you. Only you know how to be you, and that will be different than any other "you." Roles are the result and cause of so much of neurosis. For example, a "dutiful son" does so and so for his mother, never sasses, thinks first of her and has an obligation to see that she is happy. A real son does what he feels. When he is a feelingful person he will love, with the full meaning of that term, his mother. Anything but that will be an act. One can make a boy *act* like a dutiful son but that act may be a role in direct contradiction to his feelings.

People used to living on the surface, having buried their deep feelings, are content with surface roles, surface behavior and appearances. They are easily taken in by surface behavior because not feeling makes them place such emphasis on it. People in a real family have no roles. They just function in terms of their abilities and often those functions are interchangeable. Almost any member can garden or cook. It depends on who feels like doing what, not on who has the role.

The most common role adults slip into is that of being a "grownup." There are ways that grownups are supposed to act. When we think about it, those ways are neurotic—inhibited, ponderous, reserved, cautious, unspontaneous and unemotional. When we think of someone as grown-up, we usually think of someone uptight, who weighs his words carefully, speaks sparingly, and never loses control. Primal patients learn that there is no such role as "grown-up." Maturity should mean to be what *children* are—honest, free, open, feeling, spontaneous, and direct. People who must act grown-up to please their parents (the "little lady and gentleman") lose those precious qualities. They merge into the role of a grownup. They put on an act because unless they have had a fully indulged childhood they cannot be grown-up. They cannot mature at a proper pace because they grew up too fast. They become rigid, inflexible, and miserable because they were forced out of touch with those precious qualities of youth—qualities that have been defined as "immature."

Those who have easy access to their childishness and spontaneity are the truly mature ones who will survive. Being "grown-up" and "mature" are concepts, not realities, and the most frequent connotation of those concepts is to be inhibited. Thus, if a person is in conventional psychotherapy and is too "emotional," he will be thought of as an "hysteric." If he can not delay his gratifications, put off his happiness, he will be thought of as immature.

There is no such thing as "grown-up." We grow bigger and taller but not "grown-up." We grow up into ourselves, whatever that is, and it can be different for each of us. I have often wondered why the President is seldom seen acting freely, even laughing uproariously. I think that in part it is because we can't allow the President to be little; otherwise, how could he take care of all of us like a good father? He's stuck in his role and the amount of latitude he has in his behavior is severely limited. By definition, he cannot be himself. If he were to expose the child inside him, we would all see that all of us are children in need; and we spend a lifetime hiding that fact.

THE STRUGGLE

The counterpart of parental need is the child's struggle to fill that need. The struggle has no point of climax where the child realizes there is no love to be had; it is the way the child keeps from feeling unloved. Deprived of a struggle, he can become depressed and suicidal because the struggle always implies a possibility of love. A child's hopes are most cruelly dashed when his struggle is rewarded with coldness, displeasure, or outright viciousness. Often, just the arching or knitting of brows, or the aloof stare is subtle enough to make the child struggle even more for the smile, the caress, or the kiss. The insidiousness and sophistication of the ways that parents throw their children into the struggle cannot be overstated, and I now want to indicate how we can identify this tragedy.

If a parent cannot laugh, it automatically puts the child into the struggle. Perhaps the child is genuinely amusing but sees no expression on his parents' face; he may then struggle harder to be amusing and "press" his parent to show emotion. Later this struggle may be acted out in the world on a real stage where the child becomes a professional comedian. He is in the symbolic struggle to make his parent show some feeling. He will seek out those in his "audience" most like his parents—those who do not appreciate his act—and play his heart out to them until finally they laugh; then he can temporarily feel loved. But because the love is symbolic and does nothing about filling his real need, the act goes on and on.

If the parent had to be "hard" and tough in order to protect himself in a brutal household, he may grow up with "hard" and cold eyes. His child, wide open and sensitive, recognizes the hardness, realizes that it isn't safe to be soft and open, and must also begin to protect his little vulnerable self. Those "hard" eyes of the parent prevent the child from being real.

A parent with a deep, residual unhappiness, shown in the sadness of his eyes and droop of his mouth and in his generally "beaten" look, automatically puts a child in the struggle to make him happy. The child early comes to feel, perhaps, that something is wrong with him because his parent is so unhappy around him. Then the struggle begins to make a happy parent. The haggard face of a mother cannot help but make a child uncomfortable and more attentive to the mother's feelings than his own.

Such a simple thing as telling a child to "look it up" when he asks the meaning of a word puts him into the struggle. Hesitation when a child asks a question puts him into the struggle. That is, indecision in a parent keeps the child struggling to make his parent spontaneous and decisive. The child has to talk faster and harder, more dramatically or whatever to "convince" his parent that he should go to this place or that. The child is unconsciously learning that nothing is given to him easily, that he gets nothing without a struggle. He may grow up not easily accepting anything if he doesn't have to struggle for it; he may even rationalize that struggle is necessary for building character, since his whole life was one colossal struggle. We can see this attitude extrapolated socially when people inveigh against dissenters with, "This is the best country on earth. You've had it too easy. You can make it if you're willing to work hard enough. It's your fault if you can't make it." Such attitudes are produced by those who have to struggle away from their feeling of need. In short, they deny their own need and then admonish others to deny theirs. Recognition of need is a danger to unreal systems, both personal and social.

Let us again consider how a parent's facial expression puts the child into the struggle. A patient who underwent a deep Primal was asked by the therapist afterward how he was feeling. He shrugged, and looked disgusted. The therapist pointed this out, and the patient went through another Primal, feeling how his mother's perennial sour facial expression made him feel she was disgusted by him. He then became disgusted with himself, and this was evident in the chronic set of his own facial expression and the way he carried his shoulders. Believing he was a disgusting person (and wearing a disgusted look), he withdrew from contact with girls. Thus, a major factor in this young man's struggle was his mother's facial expression, which was not entirely unlike her sour, sarcastic, and acid treatment of him.

There is a look in a parent's eye that can say, "Shape up or else"; another look of chronic "disappointment"; still another highly destructive look—looking at the floor instead of the child so that the child never has his existence verified. Fearful parents have a difficult time looking *straight* at people, and children sense it. Children grow up receiving these looks and they really don't know that it should be different. So later they are unable to point to any one thing and say, "That caused my neurosis." There is, of course, the "martyred" look of long suffering which makes the child feel constantly guilty over some crime he may have committed. Each of these factors takes its toll: the look, the parent's posture, his tone of voice, whether he is obese or scrawny. There are even Primals dealing with "I want a pretty mommy—my mommy makes me so ashamed she is so fat." Not only can an obese mother put a child into the struggle of wanting a thin and pretty mommy, but it can also make him afraid to eat because he may turn out to look like her.

As I have said, the struggle generalizes later on to the world. A businessman comes into his office in the morning and, not finding the usual number of phone messages, becomes upset. Why? Because he is beginning to feel the stirring of an old feeling: "No one wants me." The flurry of business activity—the phone calls and meetings —prevent his Pain from erupting. So when there's little activity the Pain begins, only the businessman is feeling it in the wrong context. Instead, he suffers a vaguely anxious feeling, covered over soon enough with more activity. From this we can see that it is more than the threat of reduced profits that sends businessmen into paroxysms of panic when "business is off."

To feel totally unimportant to parents—and to *know* it—is intolerable to a fragile child, so he struggles to be important to them in some ways. That is, he struggles away from the feeling of being "unimportant." When he grows up this may take the form of fleeing from unimportant jobs; he will insist on starting at the top in order not to feel unimportant—the old "unimportance." In school he may frequently fight with other children for leadership positions. His unfulfilled need and its Pain will cause others to dislike him. He will be unable to ever begin at the bottom, and this will only insure future failure and the feeling of unimportance. This person will not learn from his experience, but will rationalize his failures, never ever able to see the reality of his life. His real struggle is hardly with his present circumstances, but with a lifelong feeling of wanting to be important to his parents.

Children must struggle, because if their own parents do not like them, who else could? As they grow up they recreate the struggle everywhere, so that a man may force an involvement with someone who doesn't particularly like him. Or he will struggle with someone who is cold to extract warmth. Or a girl may marry a "loser" to continue the feeling that no one who matters could seriously want her.

The tragedy of neurotic life is that so little of it ever makes sense. For a child, it never makes sense not to be allowed to talk at the dinner table or to go to the show with friends; it is never right to be criticized for just lying around listening to music. Perhaps worst of all is a father's seemingly unprovoked rage and the beating that follows, or a mother's uncontrollable yelling, or the senseless ordering about from any parent. Children are forced to make sense out of all this nonsense in order to keep life tolerable. It would be intolerable to be constantly beaten and hushed for no reason; the child would become wholly inundated with the oppression of it. "It must be me. Something is wrong with me," is the child's usual rationale, and so he struggles. Having to struggle practically from birth keeps him from knowing that he is even struggling. It is "natural" for him. Yet he is struggling with his parents to make them do what they already should be doing—loving him.

CONCLUSIONS

I would be less than candid if I left the impression that post-Primal people want children. Most of them do not. This is really unfortunate because it reverses the whole natural selection process; those most fit to be parents do not become parents, and child-rearing is left to the neurotics. The reasons why they do not want children are many, but usually it is because they realize that they gave up most of themselves for their parents and that having children would require more self-sacrifice—there is no question that a child's needs come first. These post-Primal people know what it takes to be a good parent and are loath to do what they know they would have to do if they had children. They know that they could not compromise on the child's needs without feeling Pain in themselves; they could not run from their children as many neurotic parents do without any sign of discomfort.

Post-Primal people know, too, that in this society there is no way to bring up a normal child. The school situation alone militates against it, to say nothing of the child having to deal with neurotic children every minute of his life. How can a child be normal when parents must leave him for so long a time to work and earn a living? How can he be normal when the whole society is geared for unreality—from what he learns in history books to what he will see in politics? How can he be normal when he could easily die in a war; or where his self will be taken away for years in the military draft?

Normal parents would constantly be involved in the torment of trying to counteract all those influences. I believe that children were meant to be born into a natural environment—pretty much the kind of agrarian life the early Sumerians had. But it is not natural to have children who must live surrounded only by concrete and plastic, without decent air to breathe. It is not natural to have children who must eat plastic food which has improper nutrition for a developing body. Nor is it natural for a child to attend a school where at the age of six he must sit still for seven hours of his day listening to someone talk about things that do not relate to his needs. We have built an unnatural environment so that the most natural process of all—having children—becomes an anathema. But there are children in the world, and we must deal with their problems.

How does a parent know what is right for his child? How does he know how much allowance to give him; how much he should be allowed to say; how much freedom he should have? The problem is with the question. How much allowance, or freedom, or speech is a matter for *both* the child and the parent. Normal children do not want excess freedom, for that is anarchy and is only symbolic acting out of an unfelt feeling. Normal children won't ask for too much allowance. The idea of doling out an allowance may not always be applicable. There are those who prefer a common pool of money. Depending on income, it would seem that healthy children would take only what they need and when they need it. How much should a child be allowed to say? Whatever the child wants to say. You see, most questions about child-rearing are already taken care of by making a child real. It is no different from questions one could ask about normal adults. How much should they spend, or say? The question is irrelevant because normal people spend what they need, and neither say too much nor too little out of anxiety, but only say what they feel. Normal children won't need to curse and scream with every word to prove how rebellious, or liberated, or whatever they are. They won't need to cut class (assuming school is interesting) to prove their freedom. In short, children know what is best for them and freedom is not something handed down to them by an authoritarian parent.

Because neurotic children do not recognize their needs directly, they want; want is symbolic of need—money, clothes, candy. Nothing will be enough for them, just as nothing they do is enough for neurotic parents.

Let us take the subject of money. If money is given as a substitute for love, then it will be used symbolically by the child in an attempt to fill his need. He will want more and more money because he is filling the need symbolically. He can be deluded into taking substitutes which temporarily calm him. Soon, he will want more again.

The same can be said about how much a child should eat. In the first place, he should eat when he is hungry and then he should have what he wants. Isn't that what normal adults do? Parents simply do not need rules for child rearing. There aren't enough rules in any child-rearing book to teach a parent how to be a good one. A feeling parent will automatically say to his child, "How did you *feel* about school today?" while a neurotic one will want to know, "What did you *do* in school today?" A straight parent is interested in a child's feelings, not in his productivity.

I have used the phrase "letting a child be," and possibly some may interpret this as anarchy. Indeed, I mean quite the opposite. It is unloving parents who foster anarchy because they can't be bothered limiting and protecting a child. A young child needs protection so that he can feel safe. To allow a child to sell newspapers all alone at the age of eight is not loving him. If parents engage in loud shouting matches when the child is trying to sleep, they are not letting him be. If they make him eat food he does not like, they are not letting him be. If the child is fed on a schedule or made to go to bed by the clock, he is not being himself. Is it anarchy to allow a child to do what he feels? I think not. It is freedom, and freedom produces children who never abuse it. They do not want what they don't naturally need.

All of this does not mean that a child never needs guidance. Once a child is neurotic, with neurotic wants, he will need limits. Once he has been made impulsive by his upbringing he may require some curbing. When he is young he will obviously need certain kinds of guidance. The point is to guide him within the framework of his development and his needs, and not according to the warped values of neurotic parents.

Children need a lengthy, indulged childhood and then they will be ready for each new stage of development. Further, they won't become adults who have to be indulged. There won't be anything missing in their lives to drag them back. Girls won't suffer from menstrual cramps when they start menstruating because of an inability and an unwillingness to be "women." Boys won't be retarded in their physical development so that they have a delayed pubescence. This does not mean that children should be "babied," for babying a child also means that he cannot be himself. Babying a child, even when he is no longer a baby, is a neurotic mother's way of keeping a child under control. Immaturity rarely comes from being "babied." It is from parents who force their children to skip over their childhood too quickly; the result is that many of us run about the world looking to be "babied." *good point!*

There is a myth in a vengeance-oriented society that criminals—and children who misbehave are often treated as criminals—learn through punishment. Punishment teaches nothing except how to avoid it; it only blocks misbehavior. Children do not learn from being punished, but they do learn from feeling and insight into their misbehavior. The reason that emotionally healthy children are well-behaved in the real sense of the term is that they have no reason not to be. "Well-behaved" in neurotic households means giving in to the parents' neurosis. For a child, it means helping "them" destroy him. A "bad girl" too often is one whose room is not neat and orderly, or one who doesn't wash the dishes without being told. A "bad boy" is one who is lax or "lazy," one who isn't busy hauling rubbish and tearing out weeds. To neurotic parents a bad child, by and large, is one who is acting upon his feelings. Neurotic parents "tame," and thus destroy, their children.

The good child in a neurotic household does not attend to his own needs. He doesn't complain or cry out when he is sick. This same "good" child is the adult who dies early because he kept in all that sickness, only to have it ravage his body. Being unreal is a fatal disease because for a lifetime the body has to cry out its needs. That internal, painful pressure from not being spoken to, not being looked at, not having one's existence acknowledged finally kills the "good" child-adult.

It should be obvious that children never "grow out of" their early symptoms because they do not grow out of their history. The bed-wetting, nail-biting, allergies, or headaches are the result of an over-load of Primal feelings, and those feelings remain even when the symptoms become more subtle and sophisticated. A shock apparatus may, indeed, halt bed-wetting but it only serves to build up the ten-sion in a child bereft of even that "unconscious" outlet. Neurotic parents often overreact to symptoms in their children because they are the obvious signs that something is wrong. Those signs an-nounce to the world that something is amiss, and neurotic parents want an end to symptoms, not so much for their child's welfare as for their own vindication. Eliminating the symptom, then, is tanta-mount to proving that it was the child's problem and not the par-ents'. If the child begins to learn better or stutter less, no matter how miserable he still is, the neurotic parent is absolved.

I have often thought that elaborate psychological tests for par-ents (or even for children) are unnecessary. By and large, one has only to look at the children to see what the parental needs are. No matter how charming the social front of a parent, we get a much truer picture of him in his relationship to his children, for they are defenseless and powerless, and the parent is more likely to "let go" and be himself around them. A parent made to feel powerless with his parents, for example, might well abuse his position of power with his children and use them to regain that feeling. A good meas-ure of how one's friendships will turn out with people is found by looking at their children. That is how we see the true needs of the person.

Not only are psychological tests largely useless, but the whole field of child therapy is suspect. Having been a child therapist for years, serving on the staff of a children's hospital psychiatric de-partment, I think the field ought to be replaced with Big Brothers or some other kind of group who can just befriend rejected chil-dren and ease some of their hurt. Subjecting damaged children to loads of insight not only helps little but may be damaging. Too many child therapists try to get young children to "understand" their parents. This usually means children who have to deny their feelings about their parents and act like the adult in the family group, the one who knows more than the parents do. This is too heavy a burden for a child, who doesn't need to have all that insight if he can have a friend to talk to about his hurts. Too many child therapists think they have to justify their existence in some way by being other than a friend and by filling the child's head full of elaborate psychological notions and then sending him back into the family zoo to sink or swim. The child's life is even more intolerable because he feels he is supposed to cope with the chaos in the family when such a thing is impossible. He needs loving parents, and a child therapist isn't going to make that happen. The next best thing for a child therapist to do is to see the parents and help them stop hurting their child.

Fortunately, there is a way to undo some of the harm done to children. A child can be allowed to feel his Pain, bit by bit, until he is no longer split. Often, this means letting him be the baby he never was, the baby who was so hurt that he had to emotionally seal himself away from the world. It means allowing the baby to explore his physical self, something usually castigated by parents; it means permitting him to express the taboo words and feelings. In short, it means allowing him to experience his Pain rather than blocking it. Pain is the liberating force; to feel Pain is to feel again.

All of this does not mean that neurotic parents are going to give Primals to their children. But when parents are suddenly warm and kind and offer their child a feeling of safety with them, then the child will begin to feel his old hurts. Just feeling safe to express his fears will bring up his old terrors; just feeling new-found warmth from a father will bring up the hurt of no affection before.

The reason neurotic parents should not give Primals to children is that first, being neurotics, they will botch the job. Secondly, they will force a feeling child to contend daily with living in a neurotic environment. The young child is too fragile and too dependent to be forced into Pain prematurely. Primaling children is something that can only be done by Primal parents, and even then there are reservations. (See Primal Parents' Seminars section.)

Once a parent can allow his child to experience himself, a bonus occurs. The child, now open, can feel all the rest of his Pains without effort. He can make himself well. His Pain will keep him real because he will feel it instead of blocking against it and acting it out. Once major Pains are felt, whether by the parent or by the child, change becomes automatic, just as not feeling Pain automatically makes neurosis rigid. For example, a child may always leave something on his plate at every meal. If he always had been made to finish everything on his plate, leaving a bit of food may be his acting out of "I won't give all of me to you." Once this feeling is felt, he will not have to act it out. Feeling parents would never make a child eat when he didn't feel like it. Too often families are run like the military, where children eat what the parents feel like serving and when they feel like putting it on the table. The child's feelings are ignored. In this way, suppression of a child's feelings is not an active process. Simply not catering to a child's feelings subtly inculcates in him that his feelings and desires don't matter. Never having had the experience of having his feelings valued, he becomes a robot, unaware that there is even such a thing called feelings. The military and military schools in this sense are the worst places for human beings. Feelings are completely denied and discipline is substituted; people become mechanized.

In a production-oriented society there seems to be a great anxiety about children who don't produce. The idea that children who just enjoy life are spoiled is so ingrained that it is difficult to get parents to see what life is all about for them and for their children. It can be rationalized that nonproductive people do not enjoy life, but this too often comes from people who cannot relax.

Neurotic struggle is insidious. We see it in our attitude toward education, where the difficult school is supposed to be the good one and the easy school, where children do what they want, the poor one. The idea that school can simply be fun is out of the question for neurotic parents with aspirations for their children. These are the aspirations which destroy because they don't allow the child to enjoy himself but force him to try harder and harder to produce. No matter how much parents think they are doing it for their children, the Pain will be there if a child is disciplined into his skills. If a child wants to play, then let him. After he has played *first*, then he may want to study or practice. It takes faith in a child to let that happen, and neurotic parents are short on faith.

If a child is forced to perform in some way in order to get along with his parents, then his need is being perverted. To pervert the need of just wanting to be what one is, means that both the body and the mind are being perverted. The mind becomes perverted because it cannot recognize the body's needs. Sexual perversion is only an extension of this process because sexual perversions are aspects of physiologic functioning where the mind puts the body into bizarre performances in order to achieve satisfaction. Children forced to be unnatural do indeed become unnatural—they are "perverts." Perversion is a total event, not just a confusion of mind. A child who receives love only if he studies, may come to "love" to study because *not* studying is painful. He has perverted his need for love so that studying brings some relief.

As I see it, the job of parents is to help children enjoy life. If children are happy and well integrated they will want to produce and to take part in society. If they are not, then they produce not out of feeling but out of a need to get love. There is a great deal of anxiety about children who cannot produce in school; they are called underachievers—meaning that, according to someone else, they aren't achieving what they *should*. Achieving what they feel like achieving is considered being a failure. The best rule of thumb for rearing children is to do what makes sense. Children should go to bed when they are tired, for example, instead of by an arbitrary rule. With enough faith and patience in them, children will select a proper bedtime just as adults do.

Psychologic theories ought to make as much sense as the rules for child development. Inborn jealousy and Oedipus complexes do not make sense. They are not natural states. There is no innate reason why a boy at a certain age should turn against his father and to his mother for love. It is when we superimpose artificial theories on children that child-rearing becomes mystical and mysterious, when all it really takes is being one's self around them.

Loving a child should be as natural as breathing air. Children take both for granted, but when love is missing there is a frantic and usually unconscious struggle. Imagine the desperation, the panic, the unbearable Pain that would occur if breathable air were suddenly not there. It is no different for an infant or child when love is not there. Love, as Primally defined, is necessary for life.

Letting children be natural is quite simple. It means cooking what they like to eat and allowing them to dress the way they feel. Most children grow up not even knowing that their mothers should cook what they want. They just have to eat what is set before them, and the "good" child never complains.

The problem with unloving, "dead" parents who never really lived themselves is that they live forever inside the child. It is their values and judgments that twist his mind and the shape of his body.

What is confusing is the way that parents will tell a child ever so often how much they love him, and the child believes in his head what he is told; but his body cries out to be held more, to be talked to and understood, to be looked at. Mother might say, "Daddy loves you, you know; he just isn't demonstrative," and the child is supposed to "understand" that he is loved. Knowing about love is far different than feeling it. But *understanding* that one is loved is one of the ways children become unconscious of need. The need is covered over by "understanding" that "they really love me, but they have to go to work and leave me." If children say, "It's all right, I understand; don't worry about me," they are praised for their maturity and self-reliance. Far better off is the child who lies down and cries, "Don't leave!"

Neurotic parents seldom see the horror of what they do because their children often become what they need. In short, the child fits comfortably into the parents' void and is no longer an entity unto himself. Parents don't feel their needs or the child's struggle; they both just act it out. It is only when a parent is open to himself and to his own Pain that he can see what he has done to his children, how he has used them as symbols to fulfill his unfelt needs.

The parent who finally sees what he has done to his children may be tempted to ask the child to "forgive" him. But he ought to forego this effort, because it is one more way the parent tries to get his child to "give." There is no real feeling such as "forgiveness." It is like asking a child to forget the hurt the parent has inflicted on him and that is pretty much impossible. Nor should he. No words can wash away that past, and in getting a child to forgive, the real feelings simply become covered over and the child must pretend he no longer hurts, when that hurt is very much lodged inside and can only be felt in all its Primal intensity for it to go away. Then the child will be over it without any words about forgiveness having been spoken.

If a parent can't feel, he will go on hurting his child unconsciously, and lectures won't stop that parental destruction. What good is it anyway to lecture someone about being a parent when he is already drowning in despair? What good is it to tell someone not to ignore his child when *he* feels like the child who needs attention?

The thing that constantly strikes me is what innocent victims children are. Whatever the parental whim, that's the child's life. This is brought home to me in restaurants. I find it excruciating to sit next to families. Rarely, if ever, do I see anything but constant subtle (and not so subtle) harangue, humiliation, pressure and hurt. Parents can't seem to allow children to talk while they eat or to speak at *their* normal pitch. They seem to have a universal anxiety about food and eating, and children just have to eat . . . and eat what parents decide they should eat. They won't allow their children to move around. They are constantly at them for their manners until the last bit of pleasure at mealtime is squeezed away.

Children can shout "Mommy, Mommy" for hours and parents go on talking to other adults or looking in shop windows as though the children didn't exist. They wouldn't think of treating other adults like that. But to neurotics, children have few rights. They are supposed to wait until they are grown up to live. No wonder so many children can't wait to grow up. Rare, indeed, is the parent who enjoys himself around his children. Some neurotic parents enjoy children when they perform, but few enjoy *themselves* in a relationship where the child is just himself. Grandparents are more apt to enjoy the children because they have already lived out their needs with their own children. They can afford to be less demanding with someone else's child.

It is becoming clear, I hope, that actions and interactions between parent and child are only important insofar as they reflect feeling.

The fact that there are hundreds of books written on child-rearing implies that children are a separate species requiring special treatment. They are just people needing exactly what parents need. The question is not "How should I *handle* my child?" It should be "How do you treat people you love?" A parent isn't someone who lays down rules. He is a loving friend.

Feeling is what relating to anyone is all about. Children are just people. There are no special rules about relating to them that do not apply to any and all relationships. There's not much you have to do to children. You don't have to discipline them, lecture them, punish them, or lead them. All you have to do is talk to them, listen, hold them, be kind and free, spontaneous and easy and just let them be.

But after all is said and done, what does role matter anyway when it is obvious that all of us are acting out our little selves and it is those selves that dictate how we'll act toward our children and does not derive from any title we have been given. When our little self has been humiliated for a lifetime, then no child of ours is going to sass us without feeling our wrath. When our little self has been commanded and ordered about for years, then our child won't be given the leadership and decisiveness he needs from a parent. When that little self inside us has never been touched and caressed, then our child won't know what physical warmth is about.

XV

Learning From

My Children

BY VIVIAN JANOV

I am a post-Primal patient, a Primal therapist, and the mother of a teen-age boy and girl. I have listened to patients for many years, hearing their Primal grief: "Let *me* be the baby" . . . "Mommy, be nice, don't hurt me." Many times as a therapist I have sat with my own children, who are calling the "Mommy" of their babyhood —me! This has been amazing, painful, and yet a rewarding experience. My children's pain goes back to their formative years and by reliving those scenes they are relating to the mother I was in the past. They are not afraid to say the truth, even though I am there. I cannot deny that these are more than just ordinary sessions to me. They are often the prelude to my own Primals.

Sometimes, scenes that I thought of as insignificant in their lives were the cause of extreme pain to them. I learned something very important: *My intention was not always their reality*. Well-meaning parents, in their attempts to civilize their infants, often create a reality that is terribly hurtful to their children. A good example of this lies in early toilet training. The mother's *intent* is one of establishing good habits in the baby. They baby's *reality* is hurt bewilderment at the punishment for performing a natural function. Furthermore, parents who cannot feel their own pain will often stop their children from expressing pain. "There, there, don't cry;

it doesn't hurt." The intention is a soothing of both parent and child; the reality is learning how to suppress feeling because it isn't acceptable.

Perhaps it would be helpful to parents if I generalize some "horse sense" I have learned from my children, both of whom have had terrifying Primals that have taken them back to the crib in the early months of life. In these early scenes they were crying for Mommy. I didn't come when they cried, and the feeling for them was "I knew I would die if I didn't keep crying for you to come." I remember the pediatrician saying we would have to "break" our children of crying for feedings in the night by letting them cry it out. I felt like "breaking" his neck when I realized the terror and pain I inflicted on those helpless infants on his advice . . . the advice he is probably still giving. Of course, I am to blame for not feeling their need despite any advice. I firmly believe that young babies have only one way to survive and that is through their crying. If it is ignored, they experience the same dreadful fright that an adult might experience as he drowns. Mommy is the only link to life. Mommy's not coming is *death!* I have observed this exact Primal in many other patients and I know it is tied to the belief that babies have to grow up fast and be little men and women for people who cannot bear the responsibility and caring of parenthood.

It is time to return the cradle to the parents' room, so that the baby's needs can be met quickly. I can hear all the grandmothers grumbling about spoiling the baby. There is indeed a whole school of pediatricians, psychologists, and unfeeling parents who have given babies the magical quality of being cunning, power-mad schemers who must be taught discipline and self-control from the moment they are born. I believe the baby will be content, relatively pain-free, undemanding, and unspoiled if you always pay attention to the cries that say "I need." All this presupposes that Mommy and Daddy really want the baby and that they understand how much time and patience it involves to be a really good parent. Too many parents have an image of a pretty baby "toy," all dolled up, that they can put away when they're tired. Babies require hours of tender handling and devotion to prevent neurosis.

As my son grew out of infancy he would always ask to have a

light on in his room at night. We knew that there was a generalized fear there and we went along with his request. Of course, I would assure him that no "robbers" were coming, and intellectually he understood this, but he still wanted the light on because his *feeling* told him otherwise. This troubled me because I felt helpless to get to the real fears. There was nothing I could do about it until the day he had the Primal that made the connection to his night fears and led to their disappearance. He was really afraid that the "robbers" would smother him, and that if he called for help they'd get Mom and Dad too. We, his parents, were his lifeline and protection. The fear of losing us became magnified in the dark. How many times has a parent said, "Big boys aren't afraid of the dark." Many big boys as well as lots of little boys are very *much* afraid of the dark. Parents heap insult on injury when they cause a child to be afraid of being afraid!

The origin of my son's night fears may be rooted in the times I let him "cry it out," or in a brief hospital stay at the age of 5 for a tonsillectomy. I was not permitted to stay overnight at the hospital. When I arrived at 6 A.M. the next morning, he was already crying for me. To him this overnight stay must have been like a horrible nightmare . . . strange people in white, a stark hospital room, being strapped down, a black mask being pressed down on his mouth and nose, awakening with a burning throat and no Mom or Dad. I shudder as I write this. How could I have subjected my baby to that trauma? Hospitals and doctors have got to recognize the deep harm they can cause and not only allow parents to be there but *insist* that they stay. A child's reality is all that counts. When things feel dangerous he is not apt to relax with the thought that Mommy is coming back. He wants safety, and parents are the only safety he has.

We are so used to the way things are organized that we have come to believe that is the way they should be. An example of that is putting infants in their cribs. Maybe they should be sleeping between their parents, safe and secure, as the Eskimos do. Perhaps the preponderance of night fears we see in children come from the unnatural early habit of having small infants sleep apart from their only source of life.

Recently one of our Primal families moved the beds of their pre-school youngsters into the master bedroom with them. The great happiness and security this brought to the children cannot be measured. It took some readjusting of the parents' sex lives, but it did not create a major problem for them.

We often think we have to be strict and punish our children for their misdeeds or they will end up as unAmerican, psychopathic criminals. One evening, our son and his friends experimented secretly with liquor and cigarettes. We were horrified and scolded him with such gems as "can't trust you anymore" and "thought you were responsible." He suddenly started crying very deeply and, after an hour of Primals that recalled similar incidents in his life, I realized that in our righteous indignation and anger we had hurt him badly. These pronouncements were only heard as one recurring echo . . . "Mommy and Daddy don't love me anymore." Out of our own fears we had made the incident much more important than it was. His reality was that we were disappointed in him as a son and it would alter our relationship *forever*. It is profoundly important for us as parents to recognize that our inability to accept off-beat behavior in a child can result in that child's feeling completely rejected as a *person* with no chance of wiping the slate clean. How soon we forget that as children we experimented with grown-up diversions.

Actually, when the neurotic parent faces the failures of his children he really is facing his own failure. His children exist as an extension and reflection of himself, instead of existing as separate human beings with distinct personalities. Perhaps this is why I could not understand or readily accept my children when they did not conform to my expectations. I could not face *my* being "bad." I agonize when I hear parents in public places reprimanding their children for being "bad." I look into angelic faces and see mournful eyes looking at a scolding mother. There are really no bad children; only children with unfulfilled needs—victims of parents with unfulfilled needs. John Lennon in a song called "Mother" says it: "Mother, you had me, but I never had you . . . I needed you but you didn't need me."

If I could address a neurotic parent with any hope of reaching him or her, I would say that unwarranted anger, scolding, strictness or rejecting punishment are felt as *no love* to a small child, even though you think you love him and are doing it for "his own good." For his own good, find out the real cause of his behavior before devastating him with cruel put-downs. Get to see your child as a real person. Children can and will talk to you about their *real* feelings. When everything is accepted, nothing can be thought of as bad or punishable. Your child is human enough to choose satisfying behavior when he is permitted a free range of choice. Why should he be sneaky when everything can be discussed in an open way? Freedom is the answer to the healthy development of the self, but it can only be granted by feeling and accepting parents. Allowing freedom is giving love.

Sometimes my children have Primaled about being left with babysitters and watching us leave for work or for a movie. I know now how wrong it is to leave a child when he is afraid and needs his parents. If children cry in fear over being left, *they* are right and shouldn't be deserted. No well-meaning assurances from a kindly babysitter can alter that fact. I know that many mothers have to work and must leave their children, but at least they should know about the effects of this.

I have often heard professional women who are pregnant planning for their return to work soon after the baby is born by hiring competent household help. I cannot express strongly enough my contempt for this sort of motherhood. If a woman is not planning to do mothering in the true sense, she shouldn't become one! This is not an achievement to be placed alongside the diploma and the marriage certificate. This is the *life* of a human child that definitely needs his real mother close to him, nourishing his body in much the same way as she did before he was delivered.

The Women's Liberation Movement has many important things to say about equality between the sexes. But there is no way a man can truly "mother" his child. He can certainly share and contribute a great deal, but he cannot breast feed the baby in the first year of life, and I believe this experience, with all the softness, holding, and love surrounding it, is crucial in the prevention of neurosis.

In these times of efficient birth control and relatively simple access to abortion, I believe that no one has the *right* to bear and neglect an infant. The choice between motherhood and a career must be made before pregnancy. There is also the same choice to be made in favor of the *small* family where attention and love can be given in a realistic way. Yes, I am saying if you are not prepared to *give* a great deal, or if you do not have a lot to give, don't become a parent. Too long have we passed neurosis on from one generation to the next, having babies for the wrong reasons. Some of those reasons are wanting someone to love us, wanting to hold a marriage together, being bored with work, wanting to make up for a bad childhood, and giving *our* parents a grandchild.

Another important message I got from my children's Primals concerns talent. At the first sign of our daughter's inclination to sing, dance, play tennis, write poetry, etc., we were signing up for lessons, checking on progress, and arranging for performances. Pretty soon her joy and delight turned into *our* thing with her tuning out. And she is angry that we have spoiled something that she used to love to do. I am deeply grieved as I write this, to think of the many ways we intruded on the great talent and creativity of our daughter. Our intention was to give her all the things *we* didn't have; to "develop her potential" and to fill our needs. Her reality was the pressure of performing and not being allowed to be herself. There is no way we can ever make this up to her.

There must be millions of ways that parents can hurt their children by not letting them be themselves. I am talking about the mother who wants a girl but gives birth to a boy. This does not daunt her; she makes him into a girl and a young sissy, and a future homosexual is the result. I am talking about the father whose son must be an athletic giant. The boy is incapable; the father pushes anyway, and a very neurotic loser is developed. I am talking about the child who must bring home "A's," and who becomes an intellectual recluse and loses his feeling, spontaneous self. I am referring to all the preconceived plans, demands, standards, ambitions, achievements, accomplishments, talents, goals, and hopes that parents invest in a helpless child long before it even enters the world. The parent is anxious to make up for all the failures of his own life through his child. The child is never thought of as a separate human being with separate talents and desires. He is scheduled to relieve the tensions of his parents and teachers.

You may wonder how a "Primaling" family gets along in day-to-day living. There have been historic days where the four of us have had simultaneous Primals, each triggering the other. The effects of Primals have been to give a great deal of freedom to all of us. The children have much freedom in governing their lives because they are often able to make sensible, nonneurotic judgments. Since they are not motivated by repressed old wants, they can act responsibly and spontaneously. At times they will have irrational wants but they can connect them to an old feeling. Primaling is a *process* of feeling what is real, and goes on and on. It is not the "quickie" answer to all problems.

Recently my son decided that his school was crowded and that classes were taught in a boring, traditional way. He decided that he would like to attend a "free" school and found one that sounded ideal to him. My reaction to his decision was a direct result of my therapy. The old me would have been full of objections: What about college? homework? study habits? the establishment? my friend's son? curriculum? his future? My new response was open to a free learning situation where he could learn what he really wanted to learn without the hassle of public-school conformity. I felt he would be able to serve *his* needs . . . not mine or society's.

Both children decorate and arrange their rooms as they please. That is their private domain and an expression of their individual personalities. I think parents often neglect this right to privacy in the same way as they ignore other rights of children.

Our family may seem unique when it comes to free expression. *Anything* may be expressed and is. Anger, profane language, disgust, love, hugging, screaming, crying, or laughing is safe to let out. Whatever anyone may be feeling at any time is allowed and accepted. Perhaps that is the true definition of love. By clearing the air at the scene, we try not to add to the storehouse of hurts and frustrations. If the painful scenes of today are allowed to be felt for what they are, they will not become future "Primals" in a psychiatric clinic. The truth of every situation remains in the body and no amount of denial can take it away. The jealousy between siblings is often a fact. Telling a child that he really loves the baby denies the reality of the moment and causes him to repress his pain.

When I heard my daughter crying in a Primal that the arrival of her brother meant "she couldn't be the baby anymore," I knew how much of her reality I had denied at the time. We had tried to make her feel how much we loved her and how important she was as a big sister. We did everything but make it acceptable to say the underlying feeling. How could she admit she hates the idea of a new baby when everyone else was so delighted? Her first fear was losing love to the rival; the second was verbalizing it, because that means even less chance for love. So everyone pretended and "said" the right things. "You're going to be big and help Mommy with the new baby, aren't you?" asks Grandma. There are about five levels of pain in that question.

The relationship in recent years between the children has changed. One memorable night they wept together and exchanged all the resentments that had built up between them. They were able to see each other as people for the first time and not as rivals for parental love. Out of that experience has grown a close, loving friendship that I'm sure could never have happened without Primals.

I know I can't make up for the damage of the past. There is no way to start all over again. I am often saddened that my unreality hurt my children, but I am thankful that Primal Therapy can help. I can at least do something about my mistakes through hearing and accepting their pain. Of course, I am only able to do this because I am constantly exploring my own pain so that I can be open to the present and stop the poison of the past from permeating all of our lives.

Perhaps part of the answer to raising nonneurotic children is a return to more primitive ways of living. I think there is a lesson to be learned from aboriginals, who carry their children in holders, who let their babies sleep in the parental bed, who breast feed their babies on demand for years, who allow free play and learning, and who surround children with a secure community of surrogate parents.

XVI

Rick's Night at the Movies

Last night my son, Rick, who is fourteen, my wife and I went to
see *The Search*, a movie made in the forties with Montgomery
Clift. It is the story of a boy separated from his mother in a Nazi
concentration camp and the search to find her. Montgomery Clift
is the American soldier who finds the boy and helps him locate his
mother. After we got home, Rick said, "Boy, there was one scene
that really got to me. It was when the soldier on the river bank tells
the boy that his mother is dead and that she is never going to come
back." My wife, Vivian, was sitting beside him as he crawled into
bed, preparing to go to sleep. She pursued that feeling: "What do
you mean it got to you? What was there about it?" Rick said, "You
know, sometimes I worry that you'll both die and you'll never come
back. It's something I'm afraid of pretty often." My wife said that
it's probably a Primal feeling, but Rick discounted it. (None of us
enter into Primals without some prodding.) She said, "Why don't
you give in to that feeling." Again Rick said it is a natural feeling
that anyone would have. "After all, it would be bad if you died."
Vivian pressed. She made him repeat the words that the man in the
movie said to the boy until he became locked into the feeling. Then
silence. He started crying softly, saying that even if he were fifty
he would still be sad when we died, how much he loved us, etc.

His sobs became deeper. Vivian continued her silence. After five
or ten minutes of crying his legs began going up and down involuntarily, knees flexed and then straight, very much like an infant's movements. His hands were in the air, bent and turned in,

again like an infant's. His sobs became more opportuning and also more infantile, until he was moving and wailing like an infant, uncontrollably and without effort. Then his wails turned into "Omi, Omi." (He later explained that he hadn't learned to say "Mommy" yet.) His wails and writhing continued for one hour until he was totally exhausted. He alternated between awareness of where he was, in his bedroom, and being in a crib in a pitch-black room as an infant. As the infant he was totally engulfed by the terror of dying because he was not getting enough milk and was allowed to "cry it out" as per the doctor's orders. We had no idea then that he was not being fed adequately. He was being breast-fed and, because he was such a big baby, needed supplemental feeding. His infantile cries were out of starvation, and the fear that no one was coming to help him. He felt as though he were actually in that room and in that crib struggling for his very life. Then his loud wails turned to soft moans and he felt "hopeless" (his later concept of giving up hope of anyone coming). Here is where he began to turn off the wanting and the hope. During all of this his breathing was very intense, as though he was running a race for his life. As the moans subsided he began shivering uncontrollably, teeth chattering like, as he put it, "the double case of the chills." After fifteen or twenty more minutes he came out of it and had the sensation of coming out of a bad dream. "It was exactly like that. Like coming out of a different world. My head was spinning around." Then he exploded into insights. He talked for another hour, making connections. He kept saying, "It's amazing." No matter how many Primals any of us have we always come out of them saying, "It's amazing!" Because it really is!

Rick knew from his Primal that he was left totally to cry all alone while hungry. He knew the reason why he had to have the light on in his room and his door open when he went to sleep . . . to make sure we were there, ready to come in in the dark. In the dark as an infant he couldn't tell where we were; if we were near or far or gone completely. Later, he needed to hear our voices to feel safe at night.

His insights went on: about having to have us awake in order for him to fall asleep—the feeling being that in case he needed to reach us we had to be fully awake and ready to come in. After his insights went on, he felt exhausted and decided to go to sleep. We left his room. Ten minutes later he walked into our room and said, "As I rolled over something popped into my mind. You know how there's always something I want, some toy or something? Well, I have to want because I never got. I mean, that early want just stayed on and I attached it to other things. That's why when you got me a watch, I then had to want something else, and when you got me that, I then looked for something else to want. I had to keep that want alive because my life depended on it. That want kept me alive. This Primal is going to save you a lot of money," he said. He then went back to his room, needed no light, and promptly fell asleep.

This Primal involved a crib experience which occurred at about the age of three months. Rick explains the Primal experience as follows: "In the movie scene where the soldier is explaining to the boy about his mother not coming back, my present brain triggered off my infant brain and started it working. It triggered off a feeling I didn't know about. Except I began to worry again about Mom dying. I forgot about it after the movie until I got home. If Mom hadn't pressed me I probably would just have had a dream with that feeling in it. Because she made me have a Primal, because she made me repeat that scene, 'Your mother is dead and she'll never come back,' I could connect up that feeling with the infant brain. And then I could connect up that infant brain to all the fears I had later, like of the dark, of being locked in a dark room, etc." Just saying those words that the soldier said opened up all those feelings.

He understood the "whys" of a lot of things. For example, he understood that if he thinks about our dying in the daytime, it doesn't bother him, but if he thinks about it at night (in the dark) he is scared. He reminded me that whenever he said he feared our dying, I would always answer, "Don't worry, you'll be sixty when we die. That's a long time from now." But he was still afraid, because it wouldn't matter if he was one hundred, that fear would still be there exactly as it was at three months. He also understood that he wasn't really afraid of *us* dying. He was afraid that *he* would die if his connection to life (Mommy) died. That was why he worried so when we took a trip or left town for a few days. This was the source of his separation anxiety. This was a big Primal, in his estimation, because so much got connected—all of his fears, his false wants, etc. He sensed that his wants were false even though what he wanted was real and not wasteful, because he had an "overreaction," he wanted too badly. That's the tip-off. Overreactions are driven by Primal feelings.

Rick defines a Primal as when the present brain connects with the past brain. He discussed heart attacks: "The way my heart was pounding during my Primal, I thought I was going to have a heart attack. I bet if I didn't connect and get that out of my system, I'd keep on having scary dreams where my heart would pound until one day my heart would give out."

Rick and his sister, Ellen, are unique beings. They are being "cleaned out" as they grow up. They have no devious motives and none of their motives are a mystery to them. If they can't concentrate in school they know why. If they start to get a symptom, they immediately understand its source. The result is that they are both extremely healthy—and well-proportioned. They have "together" bodies. So many neurotics' bodies are distorted. Their lack of unity shows up in torsos or legs which are too short, too long, or whatever.

Rick's Primal makes me wonder about how many children have night fears as a result of growing up in an era of "letting them cry it out." The fear isn't anything that is carried forward consciously. Rather it continues its life as a viable entity, a generalized background of fear or apprehension which becomes attached to this or that. It begins so early and is so prevalent that some neurophysiologists have even tried to prove its genetic quality—the primordial fear of the dark.

What is to be learned from this? Irrational fears are always rational, only the child cannot plug into the right context or connection. Anything out of keeping with present reality refers to a real, past reality and is still rational. Keeping a child open to himself, not comforting a child away from his feelings, is the greatest gift of love a parent can give to his child . . . to give him himself.

XVII

Primal Families

The following are excerpts from meetings which took place at the Institute with Primal parents. These people are making history, for they have set about putting Primal Theory into practice, and are undoing the harm they had previously done to their children. They will continue to meet and share experiences and to hammer out new techniques for helping children. These initial meetings only hint at the possibilities. What is clear is that Primals in children make an *immediate* difference in their behavior. This process is not recommended for anyone but people who have had their Primals. A parent has to be open to allow his child to be open with his feelings. He cannot, and must not, defend against what the child brings up, and because the child will be in Pain, there will be a great temptation on the part of the neurotic parent to soothe rather than to dig.

PRIMAL PARENTS' SEMINAR
February 3, 1971

ART: One of the purposes of these meetings is to talk about something that is world-shaking in its implications. There is no way that Primal Therapy is going to cure the world. What can happen is that people can learn about Primals and then give their own children Primals and reverse some of the harm they've done. That can be widespread. It's an enormous concept. And the question is how you do it, and what happens.

SUSAN: Art, I had a Primal the other day and my six-year-old said,

"Oh, Mommy, give me a therapy." I mean, she couldn't get down on the floor fast enough. And I asked her later what she felt it was, and she thought about it and said, "To be true." It's so heavy. She knows what it's about.

ART: Well, what happens when she has a Primal? What does it look like?

SUSAN: Well, with my younger children, they've much more physical than I think adults are. With my six-year-old, I've had a more difficult time. She was always very withdrawn and very controlled, a very good girl, always pleasing; she could never be bad. Lately, when an incident occurs, her rage just comes out. I don't know where to start. With my children it started with them observing me. I just started lying down one day; as I said, my six-year-old is at a point now where if I take her at a calming moment, she will intellectualize a lot more than if an incident occurs, in which case she will act out and then immediately it's anger. It's been difficult; she has been throwing furniture. I'm the greaest scapegoat, I mean, I'm the worst mommy in the world. I took away her daddy. [Susan is divorced] And she's had a couple of Primals like "Why can't we be a family again? I want to be a family."

ART: What does it look like, those Primals? How do you get her there?

SUSAN: Oh, it's just with her whole body. "I want my daddy!" and I just guide her along, "Call Daddy. Tell Daddy." And she's done it. And she has another thing. It's immediately when she's deprived of something, she wants something special, and I know it's the need. Because of having four children, they've all lost their identities. Three of my kids have had Primals that said "My mommy. My mommy. Only *my* mommy. Nobody else's mommy."

PAT: I was babysitting for Bryan [age 4] while Linda and Ben were out of town for about six days. He was accustomed to them being gone for a weekend, but had never been away from them for any longer than three days. In fact, he still will hold up three fingers and state that it's okay for them to be gone that many days, but any more than three days—forget it!

He got along fairly well the first five days, as Jim and I kept him continually busy and he really enjoyed being outdoors on the ranch all day. On the sixth day I kept him home because his mommy and daddy were supposed to be back in the late morning or early afternoon; he usually got up and went out for the day with Jim. Between ten o'clock and noon, he must have asked me literally twenty-five times when his mom and dad were going to be back and *if* they really were going to come back. By twelve o'clock they weren't back yet and Bryan was really beginning to act fussy. He would chase the cats, throw things around the house, and generally just be shitty. Finally, I was able to get him slightly into it, and he said that he was just a little boy and needed his mommy and daddy. He was crying slightly and the phone rang. I answered it and the minute I said, "Hi, Ben," Bryan started really crying and demanded that he talk to his daddy. I gave him the phone and he asked Ben to please come home *right now*—he was tired of waiting all day for him. (It had actually been two hours.) Ben told him "No," that he couldn't get away right then, and that it would be later in the day before he could get home. Bryan really started yelling and saying Ben was stupid, stupid, and that the little boy hurt. I hung up the phone and just let Bryan cry. I was sitting on the piano bench and Bryan sat up and stopped crying and asked me to play him a song. He started really sobbing. I told him sure, and asked what he wanted me to sing about. He told me to sing a song about him talking to his daddy on the phone and how his daddy wouldn't come home and how much it really hurt him. I started playing the piano with one finger and simply saying that Bryan wanted his daddy but his daddy wasn't coming home. Every time I'd get through that sentence, Bryan would just really cry and say, "It hurts me, it hurts me." I'd stop playing and wait for him to finish the feelings and then he would look up and ask me to play it again. This went on for about forty-five minutes of really deep crying and coughing up all sorts of junk. He finally asked me to stop playing; he'd had enough. Afterward, he just wanted to sit in my lap and have quiet.

On another occasion, I asked him if he'd like to go visit a friend of mine who had a new baby. He vehemently said, No, he didn't like little babies. I asked him "How come," and he said that he didn't like being a little baby. I asked him what happened when he was that little. He said that he had to take all kinds of naps and that he'd always cry and that his mommy would close the door on him and leave him alone. I said, "Your mommy did that?" He said, "Yeah, my daddy, too." I was quiet for a few minutes because he didn't want to talk anymore. Finally I said, "Bryan, did you ever tell them how it made you feel to be in your room crying and alone?" He looked me square in the face and said very softly, "Patty, I couldn't tell them—babies can't talk."

MIKE: Our boy is stuck. He's three and a half and he can't verbalize enough to know. He cries and breaks out in total body spasms. I don't know if that's just a present feeling or if he takes it back; I doubt if he does it. It's just a present-day hurt. It's not going back anywhere. It's as though he can have a feeling right now. If I leave for work and he doesn't want me to go, he starts to cry. He goes all the way through that feeling. He's not shut off. So what I think is he's just not getting new pains each time. He won't be able to until he can verbalize and go back by himself.

ART: I'm not sure of that.

DIANE: I had that same problem with Fred, who is seven. He never cried in his whole life when I left him, and he was left a lot. When I was in Spain he was taken care of three days a week by somebody else, just because I didn't feel like taking care of him. He could be left for a week and never shed a tear, and for the past two months I can't go any place without him, just nowhere. If I go to the store, "I want to go." I tried to arrange work so I could have two days off——

ART: Give an example of how you give him a Primal.

DIANE: He had his first Primal last Saturday. I have been trying to do everything with him, not leave him alone, so I took both of the kids on a Saturday to a Saturday matinee, which just freaked me out. Fifty million kids throwing popcorn [group laughter], you know. I sat through The Aristocats three times [group laughter] and you know, I got home and I had a date for that night and I really felt that I had to go out. And we got home and I said, "Okay, Fred, I'm going out," and you know, he just screamed and yelled and he said, you know, "You can't go out." And I said, "I'm sorry, I have to go out." And so I went and I sat down with him and he just started crying. He's also never cried, never, and he cried and screamed for two solid hours. "Please don't go, please don't go." If I even go to the store, he'll cry about it. He doesn't go back and say, "I'm a baby."

ART: He went back.

DIANE: He's feeling it all right now. His body went back.

VIVIAN JANOV: I still don't know how some of you give your children Primals.

SELMA: With Sam [age three] it was getting to the point where it was impossible to go anywhere alone, even to the bathroom. I tried all kinds of things, and he didn't want to talk, or he'd be distracted by something else. I decided to bring out old pictures and talk about what happened in New York, and I said, "You know, Mommy did leave you for a long time," and he looked very sad and he sat thinking about it for a long time and then he talked about it to me and to the neighbors. He said, "Yeah, my mommy left me." It seems to have helped. He's still very clinging, but it seems to have helped. He couldn't make the connection. I made it for him.

GROUP MEMBER: But you didn't lay him down and——

SELMA: You can't do that with children. They have their bodies. When you don't have your bodies you have to lie down, concentrate on feeling, and it'll happen. But you've got to be ready when it happens.

JANE: We've got a situation with our four-year-old, who's been like, in a bad place for two weeks. He's been feeling a lot. He's just been terrible. Mean. But he's been him.

ART: What does he do?

JANE: He doesn't want to go to school. He doesn't want to leave the house. And he wants me with him, like if he goes some place to play, I get the phone call ten minutes later, he's ready to come home, and as soon as I show up, it's five more minutes or ten more minutes, and he wants me there and he doesn't want to go to school. He wants everything with us.

MIKE: So we let him spend the weekend in his pajamas, that's what he wanted to do. He didn't want to get dressed at all.

ART: But you see, that's not the Primal.

JANE: We didn't know what to do. Maybe you don't understand.

MIKE: We sat down last night and tried to figure it out, and we sort of pretty accurately traced it back to a couple of weeks ago when our son stepped in some dog shit and he was left alone with the kids in the park in the nursery school, and Jane came to the park for five minutes and then went away from him. He wanted to go with her. She didn't take him. We knew that. We sort of felt very strongly that that is what it was and has been going on for two weeks, and we didn't know how to get into that.

VIVIAN: But, Michael, it's not that. I mean, it is that and it isn't. It couldn't be that from one five-minute incident that your son is holding on to you twenty-four hours a day.

JANE: Where do you draw the line about acting out? Like my six-year-old is not going to school. This is the third week now she's staying home.

ART: That's all right, but you've got to get to the feeling.

JANE: Well, the teacher yells at everyone——

ART: Well, let's take this one example of Michael's. Let's follow it and see how you do. What do you do?

MIKE: When he's really sad about something, then the door is open to everything.

JANE: Like you have to get at it like you said, at the time that they're crying, because I can't deal with a four-year-old. A nine-year-old will get sad in retrospect. So get them when they're upset when Mommy leaves.

LINDA: If Bryan is crying and saying: "Mommy did so and so to me," I'll say, "Well, tell her." He can tell her right there or he can go out and tell her.

VIVIAN: You see, that's what happens to our children after they have been kind of shown the way. They can be free human beings. Like my children can tell me off twenty-four hours a day. With Bryan, he's able to do the tantrum and then it's not going to be a stored hurt. Before that freedom happens, before children feel free enough to yell and scream at the moment, it's liable to become a stored pain.

LINDA: I can only think of Bryan before he got to the point where he is now. You can't get him back there; you have to wait till something else happens, when he starts to cry and holler, and right then catch him, then let him get it all cut at once.

ART: What would you do, though? Suppose she starts to leave, what do you do? You're leaving and he's crying. Now, what do you do?

I think it's really simple. You tell them what the feeling is. You say, "You don't want Mommy to leave." You teach them, "Say it to Mommy." You trigger the feeling. One parent leaves, but you both don't leave. If he is crying, "Mommy, don't leave," the other stays back and gives the Primal.

GROUP MEMBER: What if it is one person?

ART: Just look at how we do it in therapy. Sometimes I will get furious at a patient and leave him. Why? To reactivate the feeling. The minute he is locked in, I come right back and give him the Primal. So that is easy to do.

JANE: In working with a child, the child has the Primal over your leaving, okay, and it is seven-thirty and you have got your dinner date. Then you walk out and leave. And the fact that they felt all that shit——

ART: Will help.

BEN: Just the other day, we were together and Linda was leaving. He didn't want her to leave. He was crying and all that. He stayed with me and she went out and got in the car, and as she was driving down—he was at the window—and he was crying, "I don't want her to go." I said, "Tell her," and he just freaked out. And after he did, then we played blocks and it was a great day.

JANE: Talking about building up hurt and fucking over your kids, every time you leave, therefore, aren't you fucking them over?

VIVIAN: No, because that feeling of not wanting you to leave is a very, very deep feeling, which may come from a thousand deeply hurting things back there, and it really is not realistic. It may be connected to somewhere in infancy—not coming with the milk, and it's feeling, life or death. Whether you think it is farfetched or not, it is really where most of it's at. Rickie's fears about me leaving, I know in retrospect, came from not being fed or from a hospital scene; my not being there when he was in the hospital. A Primal Scene.

BEN: I pretty much know where our boy's came from. It was my mother when she had me. Her thing was, "Let him cry, it's his fussy period." Well, I picked that up and at noon time, or around when Bryan was tired, I would put him in his play pen, or Linda would put him in his play pen, and we would go out and let him cry himself to sleep. And I have had Primals about just seeing in his eyes what happened to him as we walked out when he was crying and screaming.

VIVIAN: You know what it is—it is death. Believe it or not, it is death. "I am going to die." It isn't that you are going to come back later, or that the child is lonely. It is death. It is the feeling when you are a baby; the hunger, the need—and it is a life-and-death struggle. And every time the life-and-death struggle isn't met, there is one more piling on of these awful feelings.

ART: But teach them. Teach them how to lie down and scream and yell. Tell them what the feeling is. Encourage them to scream it out.

DIANE: Fred is crying like almost every time I go out of the house to go to therapy, that he wants me to quit therapy.

VIVIAN: Well, he doesn't even know what it is.

DIANE: No, he just screams, you know, "that therapy."

SUSAN: My kids want to come.

ART: It is the same feeling. They are acting out "Mommy, don't leave," so you have to get them to that feeling. Always think of the feeling under it.

MIKE: All of these things seem to work when you are dealing with one kid at a time. It is a complication when kids interact on each other, and sometimes what one really wants and needs is in direct violation of the rights of the body. I mean that. Well, like they try to kill each other, or they want something—a toy right now, and it isn't their toy, but they want it.

ART: What is the scene—give us the scene.

MIKE: Well, there are so many of them I can't think of them. One kid has got a toy and it was bought for that kid by a grandmother, and the other kid's four and says, "I want it." And he is bigger than the five-year-old. When she is not looking, he gives her a clobber and then grabs the toy. So she starts to scream because he has taken her toy. He starts to scream because she pulls his hair to get the toy back, and we start to scream because we don't want to be parents. I know what I used to do when I was in that situation before.

VIVIAN: Which was what?

MIKE: I would come on like Adolph Hitler. I would say, "Give the toy back to Hugh and do this and that or I'll hit you." And I would hit the kids a lot. I would just go crazy; it would make me crazy. I would want peace at any cost. I would just make an arbitrary decision and nobody, including me, would get to any feelings behind it.

ART: You have two therapists there, don't you?

MIKE: Yeah, but it is hard to tell a kid, "You really don't want that toy, you really want me."

JANE: What do you do when a child is crying over the physical object? Like the sailboat that he wants. Mine will freak out because I went to the store and saw a bargain and I came home with a present for one and I didn't come home with a present for three, so when I come home two kids are freaking out because they want something. How do I keep them from crying about a deck of cards?

ART: How would you do that as an adult for your own Primal?

JANE: I would just feel the hurt.

ART: Of what?

JANE: Of not having.

ART: What? Where would you start? You start there, with the boat, and say, "There's more to it now, feel it all." Just get them into the groove. They may not do it for three months.

BETTY: Art, I have a different feeling about it. I tried that with Joey and I had the feeling that I had to be straighter before I could do him. He is fifteen, which is way out of the category.

VIVIAN: It is sometimes easier to do older children.

BETTY: With his second Primal he went back to three months.

ART: How?

BETTY: He was in the bedroom and he came out. And I can tell when Joey hurts by his eyes, and I said something to him, and I said, "Is something bothering you with all the kids around?" He said, "No, I was looking in the mirror and listening to music." Pretty soon those eyes were sad eyes. So I said, "Well, lie down and feel it, you know." So he was there and talking and talking, and pretty soon he didn't say anything. He had his shirt off and could see his stomach bobbing. After a while, he sat up and I said "What did you see?" And he lay down and he said he couldn' talk about it. You know, just automatically he knew, and he said "I was in this crib, and three people were standing over me." One was his brother, he knew. He said, "I don't know who the othe one was, but he had these scary eyes and he had a beard and he said he was going to kill me, and I don't know who he was." One time his dad had a beard, and so he asked me if Dad ever had a beard, and I said, "Joey, I really don't know what to tell you."

ART: How did you get him back deeper into that Primal?

BETTY: I didn't. He didn't want to go back.

ART: Next time he is going to have to do it, so you are going to have to know the way you did it.

BETTY: Don't be afraid is number one. Art, I am not ready for it

VIVIAN: It is scary to do it and it brings up your own feelings and especially the first time, because your kid is crying over a specific thing that you did.

BETTY: My nineteen-year-old is the one that I wonder about because I started him on one and I didn't know what to do about it

ART: Well, tell us about it. This is why we're here—to talk about it.

BETTY: Well, he was talking about something at school in a class in a major that he decided to go into and something about art He kinda drifted away from talking about it. He said, "I don't know if I can do it, Mom." And it was a kind of sense of insecurity.

ART: What would you do at that point? It is so simple.

BETTY: I said, "Mike, you are feeling something, why don't you lie down and why don't you sink into exactly what you are feeling right now, because I can see it in your eyes." And he did, he lay down. I said, "What are you feeling?" And I have to tell you that this was the day that I had my birth Primal, and my head was just pow, pow, pow and my eyes were like crossed, and he was into a feeling and I tried to leave, you know, to get him into a feeling, and at least, you know, get him into a little bit, and he said, "I feel so little and I feel Dad, Dad. I can see him and we are playing football." And his father was a football coach and Mike is very strong for his size and, "Dad keeps bumping into me and keeps pushing me and he keeps talking about what a sissy I am." Mike is also diabetic. And I said, "I didn't know what to say." If I did it again I would try to say, "What do you want to say to your Dad?"

ART: Exactly—perfect. Remember one thing—the want is the hurt. You always say, "What do you *want* to say?" to bring it back. And then have them say the feeling.

BETTY: And then he went into another part of it where his father, when he was in junior high school teaching, his father told him he didn't want him to call him Daddy because he didn't look like the son of a football coach.

ART: So you make him call Daddy.

VIVIAN: What Art meant is that the Primal would be something like, "Please let me call you Daddy, you're my Daddy."

JANE: What do you do, though? My twelve-year-old goes through Primals trying to please Mommy and not really getting to feelings.

VIVIAN: Stay with her. Say, "Look, I know what you are doing. You are trying to have a thing like I have because you know I will give you a lot of attention."

ART: That's the feeling. "The reason you are doing that," say, "is that you want me to love you. Let's get straight about it. Ask me. Close your eyes!"

GROUP MEMBER: The Primal then becomes the acting out.

VIVIAN: I can tell you something that helps with my son. We always do it in the dark. I sit on the floor behind his back so we can't see each other. I don't have to see him, he just knows I'm there. One time we went to a movie that I knew was his thing. After a while you know the thing that hurts. Anyway, one line in the movie is about a death scene. The guy tells the little boy that his mother is dead. So we come home and he says, "Ah, that movie was crappy, there was nothing in it. What did you take me there for?" So I said, "You mean you didn't feel anything in the whole movie—not one thing?" He said, "Well, I felt a little tiny thing at one point." I said, "I bet I know when." And he laughed. And all this is taking place in his room and with the light out. We talked about that scene over and over again, and I just made him talk about what it reminded him of. It reminded him of the idea that *we* would ever die. And that went back thirty-five layers, until all of a sudden (I couldn't believe this myself—after seeing a million Primals, it is still strange when it happens to your own child) he was suddenly an infant, I mean he was just that—even in the dark, I could see him suddenly become an infant, with his legs and feet up, and he started wailing like an infant. I shut up completely, and when he came out of it he told me it was a feeling in the crib that he was going to die if I didn't come. The real feeling of us—parents—dying is that we are the link to life—we bring the milk. It is really that explicit—it is that simple. The crazy thing is that people don't feed their kids when they cry.

ART: The biggest mistake you will make with your kids is talking too much. When they are locked into a feeling, shut your mouth and don't talk again until they talk to you. Don't say a word.

VIVIAN: *He* couldn't even believe it. He said, "I was an infant—I could see the bars on the crib again."

MIKE: What do you say to a child when they say, you know, all three of our kids have gone through, "Daddy, how old are you—and how old is Mommy, and who is going to die first?" and I think an awful lot about dying. I don't know how to get her . . .

VIVIAN: She has to go underneath it.

ART: The same thing. She has to lie down, away from you in the dark, facing away.

MIKE: "It isn't going to happen for a long time," is what I usually say.

VIVIAN: I have been saying that to Ricky for twelve years—don't worry, we are healthy, bla, bla, it is just like nothing was said. It has no meaning—it was the *feeling* that was there inside him. And if they are old enough, and if you feel secure enough in doing it, set up the scene, say, "Imagine how it feels when I am not here any more."

He said, "It is like Daddy and you are my arms and legs"; he said, "What do you think I am going to feel like when you are gone?" And then he really started crying.

[Vivian crying]

DIANE: You know, the thing about crying, it seems like my son, my young son, is going in the exact opposite. Every time I sit down, he crawls up between my legs and says he wants to get back into my stomach. You know, like he really wants that. He does it five times a day.

ART: What do you do—and that is a specific kind of Primal.

DIANE: I don't know what to do.

VIVIAN: What is the meaning of it? That's what you always have to ask yourself.

GROUP MEMBER: What is the meaning of them wanting to go back inside?

VIVIAN: He feels unsafe, and he is trying to tell you it is lousy out here in the world. He doesn't really want to go back.

ART: On the other hand, he might. Let him put his head up there strong. Put an eye mask on him. You should have masks, all of you. Put a mask on, let him get up in there, and then say, "Feel it. Stay there, but feel it." And you may find some very interesting birth Primals.

DIANE: Michael was induced labor. He didn't want to get born.

FRANCIS: Patrick was born with the cord wrapped around his neck three times. He cannot stand to have anything around his neck.

ART: So that is what you do. You take one of those and stick it around and make him feel it.

FRANCIS: I would like to know if I am helping my four-and-a-half-year-old now. I read the book *The Primal Scream* in June, and from the time I read the book, I encouraged my daughter, if she screamed, to let it out. And that is the extent of it. I was coming from the doctor's yesterday, and she wanted to have dinner at the Pancake House, and I said, "No, not tonight, Mommy doesn't have any money to do that." And she really did a whole number in the back seat. She started screaming and crying, and all I did was tell her, "That is all right, just let it all out," and she kicked the front seat, and I said, "Good, let it all out." But that is all I have done. I haven't said, "Ask Mommy" yet, I have just said, "Feel it. Just feel it."

VIVIAN: What happens after?

FRANCIS: Well, she gets into a whole body thing where she—her face contorts, she is really rigid, she feels it from her whole body, and after it is over it is almost as if it never occurred. She feels good.

FRANCIS: What normal people call tantrums, I call them Primals, aren't they?

GROUP MEMBER: Tantrums are young people's Primals.

MIKE: My son said to me, "Stay with me in the bathroom cause I afraid." I just stay with him, that's all. I don't say, "Why?" 'Cause if I can't help him feel, at least he can have me there.

SELMA: What do you do when a child attacks you? And Sam is really strong—he hits me, but I can't hit him and he really hurts me.

VIVIAN: What do you mean?

ART: Use a pillow to protect yourself.

SELMA: He doesn't want the pillow. He wants Mommy.

DIANE: Fred hit me the other day, and I just hit him back. Like, it probably wasn't the right thing to do. He just punched me and I just punched him back. And I said, "If you are going to punch me, I'm going to punch you back."

FRANCIS: That makes me confused. I have taught my daughter that when she gets angry at me, not to hit me, but to say "You are bad, Mommy." And she says it.

GROUP MEMBER: Hitting is acting out anger.

ART: By the way, that is right. That is a very important point. Do you understand? Anger is not feeling the key. Let them do it, but then get them back to the old feeling. Do you know why you all always have such a hard time figuring out what to say to kids— because you are so used to lying. You never just say what is the truth. Say the truth. Just tell people the truth. It is so simple.

DIANE: Fred asks me that, I just say that I am happier living by myself. I don't love his dad very much, and he could really understand that, you know. But I used to try and figure out something to tell him.

VIVIAN: There are about twenty-five books on the divorced parent and what to say when.

DIANE: Yeah, I read them all. [group laughter]

ART: You really have to know that kids are afraid today of the simplest things. They are afraid to say, "I'm embarrassed," or it's hard to say, "I need you."

DIANE: Fred got a leather jacket for Christmas, one of the things he wanted was a leather jacket. His dad went out and bought him one and paid, like about, I don't know, about fifty dollars for this jacket, you know. It's one of those ones with the fringe, you know, with everything on it—really an out-of-sight jacket, and he wouldn't wear the jacket. He'd say, "I really like it," and I'd say, "Okay, we're going some place, get your jacket." He'd say, "How come I always have to wear a jacket?" And he'd wear it maybe in the car, but if he was going into a store, he'd take the jacket off. Finally, he just told me, just about two days ago, he said, "That jacket really embarrasses me. I get really embarrassed when I wear it."

ART: That's not the feeling.

GROUP MEMBER: What's the feeling?

DIANE: The feeling for Fred has been that he doesn't ever want to draw attention to himself, and this fringe and all that stuff really, you know—he's been the kind of kid that would never, you know, make demands or draw attention or do anything. What I think is the feeling of a lot of kids—they want attention, but then they don't get it from parents. Therefore, they think they don't deserve attention. They're shits. Then when they attract attention they don't want everyone to see they're shits.

GROUP MEMBER: Yeah, sure. [laughter]

GROUP MEMBER: It's impossible to raise more than two kids today.

VIVIAN: That's what I was thinking of before—there's just not enough time.

GROUP MEMBER: It's not natural to have many children.

GROUP MEMBER: We don't live in an agrarian world. You need to be with your kids almost all the time.

GROUP MEMBER: If you can't you shouldn't have the kids.

GROUP MEMBER: Just imagine if you lived in a little hut, and you stayed home around a big pot of whatever and the kids were just there.

ART: The truth of the matter is that capitalism is an unreal system where mothers and fathers have to work all the time. A child is born into an unreal system where everyone leaves—and it's crazy.

GROUP MEMBER: The reason that you leave is to make money.

LINDA: Well, you know schools affect kids, too. They are going to be crappy. There's hardly any good answers. You can't really let your children be free in this society. It's really hard.

GROUP MEMBER: What are we going to do? Move to an island of Primal people?

ART: You do the best you can do and it's never really going to be perfect.

JOY: You know what I think the difference is, too? I think when children don't receive approval at home, they have a tendency to go out and seek it elsewhere, in the school and other places in our society. My twelve-year-old has had some problems at school, and she's been an excellent student. And I see now how crazy the school system is—the grades and demands and everything is just so unreasonable. She sees my attitude now. Whatever she does is fine. She's no longer making this crazy effort to seek out that approval from school.

GROUP MEMBER: And then you get a call from the teacher.

JOY: Oh, I did! They wanted to crucify her and I wouldn't help them. For the first time—because I'm not afraid of disapproval any more.

LINDA: One thing I've noticed with Bryan is if I don't get into the feeling, if I let him scream and holler about what he originally starts and don't get into the feeling, then he acts out the entire rest of the day. With everything. And even something as simple—like my mother comes over and he says, "Me no like you," and he slams the door in her face [laughter] and then she comes on in and he says, "Don't hang your coat in that closet."

ART: What did you say?

LINDA: I just said, "Bryan, what?" And he repeated it. He said, "I don't want Grandma to hang her coat in that closet." And I just listened to him and he started to cry. My mother went ahead and did what she started to do. She went ahead and put her coat in the closet. She ignored him entirely. And he started to scream and holler at the top of his lungs. Then he started to cry, "I don't want

Grandma to hang her coat in the closet." That's all he would say; he must have said it maybe a hundred times.

ART: What did you do?

LINDA: I listened to him, and when he got quiet, you know, finally he got a little tired, I said, "What do you really want? What do you really want" And he didn't say anything and he just continued to cry . . . And then do you know what he said? He said, "I want my Daddy." I had no idea that that's what it was. He hadn't asked for Daddy. That's where Daddy hangs his coat. And she was going to take Daddy's space. And then he cried constantly. He cried, "I want my Daddy. I want my Daddy to come home." But before I had no idea what it was.

JANE: Well, since you bring up the subject of grandparents, I've heard a few things from my own kids that—the real harm that comes about from grandparents, too, boy! It's really crappy. [background general agreement with various noises]

My mother really said some bad things to my daughter. I said, "Well, why didn't you tell me?" And she said, "How do you tell your mother that? You don't even know what's happening." It's a devilish kind of subtlety.

MARY: My fourteen-year-old was late with her period last month and she was over at my mother's when she got it. She sighed with relief. "Ah, it's here." Mother looked at her in her puritanical way and she said, "I've never heard girls be that pleased when they got their period unless they were questioning if they were pregnant." And this is why I have never in my life had a good feeling about enjoying sex. I couldn't even touch my body to masturbate. And she's doing it to my kids now.

GROUP MEMBER: And you don't even remember that they did it to you.

GROUP MEMBER: But it's when you see them do it to your kids, it brings it back to mind.

GROUP MEMBER: It does.

FRANCIS: I have an eighteen-month-old boy. And last night, it was quite an experience, he woke up in the middle of the night and cried and I went right to him. And I know he wasn't crying for long and I'm telling you, that little boy must have been frightened so badly at something. Whether it was being alone or what, he was like a monkey. I put him close to me immediately and he, his whole body, just like locked on me. He was so frightened. And I held him and he was asleep in like thirty seconds. But you just felt that fear, that need, and it was—I was so glad I could be there. Oh, God, it was just incredible.

VIVIAN: Well, it's a twenty-four-hour job to do it right. It's very hard.

ART: By the way, if you're going to give your kids a Primal, give them the Primal within six to eight hours from the time something bad happens. 'Cause there is some research to show that after eight hours, it locks in the brain. It changes from short-term memory to long-term memory. Though I'm not certain about this, perhaps if you get them within six to eight hours, maybe you can eradicate the memory. And the Pain. [hmms]

VIVIAN: That's what Bryan is doing. He is constantly clearing his body of pain. You see, he's learned to do that because they have let him.

ART: So if something bad happens, get them right away. Say "Hey, this morning Grandma did this or that, right?"

GROUP MEMBER: A lot of parents would do some of the right things if they knew. I would not, for instance, have let my kids cry at night if I'd known it was so damaging. I thought I was training them to sleep through the night.

GROUP MEMBER: But that's all the pediatricians told you during that period of time.

GROUP MEMBER: That's what they all said. You were wrong if you did pick them up at night.

GROUP MEMBER: Many books still say that.

GROUP MEMBER: I don't think it does any good to write for neurotics on how to raise children.

GROUP MEMBER: There is a line in a baby book where the doctor says (he is talking about spoiling), "Let them cry even twenty minutes, if you can stand it." *You* can stand it. Right. But what about the *child?* And I read that book, right? How many millions of women read that book?

VIVIAN: It just occurred to me that advice does help. I just remembered one thing when Ellen was a baby. That she used to cry at one certain time and it was our dinner time. Always when Art came home from work, she would start crying. And the doctor told me, or I read it somewhere, I can't remember, put the baby on the table while you're having dinner. And I did that. And that was good advice.

ART: We stuck her in the middle of the table and we ate.

VIVIAN: She wanted to be with us. I didn't even know it.

ART: She had hold of the catsup and all the food while we tried to eat. [laughter]

STARR: My son is two and he had a nonverbal Primal. It happened over a toy in the grocery store. He wanted a toy and we gave it to him. And then he started fussing—the toy wasn't right, he couldn't get it open. And I was in the grocery store with half my basket full and he just started crying. Finally, I took the toy away from him and said, "That's not what you want." And he started crying, and then he started reaching for everything—pointing at crackers or pointing at the cookies, or wherever we were. And finally, I just stopped the basket and he was crying right here. And I said, "Do you want down?" "No." And he just kept crying and crying, and finally he stopped crying like that (snap of fingers), and he went like this and pointed at my eye, which was at eye level with him, and he said, "Ouch," which was going back six months to a time when he came up to me and poked me in the eye and I turned around and hit him. And he said, "Ouch," to me. And I held him and I said, "Yes, ow, it hurts." And it was okay, you know, that he hurt me. There were no words since he talks very little.

ART: You recreated the exact scene?

STARR: He recreated the entire thing.

ART: That's a Primal of a two-year-old. You know, a two-year-old having a Primal about his childhood. [laughter]

STARR: And before that he had been hitting everyone in the eye. Or coming close to it.

ART: I'll bet you didn't react when he poked you in the eye the first time. That was probably your dead period. Was it?

STARR: Yes. I don't remember being hurt. I just remember hitting him.

ART: And, he's like saying, "Remember that time, you know, I hurt you and you hit me back, and I feel bad about that." Either bad that he hurt Mommy or bad that you hit him. But you see, if you hit a child, you take away your hurt and their hurt, then they can't feel sorry, because you're mad and that's all they can see. It's a whole different thing. If your reaction isn't real, it makes them unreal. Instead of feeling hurt, then they have to feel scared.

VIVIAN: What do you think made him do it—because you got so close to him? Or because you let him cry longer?

STARR: Because I was just there, I think.

VIVIAN: And, really there.

STARR: And, boy, I tell you, there's more to the story. It was real early in the morning and there weren't many people, but the grocery checkers—they were all just standing there, freaked out.

I was at the laundromat today, and there was a woman with a small child on her lap, combing her hair. And the kid was obviously not wanting her hair combed. And the mother said, "Sit still, Sit still, If you don't sit still I'm going to hit you." David was on his bike down there and I looked at him. He reacted to that and I went over and I sat by him. And you could just see his anger at that mother. And I said, "That's a mean mommy and I know you hurt." You know, he still can't relate verbally.

VIVIAN: Is he a late talker?

STARR: Yeah, very.

ART: You can say something like "You're mad." Get very economical. If you say, "Oh, that's a mean mommy," it may not be his exact feeling.

STARR: Well, he wasn't involved.

ART: Yes, he was.

STARR: Oh, I think I see.

VIVIAN: By the way, don't be afraid that you're wrong. If you're wrong, you're still where you were when you started. He'll say, "You know, that's not it."

ART: What's right always is the truth. "I don't want to be with you today. I'm tired. Go away." That's the truth. They can handle that, if it isn't too frequent.

JANE: I've been doing that since I've been sick all week. I say, "I'm sorry, Mommy's sick and I can't read to you right now." And I felt bad saying it, but that's all I could say. And then I felt, well, maybe I shouldn't have said that to him.

ART: Say, "I know how you feel, you're just a baby and I'm the mommy, and you feel like I should be taking care of you—and you're right. I am the mommy, but today I don't feel so good, but I'll be taking care of you tomorrow." Just say what's real. [group agreement] They are dependent—they have to know you're going to be there.

PRIMAL PARENTS' SEMINAR
Follow-up Meeting
March 1, 1971

ART: Since last time a lot of you have had experiences that we're going to talk about, and we'll get into some more sophisticated techniques of Primaling children.

VIVIAN: Have any of you had any new experiences since we talked last time?

WALTER: Yeah. About a week after the last meeting, it was on a Saturday, and Pam [the mother] wasn't in good shape at all, and Saturday evening I brought Claudia [age three] with Pam to the Institute for a private session. Well, you know she had to go along to see what was happening. Claudia started to cry. And she cried for about twenty minutes straight, just solid crying. No words at all, just crying. I sat there with her and let her cry. She sat in the chair, and when she was finished crying, she didn't say anything, she just kind of looked at me very sadly, and I asked her what was wrong, and she said she was sad. I asked her why she was sad and she said she was sad because Mommy left. So I asked her if that was like any time before when Mommy left, and she didn't say anything. She just started crying again. And she cried for another ten or fifteen minutes, just solid tears. And when she had finished crying, without me prompting her, without me saying anything, she just hugged me and she said, "It was just like when you and Mommy left to go camping last summer." And that was nine months ago when we went camping, and we went camping for two weeks without her in Oregon. And she just went back to that and made the connection between Mommy leaving now, and Mommy and Daddy leaving then.

VIVIAN: It's the same feeling for her.

WALTER: Right. Exactly. And she made the connection without any help from me. So that was pretty good for her.

ART: How was she afterward?

WALTER: Oh, she was in a really good mood afterward. I asked her if she wanted to go in and see Mommy now, and she said, "No." She just wanted to play. She was in a good mood for three days afterward.

VIVIAN: It's amazing with a three-year-old—you can say when did that happen to you before, and it works even in their short experience . . .

WALTER: But it's really incredible that she said when we went camping last summer. Now I didn't think that she had a concept of time, really, and she's never mentioned anything like summer or winter, or the season. But she said, "last summer." I thought that in itself was incredible. So she went back to that.

ART: The feeling took her back.

WALTER: Right.

VIVIAN: Did she say what it felt like?

WALTER: No. I asked her when we got home. I asked her, "What was the feeling like?" She just looked at me dumb and said, "I don't want to talk about it." [laughter]

ART: Did she cry subsequently when her mother left her any other time?

WALTER: No. She used to cry all the time when Pam left, and now she doesn't cry any more. But I don't think it's over yet because she cries when I—well, maybe that's a different thing—when I leave, which she didn't do before either. Now she cries when I leave and she doesn't cry when Pam leaves.

VIVIAN: Do you know why?

WALTER: No, not yet.

VIVIAN: I don't think you were very attached to her earlier, were you?

WALTER: No, I wasn't. But she might be getting attached to me now and right—missing me when I do go. Yeah. Yeah. It's really a very simple thing. [laughter]

VIVIAN: She's starting to care about you.

WALTER: Yeah, she's being less afraid of me, too. She used to be afraid of me coming in at night; if she cried at night and wanted some water or something, she wouldn't want me to come in, she would want Pam to come in. And now, she'll, well, she doesn't mind if I come in, but she usually asks for one of us at night. Half the time it's Pam, half the time it's me. Whichever word gets out first, I guess. She's getting very simple. Very simple and straight-forward.

ART: Yes, she's changed totally.

WALTER: Oh yeah, God, you should have seen her at Christmas, you know, when she came back home from Pam's mother's house. She was like a zombie. She was almost in shock. Like she, she just sat in the living room and she wouldn't move over to the table and oh, sad situation. So we took all the food off the table and put it on the floor and just sat around her. Then she started crying. And she cried for about two days. And then she started to come out a little bit, playing and stuff. But it was like she had stored up all of these tears, and I guess the grandmother wouldn't let her get them out. She's a completely different child now.

VIVIAN: She's so cheerful, it doesn't sound like her.

WALTER: She's really boisterous now. She's even doing tricks now, like she tipped over the popcorn last night. Just threw it all over the place. She could no more have done that three months ago. [laughter] She's gone to some other things. She started a few nights ago, we were living in an apartment over a garage for a while, this big tree outside, and I forgot why she was crying, but she was crying for some reason, and Pam tried to get into whatever she was crying about and all that came out was, she was afraid the tree was going to take her away cause the wind was blowing the tree around. She was afraid the tree was going to take her away to a monster who was going to eat her. And the monster had three eyes and the monster made her cry and made her sad. And then, we tried for about a half an hour to see what the monster was like, anything about the monster. All she wanted to do was have cookies, have pretzels, have crackers, have a bottle, go to sleep, anything but talk about the monster. So we finally gave up because she was so terrified she was shaking, and I didn't have the heart to do any more to her because she didn't want to be helped.

ART: And that's it?

VIVIAN: You didn't get to it?

WALTER: No, after about half an hour of watching her shake in front of my eyes, I couldn't take any more.

ART: Well, what would you do ordinarily? Or what should you do if a child is really afraid?

VIVIAN: Well, what have any of you done?

MIKE: My nine-and-a-half-year-old started, you know, with her fear and she was, I mean, like this is really an extraordinary story, but I mean there's been a lot of good results, too. It started with her being afraid as we were going out. She'd say, "When you go off, I'm afraid." So, what I did was I laid her down in a darkened room, in our bed as a matter of fact, and we just started talking about being afraid. She admitted to me that she was having the same kinds of dreams now that she had when she was very little and that, like she gave me the opening, you know. This little conversation was drifting back to that motif of being very little. And so I said, "What were the dreams about?" And she said, "Dinosaurs." I recalled Kathy having been really terrified, you remember this, terrified of dinosaurs when she was very little, and I also remember a lot of times when I've really terrorized her, fucked her over, that's my own craziness. She wanted to come and be with us in our bed. And we were under some kind of, you know, plan where we would, our master plan was not to let her come into bed with us because it's *our* bed. But we couldn't chain her up, or lock her in, so we got this gate, so she could see over the gate and see us, and couldn't get to us. And she went from being afraid of the dinosaurs, and it was very dark in the room, and she saw me standing in the doorway of her room and I was so angry at her and she was hiding under the covers, grabbing her pillow, and I recall this incident too, she was grabbing her pillow, hiding under the covers from me. She was just crying, you know, she was really Primaling, and she was having deep sobbing crying, deep in her stomach. She began by hitting. It started with anger for her. She just got so angry and then it just cracked through and she was feeling very hard. And God, you know, in the middle of it she was still crying, she said, "You're the dinosaur! You're the dinosaur!" And I just said, "Right." You know, but I mean I wasn't feeling that phlegmatic at all. It was really extraordinary. And then, unfortunately, I couldn't hold on to my stuff anymore. I just went up. We held each other and we Primaled together. It made us an hour and a half late for a dinner date. But it was fantastic. And when she came out of it, her face, I've never seen her face like that. You've probably seen her. She's got a very phony little smile on her face. And it was all gone. She couldn't have cared less about us going out. Totally unconcerned. She didn't even bother to say good night. So this has happened now twice. She's had two very big Primals about going out. The second one was about the gate. And the gate going up. When she was little, there used to be a wolf in the closet. She was wailing, "The wolf is the gate, and the wolf is you!"

VIVIAN: She's had two Primals?

MIKE: She's had, I'd say, three, and she's done some crying which is sort of inbetween. I can't tell about the little ones, I'm frankly stumped. I don't know what to do. They can't symbolize enough. They can't. Our boy is four and when he is feeling it I put him down in bed, and he's mad at Mommy. So I say, "Hit Mommy." Meaning, hit the pillow. And he sits up and goes, "Where is she?" [laughter] And that is the hardest thing. You can't lead him away from hitting, because I hit him when he was little, and he was hit a lot. He comes in and just wails on us. It's hard to make him stop doing that to get to the feeling. The feeling really is that he wants to hit. He's really angry. Anger is not a feeling, but I can't crack him through that.

LINDA: I find with our son, he's three and a half, that I say, "You're mad at Mommy," he'll say, "Where is she?" I get the same response. If I say, "Tell Daddy," it brings him right out of the crying. The crying will stop. He'll look around the room and say, "Where is he" Or, "I can't, he's gone." Or he begins to give me a whole story about, "He's at work, he's not here." And I say, "That doesn't make any difference. Tell him anyway." And he'll, he kind of looks like he's not sure. And if I say, "Go ahead," I just have to keep prompting. And then he usually does.

I do find since our last meeting that I can tell him what he's feeling. And I've done that and it works much better. He gets to it much faster. He doesn't act out nearly as long. If I say, "Do you want Daddy to come home?" or "Are you sad because Daddy left?" then he says, "Yes." And then he just continues to cry and he says, "I want my daddy." Or whatever the feeling is. But I do find that you have to be very stick-with-it and just hammer away.

I guess it was yesterday, Bryan just went crazy. He was running around the house, just chasing me, beating me, hitting me, screaming at me, and his face was livid with anger and red as a beet. And his whole body was just trembling. And I was trying to get away from him because he can really hurt when he's that mad and hits. And he started going like this with his arms at the furniture and I didn't want him to hurt himself, but he knocked the phone off the table and he knocked the vase on the floor and I tried to control him. And I forcibly laid him on the floor, and I want his arms and legs free, so I usually just hold his chest down a little. And the minute I let him go, he jumped right up, and he said, "Leave me alone. Don't touch me." And he started screaming. And he went in his bathroom and he said, "I'm going to throw water on you." And I stayed in the living room and I thought it was just another number. And sure enough, he came out with this empty bottle out of his doctor's bag and it was full of water, and he ran at me, and he went like that and threw it in my face. And it went all over. And I chased him back in his bedroom and he started to crawl under the bed, and he was hitting, and screaming and hollering, and I held his ankles. And he started to pound on the floor and cry really hard. And I said, "What is it, Bryan?" And he got quiet. And I just didn't say anything. And he started to cry again. And he said, "I want my daddy to come home." 'Cause Ben has been gone since Thursday—he went skiing. And ever since we went to the airport, he started to cry at the airport, but he didn't really get a feeling. He just cried and said he didn't want the airplane to get off the ground. But he never really felt anything and it took him until yesterday, you know, to really cry for a long time, and once he said it, I just left him alone and he cried for about fifteen or twenty minutes. And when he came out of the bedroom, he just smiled. I looked at him and said, "Are you okay?" And he said, "Yeah." And then he ran over to me and hugged me and sat in my lap for a while. And then he jumped down and started to play, and all the rest of the day he was just as happy as he could be.

MIKE: When I was a little boy, the kids called me "the Professor" because I wore glasses. I told my mother that and she said, "You're better than the other kids! You're smart." And immediately split me away from it. What I wanted her to say was, "God, that must feel terrible!" So that's what I do all day long. When a kid says something to me, I say, "That must feel—whatever it is. That must really feel sad; that must really feel bad." I help them articulate it and I say that I understand. 'Cause I really do. I'm not bull-shitting them.

BETTY: Yeah. I have a son, Joey. He's fifteen and I've learned with him just when the hurt comes up in his eyes. Just—the tears will come out and I've had him lie down. It's best to have him lie down where we are instead of going on the couch, a set place. And I've had no trouble with Primaling the first four times. It just seemed he talked himself into it. But last week we came home from the show. We came in. He said, "I'm scared when you and Doug (that's his stepfather) leave." And so I said, "Lie down and feel it." And so, he couldn't. And so I tried to bring it about with him.

ART: How?

BETTY: Like I gave him a mask to cover his eyes.

ART: You gave him *orders* to feel. Don't ever give orders to feel because it won't work.

VIVIAN: Wait for the Primal sentence. You know, something we talk about in training. You listen and you listen and you listen, and suddenly he says something that has the feeling in it. And you make him stop. He'll just start crying. Or sometimes when a kid is just getting to the point and you, knowing your own child so well, can see the sign of it, like you see his eyes change, or whatever, and you can say, "Shh," or something like that. Just to stop the flow of words at that point. Say "You're really feeling that, aren't you?"

KAROL: All three of my kids love to look at their baby books. It's their favorite thing. The baby pictures are what started my youngest one. When I was going through Primal Therapy. She used to carry around a little, tiny photo album with all the baby pictures in it. Just a little, tiny wallet-size thing, and she'd have it by her bed, and she'd look at it before she went to sleep at night, and then during the day once in a while she'd go get it. She was hanging onto the babyness because I wouldn't love her as she grew up. She had to stay a baby. And her first Primal was, I said, "You can't be the baby anymore, can you?" And she said, "No," and she just burst out bawling and was the baby right then. That was her first Primal. But she doesn't Primal very often any more. In fact, I couldn't say she even has a Primal anymore. All she has now are things about when her cat gets lost or something.

ART: Is she pretty straight?

KAROL: Yeah, she's very straight.

ART: Well, that's why.

VIVIAN: Well, you know, I felt that a few people talking about Primals with their children tonight were kind of disappointed, a little bit, at the results. Are you?

KAROL: Oh, no, not at all. It's slow and that's the only thing I'm a little disappointed about, but that's not a big thing. That's just the way it is. But I am very happy with the results.

VIVIAN: Well, then, maybe we have a lot of things to find out with children. We're just going to have to wait until they're ready to do it each time.

KAROL: Well, I could no more get my children into a Primal by telling them to lie down, they're going to have a Primal, than anything. I mean, they have to have the feeling coming up and be into it before.

LINDA: Bryan talks about it afterward, like maybe two or three hours later, he'll say, "Mommy, I was crying." And I'll say, "Yes, you were." And he'll, like yesterday, he said, "I like to cry." And I said, "Why?" And he said, "Because I feel better." [laughter]

VIVIAN: He likes to cry because its allowed and it's a real need.

LINDA: Right. And then when I said, "Why," he said, "Because I feel better." And he does. He feels better, he acts better, looks better. Ben brought home this big picture that he's had down at his office for a long time up on the wall. It was taken when Bryan was not quite two, with his long blond hair. He looks just about the same except his face has lost some of its babyness. Bryan looked at the picture. And he got very angry. He just said, "Me no like that." And I said, "Why?" And he said, "That's not me." And I said, "Yes, it is." And he said, "No." And he just kept saying, "No, it's not." And I said, "Why? Why isn't that you?" And he said—he didn't have an answer. He couldn't explain it. He just kept saying that "No, that's not me." And when he was a year and a half, he was totally different than he is now.

GROUP MEMBER: We're raising a new generation of Primal kids now.

ART: This is going to be the most amazing group to follow and study and watch.

BETTY: I'd like to discuss the sort of theoretical implications of it because it seems different from what I read in your book. I have a feeling that the child, once he turns off, is unreal, and from what I hear, a child can very quickly turn back on at a very early age. For instance, you said that even if you get a good school teacher sometimes, it will never do the trick. Do you still feel that way, that other than the parent, no one else can turn the child back?

ART: Right.

BETTY: Still the parent? Right?

ART: The point is, if you get kids to direct that anger and their smacking toward you, in a day you can stop all fighting at school. If you keep blocking it every day, they fight at school every day.

RICKY: You know, you said that a straight person should be able to handle sick kids at school. I don't think they should. I don't think they should have to.

ART: Why?

RICKY: Because they don't want to live that way. They don't want to live with neurotic people.

ART: That's true.

RICKY: Neurotic kids.

ART: So what do you think?

RICKY: The best thing I'd recommend is a Primal school.

ART: In your day, Rick, maybe.

GROUP MEMBER: I'm thinking, you know, I'm not trying to just keep concentrating on this problem. I think there are real problems and Primal problems. And it is a real problem for some children to get along in school. They're actually being hurt every day somehow, man, by the teachers, by everything around them.

RICKY: Kids, too.

ART: By having to sit still for eight hours, which is absolutely insane. Absolutely crazy. A little kid? Sitting still in the classroom for an hour at a time?

VIVIAN: Primals about school are still tied in with mother and father.

GROUP MEMBER: In what way?

VIVIAN: Because you're afraid to tell parents you're so objected to by other kids. There's a lot of aspects to rejection.

GROUP MEMBER: It's a terrible loss of face in your parents' eyes to have to tell them.

VIVIAN: Right, right.

ART: If you admit that the other kids don't like you, maybe your folks won't like you either. You see, you don't want to take that kind of chance.

KAROL: My daughter got away with a lot during one class because I'd always come to school and yell at the teacher when she was cruel to her. And now, when my girl wants to do something, she just does it. If she wants to chew gum in class, she takes her gum and chews it, and she just doesn't let the teacher catch her. She knows how to get around these things because of her mother.

RICKY: 'Cause now when I look back at public school, I think of what I should have done then. How they controlled you to do everything. You wonder why you didn't do anything, because nothing would really happen to you if you did. They frightened you from when you were four or five, from when you started kindergarten.

SELMA: I remember some kids telling Sam, "I'm going to tell your mommy." And even though he knew they would tell me and it wouldn't matter, it still bothered him that they should come and tell me—so that he would come crying to me and say, "He told me he was going to tell you what I did." And he was crying right then and there. It wasn't—the fear of me, but that they used it.

ART: If you sense that something's not straight with your kids, then you can make them say the straight thing. That's what Primal Therapy is all about. The main thing about giving kids Primals is to get behind them. Not facing the kids. You lay them down. It should be semidark. Then you talk about the feeling and wait for a good opening.

GROUP MEMBER: Yeah, the dark thing is important. I've done much better in dark rooms than in a light room.

RICKY: It shouldn't be semidark, it should be dark.

ART: Yeah, as dark as possible. I stand corrected. [group laughter]

LINDA: I tried it in a semidark room sitting behind Bryan, and just the fact that he could hear my voice and kind of see me would make him get up and look for me. If it was dark, of course, it wouldn't make any difference where I was. But in a semidark he was distracted because he could almost see me.

RICKY: You can envision better what you're talking about. Your past things, you can see them better.

ART: You know, it's a miraculous concept; to go back in time and let your child know it's okay to feel. Let's face it. Not every parent is going to get therapy. Some parents think that's being a good parent, to train their kids to sleep through the night at an early age. And this is what they've learned, and this is what they do. All right, now they read that that's a very harmful, very painful thing, they'll stop doing it. Small cases, not big. That's what I mean by preventive measures. What we can do is change the standard, so that kids don't have to live within standards that box in feelings.

PRIMAL PARENTS' SEMINAR
December 12, 1972

VIVIAN: A few of you have put notes on my desk asking me when we would have another Parents' Meeting. We have had a few meetings in the past, and I think that it would be good to talk about what it is that you would like to get out of this meeting, and what you would like to contribute or find out.

DOTTIE: Well, I'm really confused as to my kids. I just never knew what to do with them before, and now since I have been in therapy, they bother me and I don't know how to handle them any more.

VIVIAN: Do you want to talk about some of your problems?

DOTTIE: I have a real big problem with my six-year-old son. He steals money. A week ago he stole a quarter from school. I don't know if I did right, but I didn't make him take it back. Last night he took some money out of the neighbor's house, and he sat and hid in the closet and was afraid to tell my husband. So he told this nineteen-year-old boy from Canada who is staying with us. I just don't know what to do.

VIVIAN: He told the boy that was living with you that he had stolen the quarter?

DOTTIE: Yes. I was at group and my husband was at home. He was really afraid to tell his father, because when he started stealing when he was four, Ron made him take the money back one time.

VIVIAN: Have you asked him why?

DOTTIE: He told me this morning that he doesn't know why he steals, and he cried and says he hates himself. I asked him how he felt when he was taking it, and he said that he just couldn't help it. He says that he says to himself, "Tom, you can't take this money," but before he knows it the money is in his pocket. He didn't want to go to school today.

VIVIAN: Do any of you have that problem?

NORMA: I do with my second daughter, only we have just discovered it since we have been in therapy and we haven't even confronted her with it. She knows about it and she knows that we know about it. Just before we came here on our way from Ohio we stopped at my sister's in San Francisco. We were all going to Chinatown to get something for all of the kids. Apparently my daughter took a bunch of her cousin's money, which I didn't know about. It was very obvious that she did take the money because a silver dollar was missing and she didn't have a silver dollar in her possession before. She knew she was kind of in the middle. I just didn't want to make a big thing of it. But I don't know what to do about it. When I bring up the subject, she will immediately try and change it; her eyes will dance; she will do anything to avoid talking about it and I know this. That is where I am now; I don't know where to take her feelings.

VIVIAN: Linda, I think you have had some experience with Bryan taking money.

LINDA: Bryan does that with Ben and me all the time. He will take Ben's wallet, or he will go in my purse and take the money and put it in his wallet in his bedroom.

DOTTIE: But does he spend it?

LINDA: No, not usually. His attitude is he wants to hoard it and he wants to get as much as he can. If we go shopping, I will say, "Bring your wallet and spend your money." "No, I can't do that. I want to save it," he'll reply.

DOTTIE: Do you take the money away from him?

LINDA: No.

VIVIAN: What is your experience with that? What does it mean to you and what does it mean to him?

LINDA: I ask him and I get practically no response from him other than he just wants money. He is five years old, and I am sure he has gotten this concept from school that if you have a lot of money, you are rich. He will say, "I want a lot of money so I will be rich." If I say, "What does rich mean," he will say, "It just means I have a lot of money and I can do what I want." His feeling is he can do what he wants. The money I don't think is important; it's just that he is able to take it and we don't take it away from him. We let him have it. He doesn't know the difference between a ten dollar bill and a one dollar bill. If he takes ten dollars at night, then at some opportune time when he isn't there or isn't aware of what I'm doing, I will take the ten dollars back and leave one dollar in its place. Ben has tried just taking it away from him, saying, "That's not yours, it's mine," and all he does is get upset and violent, and he cries and screams and hollers, and he doesn't seem to get to any feeling other than at the immediate moment he is not having his way and not getting what he wants.

BERNARD: Do you give him pocket money regularly?

LINDA: No, not regularly.

BRITT: If he asks for it, do you give it to him?

LINDA: Sure, if we go shopping, it's a dime for this and a penny for that. A penny to him is the same as a quarter.

VIVIAN: Just like when we talk about becoming a therapist around here, we always say, let's not look at the surface, let's look underneath. That is what you have to do with children. What is underneath children wanting your money or other people's money?

PAT: I stole all the time when I was small—food from the stores, candy, etc. I would even steal on the way to confession. I don't think anyone knew I stole, maybe my mother. I stole money from her purse. The fact was no one paid any attention to me. My father wasn't there and my mother was working. There was nobody.

VIVIAN: Why did you do it?

PAT: Because then I could treat my friends with candy and I could have money for myself, usually to spend it on candy at the penny candy store. I was little and it felt good.

VIVIAN: I think that there is a danger in generalizing the classical Freudian interpretation that children taking money are stealing love, but maybe basically we could say that about all children who steal. Primally, I think we have to say something more about that and get to what each child wants. In other words, your child wants love in the broad sense, but what does he want with the money? What does he want to get from stealing? What does Bryan want from Ben and Linda by taking their money, which is slightly different from taking other people's money? Let's talk about some of the ways that you can get to that. How do you get to what your children are telling you? Just like a patient tells a therapist something by acting out symbolic behavior, your child is telling you something when he acts out some behavior.

LINDA: You're asking how to get to it, you mean?

VIVIAN: Anything you want to say about it. Whether you think there is a way to handle it, or how you would go about it, or what you think are the causes for it. I think that deep down every mother knows why her children are doing things. Dottie, why do you think your son is stealing from other people?

DOTTIE: I don't know. I give him money.

VIVIAN: Then it makes even less sense for him to steal.

DOTTIE: I don't give him money every day. I don't know whether to give him an allowance so he has his own money.

VIVIAN: What does he want to do with the money?

DOTTIE: I don't know. He doesn't want to spend it; he just hides it.

LINDA: I don't think that what he does with it is the important point at all. How old is he?

DOTTIE: Six.

LINDA: Have you ever just sat down and talked about it?

DOTTIE: Yes.

LINDA: What happens?

DOTTIE: He just cries and hates himself and doesn't know why he does it.

LINDA: But how do you approach the subject when you talk to him?

DOTTIE: Last night, when I got home, I said, "I hear you took some money from the neighbor's." He started to cry and I just sat there. All this stuff comes out that he hates himself, that he doesn't know why he does it when he's taking it, and he can feel that he shouldn't be doing it.

VIVIAN: When children do things like steal, what they are really trying to say is that they want, and sometimes they don't even know what they want.

DOTTIE: Right. I said to him, "Tom, what do you want with the money?" He said he didn't know.

LINDA: He probably doesn't.

VIVIAN: He doesn't. So what do you do with that as a mother?

GEORGE: I don't think giving him an allowance would help. That would be a little bit of money, but it's never enough. He will never steal enough to be able to get enough.

DOTTIE: It's the thrill of stealing. I know that. I still feel that.

VIVIAN: What is the thrill of stealing? What do you really mean by that?

DOTTIE: I get a big thrill out of stealing. Right now I'm in a place in my therapy where I just want to steal constantly. I'll be doing without something and I feel like stealing.

VIVIAN: What does stealing do for you?

DOTTIE: I really get excited about it; it's the only thing that turns me on. I can see the same pattern in Tom.

VIVIAN: Have you felt why you steal?

DOTTIE: I feel like I get something for nothing.

VIVIAN: And your son gets something without having to be anything or do anything, and he doesn't even know that; he's really unconscious.

GEORGE: It's also feelings of anger and resentment. Taking from someone else who has something probably brings up the feelings, "I deserve something; it should be mine."

VIVIAN: Again, the surface behavior is not what we are after. We are after some way for us as Primal parents to do something different than ordinary parents, who would punish or give an allowance or do the surface retaliations for the surface behavior. We have to go underneath the behavior.

DOTTIE: Does that mean that, like therapy, you lay them down and talk with them?

VIVIAN: Yes, but you don't have to be mechanical about it. You don't have to lay them down to feel or to talk. In fact, I think I would recommend generally that you not do that to your children, because I think they begin to feel that it's some sort of ritual instead of just a human encounter. Again, I want to get to the point. How are you, as parents, going to get underneath your child's unconscious statement? How do you deal with it?

NORMA: One thing that I started to do with my daughter's stealing was to think about it. I knew it was a surface thing. My other kids don't steal. There was something there, and I started thinking back. My kids are six, seven, and eight; she was right in the middle. I was right in the middle at home. My family is exactly the same as was the number of members in my home as a child. I felt like I was right in the middle, and I felt that my younger sister was the baby, and my older sister got everything and I got nothing. I didn't steal, but I think that my daughter's basic feeling is that she is caught in the middle—she's not old enough and she's not young enough; she's kind of nothing.

VIVIAN: That may be the reason.

NORMA: What I did was think about the situation. What did I do to my daughter? My oldest daughter got a lot of attention, and then my second daughter arrived and it was okay while she was a baby. However, I still had a lot to do with my oldest daughter because she was older. So my second daughter stayed in the buggy a little bit more than my first daughter. Then my third daughter was born, and I think then it was all over for my second daughter. I think I just forgot her because there was so much going on. Just recently I started hugging her, or maybe squeezing her every time she walked by me. Before that time her body was like a board; she didn't bend.

I feel bad talking about it. But since therapy I have tried to hug her or kiss her on the cheek or have any kind of physical contact, which is what I think I didn't give before because that is what I obviously didn't get. Sometimes I don't feel like it, but I do it anyway, at any old time, and her body is softer; she bends more easily. She will sit on my lap now. I know it's just a beginning, but I think it's where it's at for her.

VIVIAN: I think you did a wise and intuitive thing, because that again matches the therapy. We reawaken in patients the things that they didn't get or needed and that is what you do with your children. The skin and body contact that babies and little children need is so crucial. It could be that when your daughter is taking money she is saying, "I want a mommy, I want something, I want." She wants, but she doesn't know what she wants. Her wanting is acted out in the form of wanting money, but she knows that that's not it. So she's trying to give herself what she didn't get.

BILL: Kids want the same things that we want. We want our Mommies and Daddies, and they want their Mommies and Daddies. Your boy in a way is getting you by stealing, because when you are sitting with him and he's able to feel his feelings, you give to him.

VIVIAN: One thing to do with this problem and a lot of other problems is to just sit down and think, "What didn't my child get that I think he needs" and try and start to do it. Another thing you can do is actually attack the unconscious want by verbalizing with your child. For example, at an opportune time you might say something like, "I don't think you really want money, I think you want Mommy." It has to be your own words. Then see how your child responds to that remark.

PAT: I know that really does work. It sounds stupid when you are saying it to your child, but my kids actually said "Yes."

VIVIAN: What did you say?

PAT: "I think you two kids want to sit in the kitchen with me while I'm doing dishes or cooking," and they said "Yes." They had been hassling me for an hour and couldn't say they wanted to be with me, because they can't say that.

VIVIAN: In other words, a lot of you have had experiences where you say what you intuitively think your child is acting out, and they grab on to it?

BILL: They get mad and the anger or pent-up feeling comes out.

VIVIAN: I don't understand.

BILL: The child may be angry and isn't getting that out, so he goes around being mean to his little brother or hitting things.

VIVIAN: What do you say?

BILL: "Daddy hasn't spent enough time with you lately, has he?" Then his feeling just flows out.

KATHY: I think that is a very good point. I find that with my son, too. I'll stop and say, "I've been a bad Mommy," and he will grab on to that so fast, or he'll get angry and I'll say, "Do you just feel like crying," and he'll stop, say yes, and start to cry.

VIVIAN: Have any of you other people had similar experiences?

BARBARA: My daughter is eight. I find what I do first is say, "Is that like something you have felt before?" and then if I think I know what it is and she doesn't, I'll let her talk herself into the feeling. She may say she doesn't know what it is. Sometimes she'll say, "Help me, Mommy; you go to the Institute and you're supposed to know about feelings." Last night she was crying because the teacher's aide who has been living with us for three months is leaving, and it's hard for my daughter to have people leave.

VIVIAN: You mean a maid at home?

BARBARA: A teacher's aide from school. We have one for two or three months who lives with us and gets room and board in exchange for taking my daughter to school in the morning and helping me out.

VIVIAN: Some people call that a mother's helper.

BARBARA: Anyway, my daughter was crying and crying because the teacher's aide was going to leave and she was going to miss her. I said, "Let's go in your room." I knew what it was and I said, "Does that feel like something you have felt before?" She said, "When my daddy left." And she cried, and cried, and cried. Then she sat up and said, "But that hurt much more," and that was the end of her feeling. I have a sense usually of what it is, but I could be very wrong. Also, I know that it could be something from five years before. Sometimes I will guess like that and I'll say, "Maybe it's like such and such," but I give her the chance first.

VIVIAN: I think that's very good. It's good to throw out such a general thing so that they can say what it is first. Yours was a perfect situation for making suggestions, but the stealing thing isn't something where you can say, "Is that something that you may have felt before?" When he says he hates himself for doing it, you might say, "Is it because?" or "Do you think it's because?"

BARBARA: You could say, "What do you want from money?"

DOTTIE: Why does he hate himself for doing it, though?"

CAL: Because he's afraid you won't love him now.

BARBARA: He's been a "bad" boy.

CAL: If he said that, you could say, "Are you afraid I won't love you because you steal?"

VIVIAN: I don't think children hate themselves. I think they only see themselves through your eyes. He's saying, "Am I going to be hateful to you now because I've done a bad thing?" It's compulsive behavior. You have to understand that he doesn't plan to do something bad and steal. He's doing something he needs to do as much as people need to eat lunch. He needs to take the money. You have to look at it that way. You can't think of it as some strange aberration. He has to do it.

CAL: Remember A. S. Neill's book, *Summerhill*? He used to reward kids when they would steal. I used to try that with delinquent kids and it would really screw them up, because they couldn't understand why you would do that.

VIVIAN: Anyone who read *Summerhill* is really impressed with it and thinks of it as the pre-Primal book, in a way. All of his ideas were very beautiful, and he was very disappointed when he took children who were older and found that his ideas weren't good for them, because they had already gone so far to the pain side of their lives that it was very hard to correct by doing things that you could do with four- and five-year-olds and not with a fifteen-year-old kid who was so hardened to his life.

CAL: Their defenses are just too strong.

VIVIAN: Has what we said helped any of you? Does any of it fit in with the raising of your children?

DOTTIE: I have tried saying things similar to those that Barbara says to her daughter to my eight-year-old daughter, and she says, "I don't want to hear any of that therapy talk. I don't like it."

VIVIAN: I, too, have experienced not being able to talk about therapy in our home. Rick warns, "If there's one more word about it . . ." He was ten or eleven when all this started. It's a hard thing for children. For my son, it's grown-up stuff and it applies to grown-ups, and he doesn't want to hear about it. "They're not asking me about me. They're talking about pain," and he doesn't want to hear about it. I don't blame him for that. What I think it might mean for your daughter is part of that, and you may also be calling on her to do something she can't do.

DOTTIE: She doesn't know how she feels. What do I do?

BARBARA: There's a really painful point here. Just like these meetings are painful for everyone here. The more you feel, the more you really feel how you have inadvertently messed up your children. It has to be. It's a direct ratio of this therapy. Each day I feel it more. I wanted my child very badly. I love her and she's the big thing in my life. We want to help our kids to make it less painful for us. It's a fact; there's no short cut for our getting straight and there's no short cut for getting them straight. You have to take the pressure off. You have to just be there and try to get as straight as you can and try to be as available as you can for your children and suffer through that pain of looking and seeing and just doing the best you can. You can't do any more than that. We can have meetings all day long, seven days a week, about who said what. It helps us because it helps reinforce us. We all have the same problems, but there are no short cuts and it's painful.

LAURA: I would like to say that I'm having an opposite reaction from yours. What's happening to me is that I never wanted my daughter; I never wanted her from birth, but I always could hide it. Now I can't hide it any more. I can't pretend. It's excruciating for me to be with her. I feel phonier and phonier. I feel I have to pretend or I'll mess her up more, even though I know she's seeing through the pretense. I don't know what to do. If she would just go away and never come back, I'd be happy. But that's not going to happen. I'm in an impossible dilemma.

VIVIAN: You will have to feel it through.

LAURA: I'm feeling it, but meanwhile I have to deal with reality and her. What I had hoped with this therapy was that after I had felt a lot of my own pain, my love for her would be uncovered, but that's not happening.

VIVIAN: Have you had feelings about why you didn't want her?

LAURA: I have had feelings about my not being wanted. But it doesn't seem to help. What's happening is the reverse; I'm disliking her more and more. I don't want to be around her more and more. As far as helping her through her fears, "Go away, I don't want to have anything to do with it."

VIVIAN: Do you talk to each other?

LAURA: Yes. It's helped somewhat with her not living with me. She comes on weekends only and it's just super phony. We do talk, and one good thing is that by being away from me this year she automatically says to me, "I feel so much better about myself," and I know why. It's because I'm not dumping on her. I encourage that kind of behavior. But it's very hard for me. She comes up to me and says, "I love you, I have missed you." She hugs me, and I don't want it. I feel like a shit for saying these things and that I don't love my own daughter, but it's the truth—I don't. Has anyone experienced this besides me?

DOTTIE: I have the same thing with my daughter. I can't hold her. I don't want her touching me. With my son I can hold him and I can feel his body. Her body is like a board. She needs it so bad; it's written all over her face. She needs me. She'll run her hands over my breasts, chattering a mile a minute so that I won't notice what she's doing. My body freezes because I can't stand it.

LAURA: Right. The need is so palpable. It's right there. If I look at my daughter, I see it and I feel worse.

DOTTIE: During my three weeks I cried and cried about her. I can really cry about her, but I can't feel my pain.

BILL: I feel that these heaviest areas are also our heaviest areas, and that is why they are so rotten hard. It's been said before—the things we can't give our kids are exactly the things we didn't get. I feel this with myself so much with my own son, and I hear other people say it, too. The biggest thing to do is get to your own pain and get straight. Things go along for awhile and then, without knowing exactly why, your child has a certain problem—it just has to be. Your problem has to be his problem; it gets passed down. That's why it's so hard to handle, too.

NORMA: I think what Dottie said I would have never had the guts to say. Now that you have said it, I really think that that's where I'm at, which is really hard to accept. I think you really had a lot of guts saying it. I think that if you never got it, if you were never wanted, how in hell can you give to your kids?

GEORGE: You can't; it just hurts.

NORMA: I can; I do it each day. My God, they walk around, I have one on my arm, one on the other arm, and one on my leg. I kind of shuffle along with them. I have started not wearing a bra, and every time a kid comes up to me they are nuzzling, nuzzling, and nuzzling all day long. It's just really painful, that's all, but they need it.

PAT: You were talking about touching and that you didn't want to touch your daughter. When I would nurse my kids (I was nursed only two months, and then I was half starved), I would cry a lot because I knew that I didn't get any nursing, and at that time I didn't know all the sophisticated things I know about that now. But I would nurse them and give them all these things and I recognized that I had never known that kind of closeness. I cried; it hurt. On the delivery room table I cried and cried and cried. It wasn't any kind of hysterics, it was just painful.

VIVIAN: I don't think you ever get to anything with your child unless you start out with the truth.

LAURA: I can't tell my daughter I didn't want her.

VIVIAN: What I'm saying is that the theory behind the therapy is that if you feel something through to the other side, even not liking your daughter and how much you don't want her, it will lead to your being able to like her.

BRITT: I think it's really hard for the children that we are in therapy. We are gone so much of the time; three nights a week, plus giving them now what we haven't given them before.

VIVIAN: There are two of you, so you will have to split your attendance at groups.

BRITT: But Bill is gone so much more than me.

VIVIAN: Your children come first. If there are two of you, one of you has to be home with the children giving them as much as you can. The first step is what Dottie and Norma said—to feel how much you didn't want them. I don't know if that ever ends or if you can go beyond that. The second thing is you have them and, as a human being knowing what you know now from Primal Therapy, you have got to be there because they want you and you had them. Maybe it was a mistake, but it's the kind of mistake you can't undo and you have a responsibility that you have got to face. There's no way to turn your back on it. It would really be insane if you would come through this therapy only to destroy your own child.

DOTTIE: I'm not quite clear on what you meant a few sentences back. Will feeling how I don't like my daughter touching me make me feel like having her touch me?

VIVIAN: If you get to all the feelings about it, the bad feelings will be gone. If you feel something enough, it dissipates.

BILL: A small example of that is I could never put our kids to bed. I would always find something else to do. I would be busy or I would be away working nights. Pat always put the kids to bed. I was acting out. One night I said I would do it, and I lay down with them and I started getting into feelings. I got to a lot. Now a good part of the time it's a pleasure (it's a kind of sequence in just one little part of my life, and I don't pretend it works all the way through), but that specific thing has gone from an acting-out thing I didn't want to do, to the feelings, and then to where it's a pleasure doing it. I don't always like to do it, but sometimes I really do.

VIVIAN: Those little people around us are not some kind of monsters waiting to get us. If they get what they need, they are really nice. You have to think about what there can be between you and your child, once you feel your feelings about not wanting to give. That is where it's at. You sort of get caught; all your life you didn't get, then you have a baby and have to give to the baby. So you are always the one who is out in the cold not getting.

KATHY: I don't know how you deal with the older ones on that, but that's really it as far as I'm concerned. Having your own feelings makes everything okay with the children. I find that with my son and me, I can go on and on and on until I have had my feelings. Then I can't imagine I had the problem before.

VIVIAN: Do you have something specific that happened?

KATHY: I had a lot of trouble because I wanted him to go to bed at night. I wanted him to go to sleep so I could have my evenings for me. It was a big deal and there was a big scene, and I caused a lot of trouble for him. I don't know if I can remember. So much came out of that one thing. It was like I didn't want to feel my feelings, so I made him carry it. He had to be the one to cry at night.

VIVIAN: You mean your feeling was that you wanted to be free at night?

KATHY: I didn't want to feel my pain, whatever the feelings were at the time. There were a lot of feelings, different ones, and I put it on him, letting him feel the pain, crying, and going to sleep. Then I felt my feelings and I found out what they were. Everything I said to my parents in my Primal was what I say to my child. I would say to him, "Go to bed, I need some time." "I need some time for me," is the feeling. When I would have my feelings, I would get to "I need." It was ridiculous, because the television was more important than my son. He had to go to sleep so I could sit down and watch TV. It was only when I got through those feelings that I just sat down and said to myself, "What is this—a television versus a life?" That's really how everything comes out to me now. There's one important thing I want to say again, "If you can try and say the first few words of whatever you say to your children, it's usually your Primal." It is for me, anyway.

LINDA: Regarding what Laura and Dottie talked about—the feeling for me still comes up, but not nearly as frequently anymore. I went through therapy for about one and a half years, just trying to be a good mommy and telling myself I knew I didn't want Bryan, but I had him and I had to be a good mommy, so I put on a show and I accepted reality and just talked to myself about it and performed for well over a year and a half. Then I realized that he was seeing through that performance, and he would bust me for everything I did and said to him, by saying things like, "What's the matter, Mommy?" or "That's not how you really feel," or "That's not what you really mean."

It took me a long time of hearing that before realizing that he was right, and me asking myself, "What is that?" Then I had to have a lot of Primals of "I hate you," "I don't want you," "You take constantly," and "There's no time for me," and then my taking that back to, "there really wasn't any time for me, and I wasn't wanted and I wasn't needed and I was a pain in the behind." I had to have those Primals for a long time and during that time it was very difficult to be with him. I had to be straight with him and I had to say sometimes, "Right now I don't want you around me"; "I don't want to give to you right now, Bryan"; and "I don't want to talk to you any more. Now go play and leave me alone." I was straight with him and he felt that straightness, and it was better than my acting and performing had ever been. He could see that I was being honest and that was how I really felt. Therefore it was safe for him to be how he really felt in front of me and say what he was really feeling.

A majority of the time now it's like he's a little boy, my little boy, and we have fun. I really care about him, and it's easy to give now. But there are certain times that I want for me and I want to come first and I do. But he is there and he's my child, and he will tell me when he demands and he sees me resisting, whether it's verbally, physically, or it's just an atmosphere where he senses vibes or whatever you call it. He'll say, "But you're my mommy." He reminds me and he's right. Then he knows that he has to come first. He's old enough and we have been in therapy long enough to where he fights (literally fights) with every ounce of energy he's got to make damn sure he comes first, which is something none of us could do. He will insist, scream, holler, and physically fight to get his way and to see to it that we take care of him and that we are his mommy and daddy and that he's not going to be dumped on. When I see him do that, it brings up a lot of feelings for me.

PAT: My son says, "I'm just a kid."

GEORGE: I told my wife, who is not in therapy, that I was leaving after Christmas. I don't know how I can take my son with me, working and all.

ELLEN: If you were a woman, you would take your child with you. I had to leave my husband and take my son with me. It's hard. I had to figure out how to get a job, etc. But it's going to be better than living in a mixed-up household. At least my son will have me.

VIVIAN: Is your wife going to give up your son just because you want him? Doesn't she want him?

GEORGE: I never asked her that. I always thought it better to have some kind of mommy rather than no mommy at all.

JULIUS: It seems to me that a straight daddy is better than a messed-up mommy.

ELLEN: Definitely.

GEORGE: She will have visitation rights and see him on weekends.

VIVIAN: All these solutions are phony ones. They are halfway things to do. The only good solution is for you both to be feeling parents.

BRITT: Maybe George's wife can't feel in front of him. I know I couldn't feel in front of Bill and I couldn't have him do therapy with me. If he would try to get me to feelings, I would resent it more and more and I would do it less and less.

BILL: I have a feeling your wife is going to hold on to your son because that is her hold on you.

VIVIAN: It's crazy to talk about who's taking your son. It's important to talk about how to get her to become a more feeling person.

GEORGE: The Institute is a threat to her.

VIVIAN: Sometimes you have to make people do things, even though it seems artificial. Maybe you have to take her by the hand somewhere to get therapy, not because you are concerned about what she does but because you care about your son. That's the only good answer—for her to get into feelings.

BARBARA: Have you left before?

GEORGE: No.

CARLOS: As it applies to me and my children (two of whom are already men, aged twenty-one and twenty, and I have a boy fourteen and a girl eleven), my feeling is, "How am I better going to help my children, and at what point are my children going to have to have Primal Therapy to become real?" Even if my two youngest children are in a feeling household, I don't think they could get their feelings out. I can't make my fourteen-year-old feel; he's hiding feelings and he denies he is. Will all my children have to have Primal Therapy?

VIVIAN: Yes.

CARLOS: I thought the two youngest ones could be handled in the home.

VIVIAN: You and your wife could do any of your children's therapy once you had enough of your own therapy.

CARLOS: I have already had a feeling experience with my second son, who is the closest to his feelings. We had a rather real confrontation in which I wanted him to lower the volume of the television. He didn't want to do it. I could feel my anger at him. I told him he was my son and I wanted him to love me and respect me. I cried in front of him. He admitted that he wanted to play his TV loud because I never had listened to him, and this was his way of showing me that I should listen to him. Then he said he had a feeling he wanted to kill me. How do I handle that? Should I let him kill me symbolically by letting him hit the wall with something, or should I let him attack me personally?

VIVIAN: I think he can get it out in a lot of ways—by yelling it, saying it, punching something.

CARLOS: Can I be the therapist in that situation?

VIVIAN: I think it's better that someone else do your children's therapy. However, if there's no other way, it's better than no therapy at all.

JEAN: You mean it's never good to have the parent be his child's therapist?

LAURA: No, better the parent be there as a therapist than no one at all.

BERNARD: You can distinguish between doing therapy on your child and being there for him in sort of a therapeutic situation. I don't think it's very successful to *try and do* therapy.

MARY: My daughter wants to do therapy very much, in the sense that she understands the processes I'm going through. She will come to me when she is crying and want to tell me about it. Almost always I start crying, too, when she is halfway into understanding what she is feeling. We will both be sitting there in tears, and I can hardly listen to what she is saying.

VIVIAN: That's because you haven't had enough of your own therapy, but once you get a little stronger, you'll be able to hold your own feelings back until you can be by yourself. That's how it is when I sit for my children; I have never sat there and not cried, but they're not aware that I'm crying. There's hardly a time you are not going to feel when your child is crying about his life.

MARY: Usually I end up lying there hugging her and letting her cry.

VIVIAN: That's good. It says a lot of things without really saying them.

PAT: Vivian, you have said before that the child will pick the parent. If the child has feelings about his mommy, he will go to his daddy, and vice versa. My kids do that.

DOTTIE: If you have two parents who have had Primal Therapy, the child's feelings about one parent could be handled by the other parent.

VIVIAN: True. If I'm sitting for one of my kids, and a feeling comes up about me, they usually modify it a bit by saying, "I know you couldn't help it Mom, but . . ." If someone else were sitting for them, they would really go into it and rip me to shreds, which they need to do.

CARLOS: You say that eventually the child will realize that he is doing that himself, and he will go to the other parent if both are available?

VIVIAN: If they get Primally smart, i.e., if they are very bright and catch on to the whole process, then they will do the right thing for themselves. A lot of the good that you can do is in "being there" for them. There are three things you should think of, being a Primal parent:

1. Be determined and a lot more sensitive about not giving your children more pain. Don't lay any more of your pain on them. Think about the ways you have given your children pain. One of the ways mentioned earlier was not touching. Recognize that and act on it.

2. Let your children actually feel past pain. If you notice how I said that, I didn't say Primal your children, because I don't like to think about an organized way to do therapy on children. In previous meetings we decided that sometimes the organized way is very destructive to the relationship and "Primaling for Mommy" may become the child's new defense. Create a safe place for your child to feel everything now and in the past, as Barbara said to her child, who was feeling in the present about the young lady leaving their home. She made it safe for her daughter to feel that, and then she made it safe for her to feel that that had happened once before about her father. She didn't say, "Let's go have a Primal." Do you

understand the difference? That's all you can do.

3. Make yourselves as straight as you can by feeling your pain, including the things we have discussed here, like Kathy wanting her TV time and feeling that, so that she could then let her son stay up late.

CARLOS: Regarding the comment you made about having one of the parents be with the children all the time, do you mean that for just very young children? I have been leaving my fourteen- and eleven-year-old children with my twenty-year-old son, who is going back East after Christmas. If my wife and I come to group, we will be leaving them alone, which I feel is justified. I feel they can take care of themselves.

SANDY: I think they're old enough to be left.

VIVIAN: I think they are old enough to be asked how they feel about it.

CARLOS: If they mind being alone?

VIVIAN: Yes. It isn't always quantity, it's quality, too. If they feel like they had a big piece of you, your leaving for a few hours is not particularly significant. It's significant when they feel that they can put a label on your leaving, "There, they're gone again, they never give me anything." That can be very painful for them. I would discuss it with them. It depends, too, on what point your family is at. Some families can say the truth all the time. You can say to your eleven-year-old, "Look, we have to go to group tonight, but one of us could stay home if you feel bad." The situation in that home could be that the child is honest enough to say, "I'm afraid tonight, one of you has to stay with me." In another family, it could be a situation where the child feels he couldn't possibly say that to his parents because the parents wouldn't let him say that or let him be afraid. The point is to make your home a place where everything hangs out.

You brought up a particular point about respect. What is that? You said your son didn't respect your demands of his behavior. What did you mean by that?

CARLOS: The feeling was that he didn't love me.

VIVIAN: He didn't fear you, either.

CARLOS: Right. If I hadn't been in therapy, we would have had a fight.

VIVIAN: The traditional meaning of "Have respect for your mother and father" usually ends up as fear of the parents, which isn't true respect.

CARLOS: I haven't suppressed my children that much that they fear me. All my children would fight me. Before therapy I would come home from work, my wife would tell me so and so did this, and I would punish him. I know what I did was bad. However, I do know that they knew I didn't have any real feeling while I was punishing them. I know they saw through me.

VIVIAN: The point you just brought up is a real "bummer" for children. They do something bad in the daytime and mother withdraws love by saying, "That's bad, I'm going to tell your father," or "Wait till your father comes home." All day long that child is terrified. That is such super punishment for a child. He does something bad, Mother doesn't love him, and all day long he waits for Dad's punishment. It's much better for the mother to slap the child and get it over with. This coming home and hitting them is insane. Why would you do it?

CARLOS: I know it was bad and I feel terrible about it. I would come home and be told what they did.

VIVIAN: But you had no passion about it. Why did you do it?

CARLOS: No, none at all. I was so busy with my work.

VIVIAN: What was your motive in hitting them?

CARLOS: My wife said it was my job not hers, and she would present me with the problem.

VIVIAN: Did you feel it was your job?

CARLOS: No.

CAL: Is that a cultural expectation?

CARLOS: No, my wife is North American. Actually, in Puerto Rico the father is the one who punishes in many things. Maybe that's the reason.

VIVIAN: No, it's happening in Jewish families in Brooklyn today.

DOTTIE: Ron and I are building a Primal room. You can hear muffled cries outside of the Primal room. Is it bad for kids to hear that?

VIVIAN: If your family is at that point, I think crying is a very natural thing and it happens when it happens, and there won't be a big deal about it. Crying shouldn't be a secret thing.

DOTTIE: You mean you can Primal in front of your children?

MARY: I have a Primal room, and when I'm not available for my son and he wants me, he comes and beats on the door for me to come out.

DOTTIE: I wouldn't use my Primal room when my kids were up. My kids have been in the neighbors' house when they have been Primaling, and my son has come home and said, "So and so was Primaling all the while I was over there." Just the way he says it I can tell he doesn't like it.

VIVIAN: I think it's very frightening for a child.

KATHY: There's something very scary about seeing your mommy and daddy going through all this stuff. I don't think there would be anything wrong being off in your Primal room and them knowing you're having your feelings. I think that's good.

VIVIAN: It depends on how much they understand about it. If it's some big mystery thing or weird process that their parent is in that is secret, their feeling would be, "I don't have any mommy any more; my mommy is falling apart."

DOTTIE: That was my feeling when I saw my therapist cry. I don't want her to do that. I don't know if that's how my children feel about me.

VIVIAN: All of these things, as I said to Carlos, depend at what point your family is at. The ideal place is that everyone is able to understand that pain is a common thing and you can do something about it. Sometimes children have to be led gently to that place.

NORMA: I just want to say that during my three weeks my husband took a walk with the kids and ended up at the Institute. It was during group, and he took them to the back of the building (outside), where the screams and cries can be heard. The children listened and then asked him if there were babies in there. It sounded like babies to them. He said no. They were people having old feelings. We have been talking about this old feeling bit in front of the kids for about a year. They said, "Yeah, they're having their old feelings." They were discussing it in a very nonfearful way. It surprised me. I thought they would be terrified like I was when I heard the group for the first time. I wanted to get out of here.

VIVIAN: You have to understand that they were holding their daddy's hand; it wasn't like they were in the living room and their daddy was in the kitchen and suddenly started screaming. When they are all alone, it's an entirely different situation.

BARBARA: You brought up a point that is very different in families. There are a lot of us here who are single parents and our problems are very specific. It's great when there are two feeling parents; one can be with the children while the other goes off somewhere else in the house to have his feelings. Where there's only one parent, it can be terrifying for the child. I don't Primal at home; I come here.

VIVIAN: Let's distinguish between crying mildly in front of your child and having a screaming Primal. I think that the child should know that parents cry, but the kind of thing that looks like Mommy is going crazy and is out of control is a bit different.

SANDY: When the pain gets that bad, though, sometimes I think it's better to Primal rather than act out on the kids. I'm at a point now where my pain is so bad that if I don't feel it, I'm crazy, really crazy, and it's better for me to get out of the room and feel it as much as I can. If I don't, I do stupid things like hit my kids.

MARY: That's the same with me, but I don't hit my kids even when I'm very angry. Sometimes my daughter starts to torture my five-year-old son and I can't stand it. I feel a great deal of anger rising in me toward her. I don't want her to hurt him. I usually try to be there for them in that situation, but at a certain point I have to put my own feeling down a whole lot and try to feel it later. My Primal room at home seems to help me become as real with my kids as I am.

VIRGINIA: The big problem in my family is my son's jealousy of his younger sister. She doesn't seem to feel it, but already she's resenting the way he treats her. I tried giving him as much as I could by babying him, tying his shoes, and cleaning up his messes more than I usually do. I resent doing all this. I realized during this meeting that I haven't been straight with him. I feel that no matter how much I give to him and do for him or even treat him like my daughter, I will never make up to him the time I give to her. I'll have to tell him that I can never make it up to him. He doesn't want his sister. He's verbalized that he wants her out of the house. I think he's at the point where he has to feel it, but I don't think I can make him.

SANDY: He sounds like he's close to it.

VIRGINIA: He knows his feelings.

VIVIAN: You have to let the anger and hatred build and build until he gets to the crying part, which usually says, "I want you all to myself."

VIRGINIA: How do I let it build and build without it hurting my daughter?

VIVIAN: You have to do it with him alone. Let him say all the stuff. Let it build by expression.

VIRGINIA: I do.

PAT: Are you saying she shouldn't tie his shoes and clean up his messes in order to let it build?

VIVIAN: That probably would help.

BILL: Just try saying, "No matter how much I do for you, it's never going to be enough."

MARY: I want to tell you a crazy scene that happened at our house recently. My nine-year-old daughter got angry at my five-year-old son, and they had a battle in the living room in which I got involved because she was hurting him. She broke down and started to cry, and I sat with her in our Primal room because she wanted to cry and talk to me. She started into the feeling of how much she hated him, and how much she wanted him to be gone, and why was he ever born. She was so angry and said, "It's because of him you and Daddy split up." She said she always felt he's the one who caused it. About this time my son was insistent about sitting on my knee. He wouldn't stay out of it. He had to be there, too, and he came and was sitting on my lap. My daughter couldn't stand it. There was nothing I could do. He had to be there. He was crying, she was crying, and I was crying.

VIVIAN: That's not a bad experience.

MARY: No, it's not a bad experience—I realize it's healthier than it's been in a long time. But the one I worry about is my son, though, because he's the one who can't express those feelings. He's constantly being hurt by her, and he hums and sings and pretends that he's happy, but he won't feel the feeling of how it feels to not have her care about him, and he wants her to very much.

BARBARA: It's the same thing a child usually feels about his mother.

MARY: He looks for crumbs anywhere. That's the feeling I get from him. He's really closed off and he won't feel, no matter what —he doesn't feel safe enough with me to talk about his feelings or to feel them.

VIVIAN: But your daughter does, so that means that something's happening. And to repeat again, that's the goal, to make it safe for children to feel, and there's no way I can tell you how. It's safe when you're safe. There are some children who can't look at you when they feel. If that's the case, then make sure the light is out and you're sitting behind them. Sometimes that's helpful. It has to feel right to you also. And not forcing the issue but letting it happen naturally. I know my son would never cry unless the light was out. It was just too hard for him to look at me.

MARY: The closest my son gets to his feeling is to express his anger to me. He'll tell me what a shit I am and how he hates me, but he won't go any further than that. He also wants very much to be a baby. He wants to feel like a baby a lot, and I know when he was younger I couldn't let him be angry. I couldn't stand it when he was taking too much from me.

VIVIAN: It sounds like everything is happening.

MARY: They are both taking so much now and I've got so little, it's just really hard, but it's happening.

VIVIAN: That's a beautiful example of your daughter attacking the object of her anger and then switching to the real feeling underneath that. Underneath anger is pain. Don't ever forget that. If you are for the first time just letting them be angry, sometimes that's as far as they can go. But you know inside that the thing is to go through the anger to the bottom, and that will happen when it happens.

BILL: One thing that's helped our family is that our kids, all our kids, act a lot older than they really are. I'm thinking that a normal six-year-old acts like a neurotic three-year-old, almost. Maybe that's an exaggeration. And doing things to let them be little. That kind of helps all of it along. It's safe then and it's given to them—it's a need that they still have, and if they're young enough, they can get from you. But then that means you have to give more.

VIVIAN: I think that's so right on. If I could classify one huge mistake with my own children, it was always making them be bigger than they were; not consciously, but like being too proud of their achievements.

BILL: It's built into this society.

VIVIAN: It is such bullshit to hurry your children along. My son went to school early for no damn reason—oh, I could give you a whole list that would put me right out, but I don't think we stop to think how little our children need to be for a long time, and the dialectic is the more you let them be little, the faster they'll be big.

BILL: Just like in our therapy; it's the same thing.

KATHY: Our kids are doing the same thing. I know Don went back into diapers after I thought he trained himself at two years old. He's proud of his diapers.

VIVIAN: Bryan still has a bottle. The implications of that one little example—like if my five-year-old child still had a bottle many years ago when I was a young mother: "God, what will the neighbors say? How can I send him to school?"—all this stuff makes you a failure, because somehow your kid's still a baby and all that. But, boy, if you can baby your children, it's good.

CAL: I read about some Indian culture where the children actually nursed when they were able to walk alongside the mother and reach the breast. They must have been eight or nine.

MARY: Your son sucks on a bottle?

VIVIAN: Bryan does; Linda's son.

BARBARA: Liz is a great note writer. Like when I come back from here at night, there's a long note on the pillow, and the other night there was one. I'm not there for her to talk to, so she'll write the note.

VIVIAN: Are you saving those for her future Primals?

BARBARA: Oh, I'm saving them for her Primals; yes, I've got a stack of them. Anyway, the other night she said, "I know, Mommy, that there are nights when you are going to go out," so she asked me to get her baby bottle for the nights that I leave, and I said "sure."

VIVIAN: Yeah, well, what's the principle behind that?

BARBARA: Well, she feels little and she wants to be treated like she's little.

VIVIAN: And also that there are a lot of gaps in their short childhood; there are a lot of unmet needs, and you have to meet those needs.

PAT: Baby books, pillows, anything—

VIVIAN: I think what Pat and Bill did with their bedroom, in case any of you haven't heard, is a great thing. Do you want to tell about that?

BILL: Yeah, wall to wall "Milners."

PAT: Our houses were always so small that we all practically slept together anyway, but now this house is long and big, and it seemed like when we heard here that people slept together, we just shoved all the beds in there. I didn't know if my six-year-old would do it, but he wants to be right in the middle.

NORMA: Well, when Joe was in his three weeks I was desperate —I was up all night running from room to room, everybody needed something. So I finally said bullshit, and when the kids came home from school, we took all the beds apart and stuffed them into one room. And it cut down on the nighttime running around. And they love it. I said, "How would you kids like to move all the beds into" —they just couldn't buy the idea at first. "What, you mean everybody? Yeah!"

VIVIAN: It's Christmas every day. You want to be with the two people you want the most as much as possible.

DOTTIE: We don't even sleep on beds; we all camp out on the living-room floor.

MARY: That's what we do, too. But I've had feelings about this. Both of my kids—I have one on either side of me, and they sort of move toward me and I get crammed in the middle.

VIVIAN: You mean in the same bed?

MARY: Well, yeah, on the floor.

VIVIAN: I think what Bill and Pat did is a little more sensible—for them anyway. There are beds for everybody, but it's in the same room.

MARY: But my kids want to be right on—my son wants to be on top of me. He doesn't want to give me room.

PAT: My son wanted me to lie by him and be close. And I said that I was right there. I said I'm right here, and he said, "No, Mommy, close is right here." [rubbing her arm]

KATHY: Don comes in every night after going to sleep in his own bedroom. About two hours later he comes in and we are asleep. He will not come and lie beside me, he comes right in between us and pushes us apart if we are together, and goes right back to sleep every night.

NORMA: I would like to know what Primal families do about Christmas. I really feel so fucked over about Christmas—

ALL: Just cry a lot.

NORMA: No, I don't mean that. I mean this schtick about Santa Claus and lying and all that bullshit. What I feel now is that they're being into Santa Claus can bring them anything that they want. "We know that you don't have the money, Mommy, but I know that Santa Claus will bring me . . ." they will say. What they're needing is certainly not ten thousand toys. But I really don't know where it's at. I don't know whether to say that, no, Mommy and Daddy are really Santa Claus. That just doesn't seem right.

DOTTIE: That's what we did, and do you know what they said? Pamela said, "We knew all the time." And you know it was a real letdown for me? I cried.

VIVIAN: You mean the problem is whether to continue the myth?

BILL: That's part of being little, that myth; I like it.

BERNARD: Continue the myth, even after you've told them it's not true. Because we've always told Sophie it's not true, but she still wants to believe in Santa Claus, so we write the letter to him.

BRITT: That's the same in our family. We told Michael for years and he knows it. I told him the other day and he said that Santa Claus is going to come down the chimney, talking to his friends. They want to believe it.

CAL: My twelve-year-old brought me a card from school that he had made: "Merry Christmas to Mom and Dad," and all that jazz, and on the inside of a little box it says, "Don't forget to send me lots of presents." I think that was the purpose of the whole thing, really, to get his message over.

DOTTIE: You know, my son sent me a card with what he wants for Christmas: "Please give me love."

BERNARD: I want to ask another question. I've always liked the idea of having the kids in the same room with you, in the same bed even, but what happens if you want to fuck?

PAT: We have a couch that makes into a bed in the living room.

BERNARD: So you creep out, do you?

PAT: It's very romantic. We lock the door—

VIVIAN: There are other times of the day when you can do that, when your children aren't in bed with you.

KATHY: Not when you have a young child, that's not true. We have a two-year-old and he's with us all day long.

PAT: He sleeps sometimes.

KATHY: No, he doesn't.

VIVIAN: Doesn't he sleep at night?

KATHY: Yeah, when he wants to, he goes to sleep.

VIVIAN: Well, that's what I mean. You just have to plan your day that way.

DOTTIE: I'd like to ask one more thing. My kids, the two oldest ones, they fight a lot. Pamela hates Tom. Tom really bugs her; he likes her, he really needs her, and she hates him. So they fight, and he fights just playing and trying to get attention from her, but she fights to kill. And I don't know whether saying, "Pamela, you go into your room. Tom, you go into your room" does do any good. You must have that problem, Pam; what do you do?

PAM: Well, I usually pick the one who seems to be into a feeling the most and try to drag that one off if I can, and we just talk about it. They usually rant and rave and cry a little bit—no big Primaling. And they go right back and start fighting again.

BILL: That's a great defense, you know, when you've got the person right there who did it to you. Bob still hates Betty; it's the same thing.

VIVIAN: It's inevitable. If a child doesn't get, and no one of our children got, then when the second child is born, there is the symbol of the rejection and the focus of the anger. If both children could feel really loved, they would be friends.

Appendix A: Dorothy

The following is part of a description of a birth Primal in a forty-five-year-old woman. It is one of the many we have seen. This particular one has been filmed. It is her fifth birth Primal.

Dorothy

I was at home late at night and felt very irritable and agitated. My body was unable to stay in any comfortable position. I again began to tremble, much as I had done in the previous birth Primals. I had no control over my bodily movements. My hands, face, arms, legs, and torso involuntarily moved. I could feel sort of a "beep" in my head, and I waited quietly and my body responded to this sensation. It was as though my brain was sending signals down to the rest of my body. I knew that I was experiencing my first movements of life. The movements were in very slow motion and I felt I was performing a water ballet. At the outset, movements occurred in my upper torso in a rhythmic pattern. Then my tongue was hanging out of my mouth and starting to quiver, then gradually drawing itself in and out. From this, I spontaneously began to suck.

The "signals" were now radiating more strongly down my spine and moving into my legs. After much rhythmic movement, body contractions began and my body stretched itself out. Slowly I began to move downward in convulsive waves into the birth canal. I suddenly became terrified, and I was aware that something was being done to me from outside of the womb. My body was no longer involved in free, spontaneous movements. I was getting pulled from the outside—pounded and beaten.* I wasn't ready for

* External manipulations performed by the physician to rotate the baby into the proper position for birth.

what was happening. I was also aware that something [the pla-centa] was wrapped around my feet and I couldn't move them freely. The violent shaking began and I was quivering all over my body. The "beating" on the outside continued. I wanted to cry out for help, but couldn't. At this point, my hand became caught over my nose and I couldn't breathe freely.* I couldn't get my hand free from this position for considerable time. My whole body vibrated with fear. No wonder I didn't want to be born. No wonder it took me so long to complete my birth Primal. [The actual process took almost thirty hours, according to those present.] This relates to previous Primals that I have had relating to my legs and the inability to move them freely.

My body was literally "beaten" before I was born in their attempts to get me into proper birth position. I often wondered why I did not feel the actual intensity of the physical beatings I received from my mother as a child. Now I have the answer. It was too much for me to endure during birth and so I stopped feeling the beatings even then.

The portion that follows is excerpts from the actual recording that was taped immediately after my birth Primal (spoken with deep sobbing and weeping as insights were made):

". . . There wasn't anybody to help me. Nobody—nobody. And nobody to see . . . nobody to see that I was in danger and that they were hurting me. They were imposing all their might upon me. Then my neck was being forced from side to side and the vibrations were setting off my whole body. Someone had me by the head and was trying to pull me and force me out† [forceps] . . . wriggling me and pulling me back and forth. Then the placenta was around my legs and I couldn't move and I was being destroyed and couldn't call for help. No one could hear and no one could see . . . these were Primal scenes for me . . .

---

* The hand in this position would cause no difficulty in actual birth, as oxygen reaches the system via the umbilical cord. However, this caused a problem in reliving the experience.

† Delivery was almost complete.

". . . When I was in the birth canal, I just needed gentle, gentle help . . . but no one was there to give that to me. It is a wonder that I survived . . . I was hurting so much and I was so scared . . . I just had to turn off and shut down . . . I had no place to go.

". . . All my life I have been running, trying to find someone who would see how much I needed and how much I hurt.

". . . I know that when my Primals unfold, they follow a consistent pattern. If they could be plotted, they would unfold in a natural sequence and natural order, but unique to me as a human being . . . my own individual way. I can see that consistency as they all link up together. The Primal scenes are basic because they are the basis for my connections. I also understand something about love . . . it is just letting be . . . I just am . . . it isn't being little, or big, or smart, or stupid, or anything . . . Just is, that's all. I just am. It was safer for Mommy to keep me a little girl. She never wanted me to grow up, and she held me back from the start with her body. She had to keep me stupid from finding out that she really hated me and didn't want me. If she could keep me from growing up, the better chance she had of keeping this knowledge from me. I had to be dependent upon her for all the answers . . . that way she was safe. I had to be her favorite child so she could control me . . . and keep me from finding out how things really were. . . .

"I know that what I experienced through my birth Primal was the beginning of my body physically shutting down. It couldn't absorb the pain that I felt. Since then my body has literally come alive in so many ways. I was taking four milligrams of thyroid medication daily before beginning therapy. I have not taken any since my first day and have a normal PBI. My normal temperature has dropped . . . how much I don't know, but I recently had an infectious virus, my body knew the symptoms of high fever, yet the doctor recorded my temperature at 97.2. He couldn't understand the discrepancy. Also, the skin over my entire body has begun to secrete its own lubrication. The dryness which was rapidly getting worse has reversed itself and my skin has taken on a real glow. I really am just beginning to be alive for the first time in my life."

We see in these Primals the subtle interweaving of birth traumas and later behavior. They are not so much cause and effect as integral wholes, interrelated organismically. Getting stuck in the uterus became part of being dumb later on for her. That is, the uterine experience, plus a need on the part of her mother to make her dumb in many thousands of ways covering many years of relationship, combined to produce "dumb," unknowing, unaware behavior. Reliving the birth experience unraveled much of the later experiences with her mother for her. Another way of saying it is her mother's need to keep her dumb later in life was just an extension of not allowing her to go her own way at birth. Someone else who got stuck in the canal might have had parents who needed to control everything, and related to the child later in life in such a way as to keep him helpless and unable to do anything for himself. Thus, his Primal birth experience of being stuck may be felt as total helplessness rather than dumbness. Feeling "helpless" is an "interpretation" of experience. That interpretation comes with the use of language and the development of conceptual abilities. But the *feeling* of helplessness, of being powerless to shut off Pain, begins with the birth experience in some individuals. That feeling is unconscious and unrecognized, but because it exists and was derived from a "life" experience, it drives behavior so that the person may act out being helpless later on in life. (That is, act helpless in a situation where he has no power.)

Appendix B: Richard

The following is an account of a breech-birth Primal. He initially complained of being cold on his legs and buttocks. He was very cold to the touch. He hunched and convulsed every few seconds and had no idea about what he was going through. It was only days later, after he contacted his mother in New York, that he was informed of the nature of his birth.

"My name is Richard. I have been in therapy exactly four months. Yesterday, in an individual session, something happened— I didn't know what. Just my body convulsing, I don't know how to tell you, and then I just started having all kinds of pains, mainly in my back. This took a good solid hour. At the end of it, my therapist asked me what had been going on and I told him, 'I think I'm being born . . .' That's exactly what I told him.

"What was hard for him to understand, because he kept telling me that babies are born with their heads first, is that my feet were cold and my ass was cold. I told him that was the way it was; I don't know anything about babies getting born. My feet were cold and so was my 'heinie' . . . The next day I visited some friends who are in Primal Therapy. Here's what happened":

Tonight, Sunday, November 2, 1969, Richard came over to our house for dinner. He said an amazing thing had happened to him yesterday; he had had a Primal about being born. From what he told me, I gathered that his had been a breech delivery. This was subsequently confirmed when Richard telephoned his mother in New York. He was born in Livonia, Italy, on April 9, 1941; the first boy born in this village (now a part of Yugoslavia) since the war began. The local Fascists showered his mother with gifts and made him an official member of the party. Richard remembers being born in a cold, large room. At 9:00 tonight, while telling us about yesterday's Primal, he fell to the floor; toppled over, really. In a fetal position, clutching himself, he started groaning. I took our infant son outside so as not to distract him from feeling his Pain. From here on my wife notes:

9:02—He's on the floor, groaning in a fetal position. The groans are rather regular and sound as if he were pushing. In fact, he's pushing out so strongly that he lets out air. Farting and burping, his face is purple.

". . . It hurts me . . . aiiiii . . . it hurts. . . ." Clutching the sides of his stomach or back (he later says that this was the part of his body—i.e., his back, that hurt him the most). His face looks like a newborn child's. His body twitches. "It's cold out . . . Ooh . . . Ooh . . ."

9:25—He lies immobile, right hand under left cheek, left arm between bent knees. Breathing is hard, convulsions heavy but slow —spasmodic. His grunts are heavy, fetal. They come at approximately twenty-second intervals. He seems to hear my pen on the paper and opens his eyes. They are red-rimmed. When he closes them again, his heavy breathing resumes—as do a series of particularly violent grunts.

Now his shoulders twitch—his face is contorted as though he were under an additional atmosphere of pressure. He is now (9:30) groaning very heavily, more rapidly. His breathing becomes tortured, his groans unrecognizable strings of sound.

"It's cold—it's col-*d* . . ." he whispers.

Now (9:32) both arms are between his thighs and he is whimpering. His legs are crossed at the ankles. He lies on his left side.

9:33—His right hand, a fist now, is under his left cheek. His face looks puffy, as though he has just gone 15 rounds of a grudge match.

The cries are deeper now (9:34), more from his chest. He whimpers, as my little boy, who is having a sponge bath upstairs, calls out for me.

I have never seen such hurting eyes. My little boy's screams appear to have brought Richard out of it. He sits up. "I don't want to do it no more."

"Just take it easy," I say.

He begins to sob. "It's cold."

After a while, he asks for a Kleenex.

When he can talk again, he says: "My groans, they're like fighting to keep me from getting crushed . . . I feel a lot of pressure from just a little bit above my ass right on up [to his armpits]—a little below my shoulderblades is what hurts me worst of all, because my hands were folded in front of me."

"And your hands hurt your back?"

"Yeah, I don't know if it's them twisting me or me just coming out. After that I'm just viciously cold. My whole body feels like it weighs a million tons. I try to move my head and all I can do is just wiggle it a little. Otherwise I can't move it."

"How does that make you feel?"

"I don't know. Like I'm a blob. It's like I'm a blob that can't move."

"Would you like to cry?"

"I don't think I know how. I like the groans—I can feel my whole body when that happens. I can feel from the bottom of my toes all the way up to the neck—but my head from the neck up feels like one body and from the neck down to my toes feels like another body.

". . . The two parts of my body don't function the same, or something."

"You mean your head and your body are not part of a whole?"

"Yeah, I guess. The bottom of me is cold again and the top of me is warm. It seems I'm stuck in the middle, and that's why the top of me hurts. . . . I don't know how to coordinate them to make them work together. I don't understand it. When I'm curled up, it feels like the upper part of me is too heavy [the head]. I don't want my head to feel so heavy. [groans] It feels like someone's muscles are crushing me to death. It only happens from the waist up and it hurts real bad. It's like my spine was twisted and really strong muscles were crushing me. It feels good when it stops and I don't want it to start again, but it just keeps on happening. . . ."

Richard returns to the rug and his convulsions begin again. Later, after he has sat up and when he can talk, he continues:

"You know a tube of toothpaste . . . when you squeeze it from the bottom up? I feel as if my whole body were being squeezed and all the pressure is going to my chest and head. Like everything was going to pop up. This is like throwing up but not being able to release anything.

"I have a pain in my right shoulder. I don't know what they are doing to me. It's as if I were stuck tightly up a chute and someone were twisting the body and my shoulders were torn. And the whole thing is tearing my back loose." (10:05) Clutching his shoulder. "Mmmmmmm, mmmmmmm . . ." Face contorting and going red, stomach muscles taking over again.

"It's like they're twisting me at the wrong time!"

"Who's they?"

"Doctors—I dunno. I don't wanna talk about it no more. It hurts. It hurts so bad! Talking about it keeps taking me back to it."

10:15—He's back on the floor in agony; left hand under right cheek, right hand between thighs; curled over on his left side. He is groaning very hard; grunting and groaning. His face contorts with each effort; his stomach is an independent agent. In contrast to the rest of his body, his face is vivid pink.

10:20—Richard rolls over on his back and stares up at the ceiling for some ten seconds. Finally, with a groan, he sits up.

Sitting on his buttocks, hands crossed over his knees, he shakes his head; his eyes are shut very tight and he looks like an urchin in pain—a Murillo subject, only painted by Goya.

He collapses back against the couch; he gasps for breath. The light in our living room is not good but his hair looks wet with sweat.

"I can't go on. Really. It hurts too much. It does."

"Now we know what a baby goes through at birth. Only we've never heard a baby *talk* before."

"Do all babies have that hard a time? I always thought it was the mother that did all the hurting," Richard says—"Tony, will ya stop lookin' at me like that!"

"What can I say? I've never seen anything like this before, Richard."

Richard's Primals went on for many, many weeks. Each time a little more of him would be out of the canal. One of the crucial connections he made with the Primal was, "All my life I've been ready to fight someone who hit or even jostled me. In school I would overreact if some kid accidentally bumped into me, and I'd pick a fight. Now I understand that I'm always defending against that early pain. Anything that hurt now would set off that birth pain and I'd lash out to protect myself against any more hurt." Who could even have guessed that this boy's hostility and fights during school could be traced to life in the birth canal?

Appendix C: The Body Remembers

This photograph shows the bruises on the leg of a forty-eight-year-old woman who had been reliving being held upside down and spanked by the doctor just after birth. The doctor was very rough in his handling and one can see the imprint of the fingers and thumb of his left hand as it was wrapped around the baby's leg. An event that occurred almost half a century ago has been relived in its entirety, not just with the brain. (The woman's family confirms the bruising at birth.) The body preserves its memories and if we can understand that bruises are the physical memories imprinted in the

This photo, taken several days after the Primal, shows the bruises 70 percent faded.

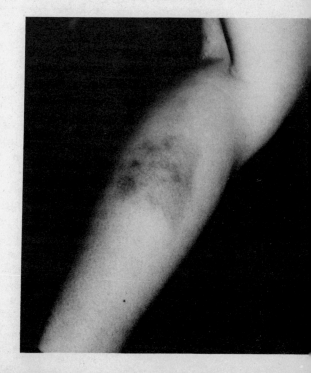

system, lying dormant, timeless, but always there, then we can understand how other memories persevere for a lifetime, exerting a force and impelling neurosis. This photo demonstrates the unity of body and mind; to remember and to feel is a total psychophysiologic event. The body is a memory bank that forgets nothing of its experience even though the mind has dissociated itself from it.

A full understanding of this photograph will lay bare much of Primal theory.

The most obvious fact is that Pain (physical Pain, in this case) that cannot be integrated early in life remains imprinted into the system for a lifetime. When an organism is unable to assimilate what is happening to it because of an overload of Pain, there is an automatic separation of the mind from its experience. That disconnecting process preserves and perpetuates the event as an unresolved, unconscious force.

The body is a memory bank which preserves all of its experiences, forgetting nothing, even when the conscious mind is unable to recall those events.

It is not only the "mind" that preserves or "remembers" experience; it is the entire body. Because the body and mind are a unit, the body constantly reacts to experience which has been disconnected, coded, and stored. In other words, Pain (and unfulfilled needs become transmuted into Pain) is a tissue state, and the tissues "remember" in a physical way. It is the same kind of "memory" as when our system "remembers" that we have taken a great deal of a certain drug and produces an immunity to it.

Experience is not an encapsulated entity preserved in the brain alone. An unintegrated early experience sets up a reverberating circuit in the brain innervating the body as an inextricable counterpart of that experience; the site of innervation depends on the nature of the Pain. If the early Pain was a physical bruise, then bruising may become a tendency of the organism, as it was with this woman, who often developed bruises that were inexplicable. If, for example, the trauma was of coming out of the womb into a very cold delivery room, then the blood system responded to that trauma by constriction. That constriction process may become a fixed one, so that there is an inordinate cardiovascular response to any stress which tends to set off the early one. Later in life, due to the reverberating circuit of early unresolved Pain, cardiovascular disease may be the result.

Here we learn something about the healing process as well. For in the case being discussed, without those critical early connections there was a continuous inadequate healing of the bruises which appeared on her body. We have found with other patients who were bruise-prone that making early connections during Primals immeasurably affected not only later bruise tendencies but also greatly enhanced the healing process when a rare bruise appeared.

So we see that there are target organs of the body which are vulnerable, not only because of the genetic endowment (which should not be discounted) but because of the nature of early trauma. An obvious example would be having been schedule-fed, often starved in the crib, and later having gastrointestinal problems. Those symptoms are the way the body "remembers." They are "translated" memories.

We must ask ourselves, "Where was that bruise all those intervening forty-eight years?" Clearly, it was coded somewhere in the system. It was always a latent tendency. It kept reminding the body in a literal but general way that there was a *specific* bruise it had to deal with and resolve. That is, the body generalizes specific Pains both physically and psychologically and this generalization process is the essence of neurosis. Being afraid of *mother* may become repressed and generalized inappropriately to all women as a class, later on.

When that bruise occurred, there may not have been an adequate cortex to interpret the event properly. Later, it would take an "adult" brain to conceptualize for the "baby brain" and tell it what has happened to it. That is the connection: knowing the source of the Pain—*making it specific so that it does not have to be generalized neurotically*.

We can make one generalization from our observations about early Pain . . . physical trauma seems to be generalized physically, and psychological trauma may generalize psychologically. Obviously, because of the unity of body and mind there is an overlap. But when there is preverbal trauma to which only the body can respond, then a fixed, prototypic response to later trauma may produce bodily symptoms. If the trauma is postverbal, the reaction to later stress may be ideational, such as paranoid ideas, for example.

A disconnected Pain exerts a force on the system. It is neither static nor inert. Connection resolves the Pain and vitiates the force. There will always be a tendency toward stomach upset or ulcers, for example, no matter how good the palliative treatment, until early starvation trauma has been relived and connected to consciousness.

In a sense the unconscious is timeless; for the woman whose leg is shown in the photograph would go on bruising perhaps for a lifetime until a specific moment in her life was recaptured—until one crucial bruise which took place at one specific time was experienced. Until that happened, "bruising" became a timeless response.

In order for that early bruise to be resolved it had to show itself again. Simply to have "remembered" it in the mind apart from the body would have done nothing. It shows us how it is total psychophysiologic experience alone that is curative. Thus insight or awareness or vivid remembering do not stop unconscious tendencies of whatever origin. They cannot control the body in any real way.

The reactivation of an observable phenomenon such as the bruise has other implications for nonobservable unconscious phenomena such as birth traumas; if the brain can reproduce an event in the body that took place moments after birth, certainly it indicates that trauma can become imprinted into the system moments *before* birth in that same brain. There would be no significant difference in that brain in terms of its ability to record events; and so we must conclude that just as postbirth Pain has an underground existence exerting a continuous force on the system, so, too, can a prebirth experience exert an unconscious force.

This discussion should clarify the distinction between a Primal and abreaction or catharsis. Abreaction is usually considered an emotional outpouring accompanying a memory. One would have to stretch the term beyond its usual meaning to include such a phenomenon as bruises at birth. The difference is one between remembering and reliving. Having bruises suddenly appear during a reliving event is not an abreaction; it is a *Primal*.

Primal Therapy has been service-marked as a protection to the public. It is available only at the Primal Institute in Los Angeles. It is dangerous in the hands of untrained personnel.